Praise for *What Retirees Want*

"If you want to understand anything and everything about the longevity revolution, from the ground level to 30,000 feet, read this timely and eloquent book. This book is much more than a source of knowledge. It constitutes a compelling call to purpose and to action. The authors conclude that the Boomers are poised to accomplish their most enduring work as they're realizing that it's more important to be 'useful,' than 'youthful.'"

Marc Freedman,
CEO, Encore.org, and author, *How to Live Forever:
The Enduring Power of Connecting the Generations*

"In *What Retirees Want* Dychtwald and Morison make a vital contribution to the public understanding about retirement and being a retiree. From knowing the demographic and financial facts about longevity, to resisting ageism, to reframing the misconceptions about growing old in this century, to seeking a purpose in the Third Age of life, *What Retirees Want* will fire up your imagination about the realities and the opportunities of a new retirement model. This book should be on every Baby Boomer's to do list."

Fernando M. Torres-Gil, MSW, PhD,
Former US Assistant Secretary on Aging, and
Professor of Social Welfare and Public Policy, UCLA

"I loved every moment reading this terrific new book by Ken Dychtwald and Robert Morison. We live in an era in which the modern elder can offer the world both curiosity and wisdom. This holistic treatise reminded me that, if we're getting aging right, we're not just growing older, but we're growing more whole and more fully integrated as well."

Chip Conley,
Head of Global Hospitality and Strategy, Airbnb (ret),
and author, *Wisdom@Work: The Making of a Modern Elder*

"Retirement conjures oscillating sensations of excitement, relief, despondency, and terror. Dychtwald and Morison address the new age of retirement, a time of unprecedented opportunity to fulfill dreams deferred and meet new challenges with confidence and joy. The pages echo with the call of Ulysses: 'Come my friends, 'tis not too late to seek a newer world.'"

Kerry Kennedy, JD,
President, Robert F. Kennedy Human Rights

"Ken Dychtwald has been chronicling the massive impact of the Baby Boom generation on business, culture and society for over 30 years. In *What Retirees Want*, Ken and Robert Morison have given us a compelling and powerful vision of how Baby Boomers are retiring our conceptions of 'retirement.' This book delivers the gift of insight into a hopeful and optimistic future of purpose and opportunity."

George Vradenburg, JD,
EVP, AOL/Time Warner (ret), and Founder, UsAgainstAlzheimer's

"In the global investment community, we look for trends that will shape how people and nations will live, work, and seek to satisfy their needs. There may be no trend more seismic and unprecedented than the age wave. Ken Dychtwald and Robert Morison present a thoughtful, hopeful, and action-packed view of how rising longevity and aging demographics will alter nearly every aspect of our lives."

Jay S. Wintrob,
CEO, Oaktree Capital Management

"In this wonderful book, Dychtwald and Morison offer us a hopeful and powerful vision of the future in which increasing longevity brings about an entire new stage of life – the Third Age. Packed with far-reaching insights about nearly every related field, from co-housing to voluntourism to AI-supported medicine, *What Retirees Want is* overflowing with potent research, compelling examples, and actionable ideas. A must read!"

Anousheh Ansari,
CEO of XPRIZE, first private female astronaut,
and author, *My Dream of Stars*

"For more than 20 years, Ken Dychtwald's groundbreaking thinking has greatly influenced my own, especially with regard to developing new ways of providing retirement plans and investment strategies to tens of millions of investors. As someone just starting this phase of life, I found this breakthrough book to be both insightful and incredibly inspirational!"

William McNabb,
CEO, Vanguard Group (ret)

"The authors challenge the age-related myths and prejudices that are pervasive in modern marketing. It's time to reframe how we think about, portray, and treat the growing cohort of retirees, and this thoughtful and important book shows us both why and how."

Stephanie Fischer,
President and CEO, Global Retail Marketing Association

"This book is a must read for those thinking about retiring – or wanting to avoid it – and for all who want to reap the best life can provide. Here you will find a real, compelling, multidimensional, and most important, practical picture and guide of what you want and need to know about the Third Age."

Michael Krasny, PhD,
Professor of Literature at Stanford and host of FORUM on KQED
and National Public Radio

"Bestselling author Ken Dychtwald has written 16 books, and *What Retirees Want*, written with Robert Morison, is his best yet. Instead of viewing 'life after work' as a declining period of one's life, Ken and Bob show us why your future will be exciting and invigorating – and just plain fun!"

Ric Edelman,
Founder, Edelman Financial Engines, and author,
The Truth About Your Future

"*What Retirees Want* explains how longer and healthier lives and shifting age demography will change everything we've come to expect from retirement. This compelling, well-researched, and hopeful read arrives at exactly the right time."

Paul Irving, JD,
Chairman, Milken Institute Center for the Future of Aging,
and Chairman, Encore.org

"*Age Wave* helped inspire me to start Home Instead in 1994, which has grown to more than 1,200 offices and 100,000 caregivers in 14 countries around the world. With its depth of information and breadth of ideas, I'm sure *What Retirees Want* will inspire new entrepreneurs and innovators of all ages."

Paul Hogan,
Co-Founder and Chairman, Home Instead Senior Care

"Ken Dychtwald and Robert Morison provide timely and sage advice for embracing a fruitful and fulfilling retirement. They make a compelling case to not let social and corporate ageism deprive us of the benefits of decades of experience and wisdom from those in their Third Age."

Dr. Rudolph Tanzi, PhD,
Professor of Neurology, Harvard Medical School,
and author, *The Healing Self*

"Ken Dychtwald's ground-breaking research and insights into the longevity and health of older adults have already reshaped the travel business for years. *What Retirees Want* offers a comprehensive and mind-stretching preview of how the travel, leisure, recreation, and hospitality industries are about to be transformed by the 50 trillion hours of time affluence that Boomers worldwide will be experiencing during the next two decades. This book is essential reading for anyone looking to better serve today's and tomorrow's older adults."

Matthew Upchurch,
Chairman and CEO, Virtuoso Travel Network

"*What Retirees Want* is a dazzling must read! Every aspect of our lives will adjust to make room for what Dychtwald and Morison call the Third Age. They provide an incomparable guide to help us all understand the challenges and opportunities of a new generation of retirees and how they can live longer, more productive and purposeful lives. And with women outliving men, this book offers a fresh and needed perspective on a wide range of hopeful action steps to improve both women's and men's life journeys."

Maria Shriver,
Journalist, Author, and Activist, Former First Lady of California, and
Founder, The Women's Alzheimer's Movement

"*What Retirees Want* provides fascinating insights into what a world with a billion people over age 60 will look like – its impact on society, business, politics, health care, and the marketplace. Anyone who reads this book will better understand how to capitalize on the new opportunities and challenges brought by the revolutionary age wave."

Thomas Donohue,
CEO, United States Chamber of Commerce

"While there are many books available about preparing for retirement, Dychtwald and Morison have taken this subject to an entirely new level. They have masterfully written a book that provides a fresh, complete, and holistic look at health and home, learning and legacy, work and leisure, family and finances – all the ingredients of a purposeful and fulfilling Third Age of life."

Nido Qubein,
President, High Point University, Founder and Chairman Emeritus of the
National Speakers Association Foundation, and author, *Stairway to Success*

"Dr. Ken Dychtwald, the renowned global thought leader on aging and longevity, and Robert Morison smartly unpack the complex trends, massive social forces and emerging innovations that are redefining medicine, culture and business in profound ways. Read this book now to better understand how to prepare for what's coming tomorrow!"

James Canton, PhD,
CEO and Chairman, Institute for Global Futures, and author, *Future Smart*

"This important new book is a 'must read' for entrepreneurs, businesses, and non-profit organizations that want to respond better to the needs and wants of a huge and growing market segment. *What Retirees Want* is sweeping and forward-thinking in its approach and chock full of valuable data, key insights, and creative solutions."

James Firman, EdD,
President and CEO, National Council on Aging

"Ken Dychtwald and Robert Morison have crafted a masterpiece that offers insights into the trends driving a new way of life, and provides the guidance needed to embrace it. This book is not optional if you want to live better longer."

Colin Milner,
Founder and CEO, International Council on Active Aging

"Entrepreneurs, investors, corporate strategists and non-profit leaders will find an encyclopedia of market insights and opportunities in this book. More than anyone alive, Ken Dychtwald knows the global market trends impacted by the age wave. He and Robert Morison have gathered the essential facts and best ideas in housing, finance, health care, grandparenting, caregiving, passion, play, and volunteering. You will definitely enjoy this must-read."

Mary Furlong, EdD,
Founder and CEO, SeniorNet, ThirdAge Media,
and Mary Furlong Associates

WHAT RETIREES WANT

WHAT RETIREES WANT

A HOLISTIC VIEW OF
LIFE'S THIRD AGE

KEN DYCHTWALD, PhD
ROBERT MORISON

WILEY

Published by John Wiley & Sons, Inc., Hoboken, New Jersey.
Published simultaneously in Canada.

For general information on our other products and services or for technical support, please contact our Customer Care Department within the United States at (800) 762-2974, outside the United States at (317) 572-3993 or fax (317) 572-4002.

Wiley publishes in a variety of print and electronic formats and by print-on-demand. Some material included with standard print versions of this book may not be included in e-books or in print-on-demand. If this book refers to media such as a CD or DVD that is not included in the version you purchased, you may download this material at http://booksupport.wiley.com. For more information about Wiley products, visit www.wiley.com.

Library of Congress Cataloging-in-Publication Data is Available:
ISBN 9781119846734 (Paperback)
ISBN 9781119651932 (ePDF)
ISBN 9781119651918 (ePub)

Cover Design: Wiley
Author Images: Ken Dychtwald © Age Wave LLC, Photo by Lisa Keating,
Robert Morison © Robert Morison, Photo by Tolga Kavut
SKY10029125_100721

From Ken:
To Alan Dychtwald, my brother and best buddy

From Robert:
To my father, Robert Morison, a most experienced retiree

Contents

Introduction

THE AGING OF THE MASSIVE Baby Boom generation is creating an unprecedented wave of retirees worldwide, and increasing longevity means that they will spend more years in retirement than we've ever seen. These older men and women are a rapidly increasing portion of the global population, and in terms of wealth and spending, they already have disproportionate economic clout. Yet many businesses and other organizations that can and should be meeting the needs of retirees continue to ignore, misread, even alienate them. These organizations mistakenly view retirement as a time of loss and decline when, for most, it's really about new freedom and purpose. It's the emerging Third Age of Life.

Let us introduce ourselves. Ken has been involved in the study of aging, health, and longevity since 1974, when he co-founded the country's first preventative health research project, the SAGE Project, and then set up similar initiatives around the world. In the early 1980s, while advising the Office of Technology Assessment – the think tank of the U.S. Congress – he became captivated by the extraordinary ways that increasing longevity, declining fertility, and the aging of the Boomer generation were creating an "age wave." He founded his company of the same name in 1986 and has advised more than half of the Fortune 500 while giving presentations to more than two million people worldwide. He is the author of 16 previous books, including his seminal book, *Age Wave*, which was published in 1989. Ken has been a leading expert, innovator, entrepreneur, and activist in the aging field for four decades. Some of his work alongside other pioneers in the field is recounted in this book.

Robert is a business researcher, writer, speaker, consultant, and authority on the intersections of business, technology, and people management. He has spent much of his career as a leader of research and executive programs in influential management consulting firms, working with hundreds of major organizations across industries. His breakthrough work has ranged from business reengineering to technology and workforce management to business analytics.

We began working together in 2000 with the project "Demography Is De$tiny" that provided the sparks for our *Harvard Business Review* article "It's Time to Retire Retirement," which earned a McKinsey Award, and then our book *Workforce Crisis*. Our collaboration has continued in a series of studies about life in retirement, and we have worked with every industry covered in this book. We are both Boomers, born in 1950, so we have lived as well as studied the topics and trends we describe – and sometimes led the way.

Age Wave's quarter-century-long research into the changing lifescape of retirement in the United States and around the world has formed a comprehensive and holistic portrait of the experiences, values, priorities, worries, opportunities, and aspirations of retirees, with special emphasis on the Baby Boomers who are swelling the ranks and market potential of retirees worldwide. We have reviewed thousands of papers, reports, and data sets, conducted hundreds of expert interviews and dozens of focus groups, and administered cutting-edge surveys of more than 100,000 nationally and internationally representative respondents. We have endeavored at every step to understand retirement in its personal, social, economic, and cultural contexts.

This book is addressed to everyone seeking a more complete and holistic understanding of today's and tomorrow's retirees in order to anticipate their needs and provide them with informed, innovative, empathetic, and valuable products and services. That includes executives, managers, marketers, and frontline employees in businesses, nonprofits, and government and community agencies. In addition, because so many retirees and pre-retirees are curious about their own options for this new chapter in their lives, we hope they find this book to be a helpful and thought-provoking resource.

In Chapter 1 we explore how retirement is transforming at the hands of the Boomers and the myriad opportunities that creates. In Chapter 2 we discuss how ingrained ageism prevents organizations from realizing the opportunity to serve new generations of retirees. Chapter 3 describes the antidote – the imperative to reframe attitudes and practices around aging.

In Chapters 4 to 10, we detail what retirees want in the key facets of their lives: work, leisure, health, family, home, finances, and purpose. In the final chapter, we'll look ahead to how the Third Age we currently call "retirement" will continue to become a larger, more important, and more rewarding segment of people's lives. And a growing opportunity for organizations that master the retiree market.

Throughout this book, we'll share data and analysis on what retirees want, along with commentary from experts and examples of organizations that are finding innovative ways to meet retirees' needs and aspirations. Many chapters end with checklists of actions and opportunities for organizations and entrepreneurs in relevant industry sectors. Much of our survey research is U.S.-based, and some major retirement issues, like pension and health care programs, are specific to the United States. But we also share international data where comparisons are enlightening, and many of our examples are multinational or global enterprises. The challenges and opportunities of serving growing waves of retirees are common in countries around the world.

While the chapters on each facet of life in retirement are of special importance to specific industries, we invite you to read them all for two reasons. First, because they are interconnected. For example, health and location shape opportunities for work and leisure. Work improves financial footing. Family and financial concerns are everywhere. Second, because we've learned time and again that the examples of situations, opportunities, and innovations in one industry often trigger insights and actions in another.

We hear from all the organizations we work with – business, nonprofit, and government alike – urgent demand for more information and better insight into what retirees want and how to serve them respectfully, engagingly, and holistically. We hope this book meets those needs and helps both organizations and retirees to thrive in the new Third Age.

***

We completed this book and submitted it to our publisher in mid-January 2020, before the devastating effects of the COVID-19 virus were widely known. We hope that by our publication date of July 2020, the pandemic will have subsided somewhat, and the ways forward will be clearer. When we talk about this book, we expect one of the first questions will be how the virus changes what we have to say. For now, we anticipate a three-part answer.

First, everything about our lives is disrupted in the short-term and perhaps the long-term as well. We've seen volatility in financial markets before. Now we're getting a lesson in the importance and fragility of our health system and supportive social networks.

Second, many of the fundamental challenges and opportunities we discuss are unchanged, while others are amplified. We more clearly see the value and power of purpose, resiliency, and (with a technological assist) connectedness across families, communities, and enterprises. And there's heightened awareness of the need for financial planning on one hand, and societal safety nets on the other.

Third, generational differences are coming to the fore. Older people are at greater health risk from the virus. But if healthy and not alone, they have stronger foundations for coping. Most are retired from work, and many own their homes. They have the safety nets of Social Security and Medicare, and many are using their experience and perspective to help them cope better than younger, less experienced cohorts.

We hope that you and all those you care about remain safe and sound and that this book provides some helpful guidance going forward.

April 24, 2020

1

The Age Wave Is Rising

How the Boomers Are Transforming Retirement

WHAT DOES "RETIREMENT" mean anymore? Literally, the word "retire" means to "leave" or "withdraw" or even "disappear." In popular connotation, retirement has become the time to end your career, kick back, and relax in a life of leisure. Today, however, retirement is in the midst of an incredible transformation, and tomorrow's retirement will have a whole new timing, meaning, and purpose.

The new retirement is not a time of gradual decline, nor is it about growing old quietly. Our studies find that increasing numbers of older men and women are not interested in "acting their age" and retreating to the sidelines. They'd rather rebel against ageist stereotypes and be productive and involved – even late-blooming – in their maturity. They see retirement as an opportunity for new dreams, contributions, and personal reinventions with new interests, relationships, and ways of living. Passive leisure is being replaced by adventure travel, "edutainment," and "voluntourism" as a vital, turned-on generation of retirees seeks new experiences and new ways to learn.

Richard Eisenberg, Managing Editor of *Next Avenue*, talks about those ambitions: "People have different dreams. For some it's about starting a business that they've thought about for years. For some it's about learning a new language, or taking up an instrument, or going back to a hobby they had when they were children, or having the time to spend with family or traveling, or volunteering." Mary Furlong, EdD, author of *Turning Silver into Gold: How to Profit in the New Boomer Marketplace* and a leading pioneer on the longevity marketplace, points out how today's retirees are on the move: "They're traveling to visit their grandchildren or their parents or they're having an adventure for themselves. Between their volunteering, part-time work, enjoying their grandchildren and, yes, their doctor's appointments, they're very busy. They want to stay in the game, even as peak performers." During the past decades, there has been a great deal of focus on helping people add years to their lives. Now, it seems, they want to also add life to those years.

A Brief History of Retirement

Up until the twentieth century, most people did not retire. The economy was largely agrarian and family-based, and all generations pitched in. You worked all your life and work served a variety of functions, as a livelihood, a way of feeling worthwhile, and a social activity, where you encountered people of all ages. If somebody was no longer able to perform a physically demanding job, responsibilities changed. Grandpa would stop plowing the fields and instead fix the fences – and pass on his knowledge of field plowing. People had no real concept or expectation of retiring. We call that the first age of retirement, and it had lasted for centuries.

By the early twentieth century, the industrial revolution had migrated much of the labor force from the family farm to the factory assembly lines, and the second era of retirement began. Older workers were let go when they weren't needed or could no longer perform at the pace or intensity of their younger counterparts. Then, in the midst of the Great Depression, Social Security was created, officially institutionalizing retirement for older workers. The program had two main purposes: first, to create a modest safety net for older adults in a period of economic uncertainty, and second, with unemployment levels skyrocketing to 25%, to provide a process whereby older people would leave the workforce to make room for the young. However, life expectancy in the 1930s was only 62, so most people didn't live long enough to retire. If they did retire, it was for an average of less than five years.[1] Early in the Social Security program, there were 40 workers supporting each retiree, and the average annual payout was $220, so it was not much of a strain on the economy.

Through subsequent decades, people began retiring earlier and earlier (Figure 1.1). Social Security benefits were increased 77% in 1950, and by the 1960s, company pensions covered half of all workers, up from virtually none in 1900.[2] The average age at which people retired plummeted from 70 in 1950 to 66 in 1960 to 63 in 1990. In this third era of retirement, people were living longer and, for increasing numbers, retirement was lasting for decades. Retirement communities and cruise lines began to promote retirement as the "golden years" of life. Many people came to think of a financially secure retirement as an entitlement, a reward for a life of hard work. But it also came to be viewed as a badge of success, and the younger you retired, the more successful you were perceived to be.

We are entering what we'll call the fourth era of retirement, driven both by rising longevity and by an unprecedented influx of Boomer retirees. With their numbers also comes unprecedented economic clout. But they have less financial security from pensions and thus more responsibility for funding their own retirements. As a result, more of them will need to – or wish to – work a bit longer

Figure 1.1   U.S. Average Retirement Age 1900–2020

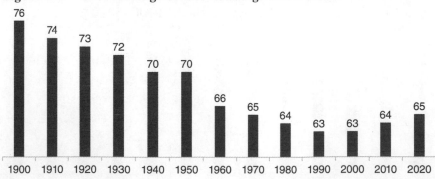

Source: Age Wave / Merrill Lynch, *Work in Retirement: Myths and Motivations*; Center for Retirement Research at Boston College, 2020

before they retire, and the average retirement age is 65 and rising. They will also have more "time affluence" in retirement and more options on how to spend it. And to further complicate the picture, they are looking at retirement differently. They don't want to be called "seniors" and they don't want their parents' retirement. They want a kind of "ageless aging" and their dream is to stay active, engaged, and purposeful. How this new, fourth era is playing out is the core story of this book.

How Demographics Are Redefining Retirement

The longevity revolution is the most disruptive trend in human history. Humans have walked the earth for 100,000 years, but our life expectancy has vaulted only in the last 100. As a result, the pace and processes of aging are being entirely redefined. A century ago, life expectancy in the United States was about 55 (Figure 1.2). Today, it is 79, and that's only good for 33rd place globally, almost 6 years behind Japan (Figure 1.3). With the possibility, and some would say inevitability, of medical breakthroughs in the near future, life expectancy could make another leap. How many decades might retirement last then?

Increasing longevity, however, is just half the story. There was a record-breaking baby boom in many countries after World War II. In the United States, we had 76 million births between 1946 and 1964. That baby boom became a teenager boom in the '60s and

Figure 1.2   U.S. Life Expectancy at Birth, 1900–2020

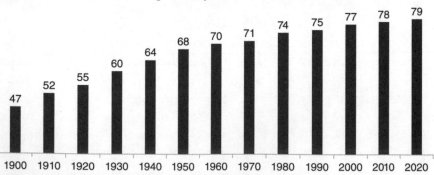

Source: Social Security Administration, 2020

Figure 1.3   Life Expectancy at Birth, Selected Countries

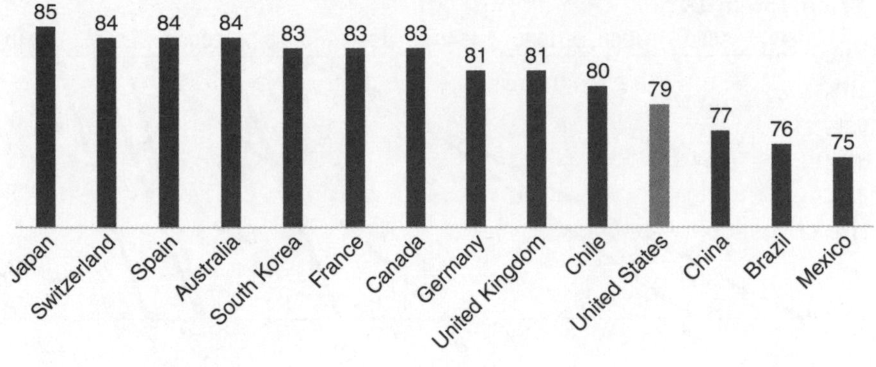

Source: United Nations, *2019 Revision of World Population Prospects*

'70s, then a labor force boom, and today a retirement boom. Every day, another 10,000 American Boomers retire. In China, 440 million people were born during the period. And while the average life expectancy in China was a mere 35 in 1950, it has vaulted to over 75 today (and rising). China's age wave may be its biggest social, medical, and economic challenge/opportunity in the years ahead.

Longevity plus the aging of the Baby Boom generation drive the dramatic growth in the number of older men and women. There are now more than a billion people age 60+ in the world, and it's estimated that we will cross the 2 billion threshold in 2048. This growth is most dramatic among the older old. In 1900, there were only 122,000 people aged 85+ in the United States. As of 2020, there are nearly 6.7 million (more than the total American population in 1800), representing an increase of 5,500%. That number will more than double to 14.5 million by 2040.

Moreover, the rate of population aging, which varies dramatically across different countries, is accelerating. It took 115 years (from 1865 to 1980) for the age 65+ cohort in France to rise from 7% of the total population to 14% (Figure 1.4). It took 85 years in Sweden and 69 in the United States. But it took only 25 years in Japan and will take 23 in China and 21 in Brazil. The next proportional increase, from 14% to 21%, is happening much faster: 42 years in France, 40 in Sweden, 20 in the United States, 12 in Japan, 11 in China. Japan and Sweden are already over 21%, and South

Figure 1.4   The Speed of Aging: Time for 65+ Population to Rise
From 7% to 14%

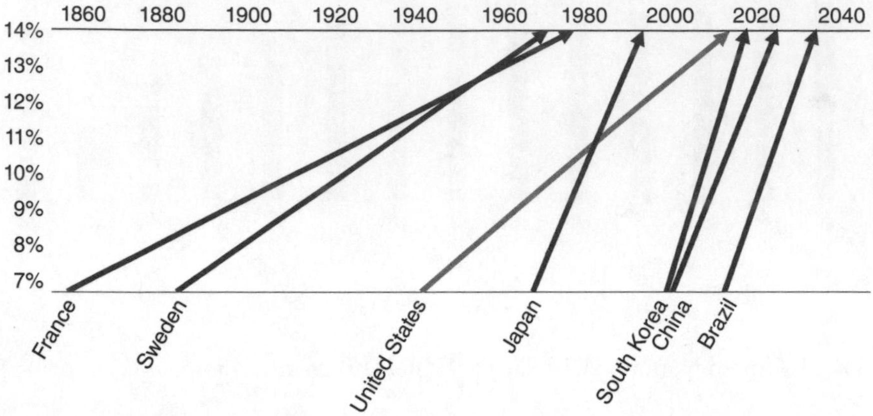

Source: U.S. Census Bureau

Korea is going from 7% all the way to 21% in only 27 years. This
population acceleration has major countries and cities scrambling
to adjust their facilities and services.

There are already approximately 68 million retirees in the
United States, or 21% of the population. The number of retirees is
projected to grow to 82 million by 2040. We say "approximately"
because the definition of "retiree" is blurry with so many returning to the workforce, or considering themselves partially retired, or
retired prematurely by health issues.

With longer life expectancy, women retirees outnumber men,
especially at advanced ages. Women comprise 57% of the population over 65 and 67% of those over 85. Meanwhile, the ethnic distribution of older Americans continues to change. Non-Hispanic
whites make up 76% of the age 65+ population today, and that
will decline to 66% in 2040. The proportion of African Americans (9% to 11%), Hispanics (9% to 16%), and Asians (4% to
7%) will rise significantly (Figure 1.5). Of course, younger cohorts
are more diverse yet – 56% of Millennials are white, 44% other
ethnicities.

These trends create today's age and retirement waves. Rising
life expectancy changes the age mix, and the aging of the Baby
Boom amplifies the effect. All around the world, populations are

Figure 1.5 Changing Diversity of Age 65+ Americans

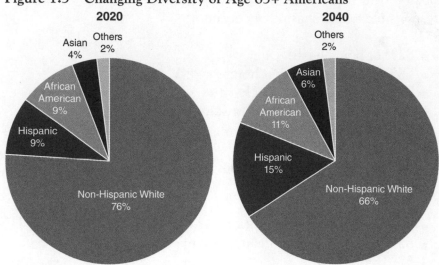

Source: U.S. Department of Health and Human Services Administration for Community Living, 2018 Profile of Older Americans and Minority Aging Profiles

rapidly aging. Nothing like this has ever happened before. We have a massive wave of retirees looking at retirements of unprecedented length.

How the Age Wave Is Transforming the Economy and the Marketplace

This story is about far more than headcount. Behind these population numbers is growing economic power. The 113 million Americans over age 50 turn out to be the most powerful and affluent consumer group in history. Representing 35% of the population, and 46% of adults, Americans over 50 control 76% of the total net worth of U.S. households. They have a combined annual personal income of over $5.7 trillion and nearly $80 trillion of wealth.[3] Median net household worth is approximately three times that of those under age 50. Ninety percent of all billionaires are over age 50.[4]

These mature households now account for $7.6 trillion in direct consumer spending, or 56% of the total. For categories including health care, they account for two-thirds of spending. They are responsible for purchasing or consuming:[5]

- 82% of home health care
- 78% of owned vacation homes
- 75% of contributions to charities
- 75% of prescription drug consumption
- 75% of landscaping services
- 74% of accounting fees
- 71% of over-the-counter drugs
- 70% of dental services
- 66% of ship fares
- 66% of magazine subscriptions
- 65% of out-of-pocket health care expenditures
- 57% of lodging
- 55% of major appliances
- 54% of airline fares
- 53% of jewelry
- 53% of groceries
- 52% of women's apparel
- 52% of personal care products and services
- 51% of new cars and trucks
- 50% of health club memberships

They also aid society and the economy in other ways. As a recent AARP study reports, the societal benefits of the 50+ population's unpaid activities – including caregiving, volunteering, donating to charities, and raising grandchildren – were worth $745 billion in 2018. And they pay 59% of all federal income taxes.[6]

Americans 65 and older, the majority already retired, account for 17% of the total population and 38% of net wealth.[7] In countries with comparable statistics available, the proportions are similar. In Canada, 18% are age 65+ and they have 31% of the wealth. In the U.K. it's 19% with 35% of the wealth, in Australia, 16% with 33%. In Japan, which is aging "earlier" than other developed economies, 28% of the population is over 65 and people in their 60s have the highest savings, double that of people in their 40s.[8]

Looking at assets and spending power generationally, Boomers are the wealthiest cohort ever. They have median household net worth of $206,700 and an average of $1,210,100.[9] They control 54% of total wealth, and they make up more than 56% of the 12 million households with over $1 million in assets (not counting primary residences).[10] However, the wide difference between median and average net worth reveals the uneven distribution of wealth among the Boomers. Half have worth of around $200,000 or less. As we'll detail in Chapter 9, that leaves many financially unprepared for retirement. Others have significant wealth, often with an owned home the major asset. And there are some with extraordinary wealth, which brings the average way up – and can distort the picture of the generation's wealth. Nonetheless, as we'll see throughout this book, financial resources enable, but do not determine, enjoyment of life in retirement.

How the Boomers Are Redefining Retirement

The Boomers have famously – or infamously – reshaped every stage of life they've inhabited. Their early years caused a market boom in baby products. Their teenage years gave rise to the hippie movement. They activated sexual and gender revolutions. They reshaped the workforce with unprecedented numbers of women. As parents, they embraced a more involved approach to childrearing. When they were young, there were three television channels; now there are hundreds. For ice cream, they had to choose between vanilla, chocolate, strawberry, or Neapolitan. Baskin-Robbins' 31 flavors was a breakthrough. Today there are hundreds of flavors and ice cream shops customize their own. As teenagers, they were drawn to the idea of "fast food" and so Ray Kroc licensed the McDonald brothers' brand, and now there are nearly 38,000 McDonald's restaurants worldwide. Now this demographically potent generation has begun to reimagine and reinvent retirement.

Interested from the start in discovering themselves and finding purpose, they grew up with major causes – civil rights, women's rights, gay rights, opposition to war – and defining events – the assassinations of two Kennedys and Dr. Martin Luther King, the rebellious freedom of Woodstock, and the wonder of the moon landing.

At the same time, the Boomers were glamorized and indulged. The story of youth's excitement was baked into them. And now they really don't want to become "old" people, certainly not by conventional definition.

In many ways, the Boomers are also the first generation to have had the benefit of retirement review and observation, watching their grandparents and then their parents be the first cohorts to have somewhat lengthy retirements, spent in a relatively quiet fashion. In contrast, they want their retirement to be more interesting, active, passion-filled, and exciting. They imagine, and indeed have, more choices in lifestyle, location, leisure, and other realms.

Because the Boomers are so different from older retirees, there's a gradual replacement going on, from one style of older person to another. The generation just in front of the Boomers grew up in the shadow of the Depression and lived through a world war. They were – and remain – far more conservative, frugal, and straight arrow-ish than subsequent generations. The Boomers came along at another time in history and had the privilege of benefiting from the postwar period of peace, prosperity, and the ensuing expansion of the middle class. Compared to previous generations of older adults, they are better educated, more high-spirited, more willing to experiment, more willing to change things. They are also more spoiled, pampered, and unaccustomed to delayed gratification. Throughout their lives, Boomers have had an ambitious appetite for breaking rules of all sorts and experimenting with a diverse range of lifestyles. We are convinced that these proclivities will be central to their retirements.

It's also critical to note that Boomer women are more educated, skilled, ambitious, and confident than any previous generation of women. They were the first generation to step out of the home-maker pattern, where the husband worked and eventually retired, and the wife managed the home and family. Instead, they pursued higher education and careers and were also willing to leave unsatisfying marriages. In retirement, they are not just tagging along with their spouses. As Dr. Rita Smith writes in *Empty Nest, Empty Desk, What's Next?*, "We Boomer professional women are the first and largest generation of women to define themselves by our work. A retirement model is needed that provides continuity and outlets for our education, productivity, achievements, sense of community, and passion for meaningful work."[11]

Boomer women's experience in decision making and financial matters will most likely serve them well in retirement, because on average the married will outlive their husbands. Many women spend much of their retirement as a primary or sole decision maker, and the scope of their decisions can include their spouses, parents, children, and grandchildren. This independence can empower them to pursue their diverse passions in retirement.

Connecting with the Boomer Generation

The times they are a-changin'. Cyndi Lauper is a spokesperson for Consentyx psoriasis treatment, Jon Bon Jovi for Advil pain reliever. Paul McCartney did a famous spot for Fidelity Investments. Not to be outdone, the Rolling Stones had as the sole sponsor of their recent North American tour the Alliance for Lifetime Income, the industry association for financial annuity providers. What's going on here? Cultural celebrities age and their needs change, just like what happens to their fans and followers.

These brands are employing the common technique of using celebrity spokespersons, as with Lauper and Bon Jovi, or simply attaching themselves to the aura of the celebrities, as with McCartney and the Stones. This is one version of "generational anchoring," connecting with a target market by appealing to their shared experiences and attitudes. It works well with Boomers because of their strong generational identity. We're shaped by both *where* we're from and *when* we're from. We are not only of a certain background and neighborhood but also part of a certain cohort – with music, entertainers, and athletic celebrities commonly enjoyed, politicians admired or despised, and language and attitudes shared with friends. We may keep up with cutting-edge changes such as new technologies (often with the help of our children), but we also remain indigenous to our cultural places in time.

When Boomers were becoming fans of the Beatles and the Rolling Stones, retirement planning wasn't on their minds, let alone financial planning and annuities. But in more recent years, financial services firms have made effective use of generational anchoring because, as bank robber Willie Sutton pointed out, that's where the money is. After Ameriprise Financial was spun off from American Express in 2005, Age Wave worked with the new firm to help them put their brand on the map through an effective combination of generational anchoring and aspirational guidance. Ads featured Dennis Hopper, co-star of the classic 1969 biker movie *Easy Rider*. In one spot, with "Gimmie Some Lovin'" by the Spencer Davis Group playing in the background, Hopper tells the audience, "Your generation is definitely not headed for bingo night. In fact, you could write a book about how you're going to turn retirement upside-down." The voiceover then takes over: "The best book on retirement is the one you'll write, the *Dream Book* . . . for retirement defined by your dreams." Ameriprise's *Dream Book* became a widely used tool for financial planning driven by people's unique hopes and ambitions in retirement.

The Mercedes-Benz 2017 Super Bowl ad had generational anchoring hitting on many cylinders, with the help of Peter Fonda, the other co-star of *Easy Rider*. Set in a biker bar full of scruffy, gray-bearded Boomer-age bikers, the action begins with a biker donning his reading glasses to see the labels on the juke box more clearly and then push the button for Steppenwolf's "Born to Be Wild" (theme song of the *Easy Rider* movie). A parody scene of biker mayhem is interrupted when someone parks outside, blocking their motorcycles. The bikers charge outside ready for a brawl, but stop in their tracks because that someone is Fonda. He compliments their "rides" and drives off in his new Mercedes convertible, leaving his awestruck fans in a cloud of dust. You don't have to be a biker or have seen the movie in its first run to get the message: free-spirited, wind-in-hair then, and a more advanced kind of free-spirited, wind-in-hair now.

The most direct form of Boomer generational engagement may be through people, often entertainers or athletes, whom the audience recognizes instantly, relates to, and ideally identifies with. Anchors can also be the music used in ads or references to movies, events, and common experiences. With today's Boomer retirees, anchoring can say, "We're talking to you," without the preface of, "Hey, old person." Anchoring often benefits from humor, and it can be sealed with a wink and a nod, the suggestion of an inside joke.

And the most engaging marketing campaigns (like the two we just mentioned) connect experiences from the past with analogs today in creative ways. They say to the audience, "This is you then, this is you now, and we understand the similarities and the differences." They elicit characteristics and attitudes – freedom and fun, purpose and hope – that persist into the Boomers' retirement years.

The New Retirement Lifescape

In this book, we'll be taking a holistic look at the various aspects and experiences of the new retirement and how so much will be both activated and transformed by the Boomers. Here's a preview of some of the major zones we'll be covering.

Work. Retirement increasingly includes some employment. Seven in ten Boomer workers expect to work past age 65, are already doing so, or do not plan to retire. Retirees work because they need the money; because they want to stay mentally, physically, and socially active; or simply because they love what they do. Many choose to work in new occupations, to start businesses, or to launch "encore" careers that give back to society. As we'll be covering in depth in a few chapters, working in new ways is becoming part of the opportunity, adventure, enjoyment, and funding of retirement.

Leisure. Retirees also have the greatest time affluence and will be looking for new ways to enjoy it. In their everyday leisure pursuits, they seek to stay active and healthy. On special occasions, they seek memorable "peak experiences" such as travel, often with family. Retirees account for a disproportionate share of leisure spending, including over $200 billion annually on travel. Worldwide, over the next 20 years, retirees will have 50 trillion hours of leisure to fill.

Health. Health is the key ingredient to an active and happy retirement. The additional life expectancy at age 65 is over 20 years for women, 18 years for men. The average person can expect to be in good health for about half that span, and is probably already managing at least one chronic condition, hypertension being the most common. Loss of health is retirees' greatest source of worry, and Alzheimer's has become the most feared condition of age. The need for care naturally increases with age: while 16% of people age 65–69 need care due to health problems or functional limitations, nearly 60% of those 85–89 need care. It's almost unimaginable what retirees will consider doing and spending to retain their health as long as possible.

Family. Family is far and away retirees' greatest source of reported satisfaction in life. Longevity produces three, four, five, even six generation families, and they will become increasingly matriarchal. Due to their superior longevity, the larger number of older women has dramatic effect on family structure. Over 34% of women age 65+ are widowed, only 13% of men. Some 9.4 million older Americans, almost 20% of the total, live in multigenerational households and generational interdependency is on the rise.

Home. Today's retirees enjoy new freedom in where and how they live. Younger retirees move to their dream locations, older ones to where care and comfort are available. Many stay in place and renovate. Seventy-nine percent of those age 65+ own their own homes, and seven in ten of them are mortgage-free. Nearly 14 million older Americans live alone, 70% of them women, and approaching half (45%) of all women age 75+ live alone. About 2.5 million older Americans live in assisted living or nursing facilities.

Finances. Less than half of Americans over the age of 60 feel that their retirement savings are on track, and on average they've saved only $135,000. So they enter retirement facing the need for financial and lifestyle adjustments. The median annual income of households headed by someone age 65+ is about $44,000, and the median net worth is over $230,000. Eighty-four percent of older Americans report receiving Social Security, and it provides 90% or more of income for 34% of beneficiaries. Retirees' greatest financial concerns are costly health issues, rising cost of living, supporting their lifestyle, and outliving their savings.

Purpose. A strong sense of purpose keeps retirees more active, healthier, and happier. They believe that retirement is the best time to give back, and they are generous. Although often portrayed as self-centered, it turns out Boomers are the most charitable generation in history – in terms of both volunteer time and money. They account for over 40% of money donated and hours volunteered to charities and causes. Still, volunteering represents a small fraction of today's retirees' discretionary time. As we'll explore in detail, mobilizing more retiree volunteers holds enormous potential for social good.

One Size Doesn't Fit All

Today's retirees want to be related to and respected for their diversity – and are weary of the stereotyped "golden agers" strolling along the beach at sunset. Colin Milner, founder of the International Council on Active Aging, stresses the importance of personalizing products and services: "The research shows that no two individuals experience aging in exactly the same way or at the same rate. Consumers expect products and services to be 'about me.' What is the solution that I need that's different from the mass solution? That's why we're seeing things like person-centered medicine and wellness. Every consumer enterprise should be looking for ways to be person-centered." Paul Irving, JD, who chairs the Milken Institute Center for the Future of Aging, reinforces the point: "Older adults are as diverse and complex and different as any other part of the population, and in many ways more so because their tastes and understandings are refined by a lifetime of experience. So a one-size-fits-all marketing approach to retirees is not going to succeed."

A first step toward customization is to recognize patterns and devise useful market segments. We have found patterns in the attitudes and experiences of retirees that fall into four different lifestyles. Our segmentation model, which emerged from numerous large-scale national and international studies, is based on the psychographics of retirees – their attitudes, aspirations, and stated needs and priorities. We have also fleshed out the segment characteristics with key demographic, financial, and other background information that aligns with the segment patterns.[12] Roughly 20%

of retirees fall into each of the first three segments, which we call Ageless Explorers, Comfortably Contents, and Live for Todays. That leaves about 35% of retirees in the fourth segment, Worried Strugglers.

Ageless Explorers

Ageless Explorers see retirement as a time of opportunity, adventure, exploration, and personal reinvention. They tend to be accomplished in their lives and careers, and retirement presents the chance to accomplish even more. Although they want to step back a bit from the burdens and stresses of their careers, they don't intend to wind down. In fact, work has typically been a source of personal fulfillment in their lives, and they often work in retirement, but more for the activity and accomplishment than the money. They are the most likely to start businesses in retirement or take teaching positions. They tend to plan ahead and have given considerable thought to their activities and ambitions in retirement.

Most Ageless Explorers feel energetic and empowered, and they tend to be optimistic and happy, active and informed, and both independent and social. They have self-knowledge and the confidence that goes with it. They very much enjoy the additional freedom and flexibility of retirement. They are financially secure in retirement through the combination of successful careers, financial knowledge and planning, and the fact of saving for 25 years (the most of any segment).

In this stage of their lives, they want a better balance between work and leisure and they especially want to focus more on family and have quality time with them. Their leisure centers on experiencing and learning new things and continuing to explore their own potential. Most of them want to give back to society, often as a continuation of the volunteering and donating they did before retiring. They tend to be healthy, and even when they have health challenges, they are determined to stay physically active.

Ageless Explorers have rejected the life-of-leisure definition of retirement in favor of exercising their freedom to choose new paths. They are in the vanguard when it comes to actively making the most of their retirement experience.

Comfortably Contents

Comfortably Contents have much in common with Ageless Explorers in terms of what they've accomplished in their careers and how financially prepared they are for retirement. However, they approach retirement with a more traditional, less driven view that retirement is a reward for a life of conscientious work. They tend to be well-educated and their work provided a good income. They are less likely to work in retirement, and when they do, it's to stay active as well as earn some supplemental money. In retirement, their focus is on recreation, fun, and relaxation. They're not necessarily winding down, but rather shifting gears and priorities to enjoy the fruits of their labor.

Comfortably Contents view themselves as responsible, hardworking, capable, self-disciplined, and ambitious. In retirement, they report feeling very positive and relatively worry-free. They are the most likely of the four segments to say they are having fun and are very happy and healthy in retirement. Comfortably Contents want to take leisure activities to new heights. They are the most interested in exotic, adventure, and extended travel. They very much want their families to enjoy life with them, and they may be especially doting as grandparents. At the same time, they feel less need than other segments to give back to society outside their families.

They have been saving for retirement for an average of 23 years (second only to the Ageless Explorers). Most have planned, invested, and achieved financial security. Comfortably Contents have played the game of "you worked hard so now enjoy retirement," and they've played it well. They now see their time in retirement as theirs to fully enjoy.

Live for Todays

Live for Todays have had active and varied lives and hope to continue with new experiences and adventures in retirement. Even more than Ageless Explorers, they seek continued personal growth and want to keep reinventing themselves. They have the biggest list of things they'd like to do and would ideally like their retirement to be an extension of their free-spirited lives. Live for Todays are versatile, idealistic, experimental, hopeful, and ambitious to do and learn new things. They are the most likely to say they never feel old inside. They like challenges and changes, and they've changed more than most – relationships, jobs, and locations. They see life as fascinating and often find it unpredictable. They're not planners. If they could, they would rather be doing it all: having fun with children and grandchildren, volunteering in the community, making new friends, taking classes, traveling, and engaging in new activities, hobbies, and intellectual pursuits.

They may have done okay financially, but it was more a matter of pay-as-you-go than save-for-retirement. Many will need to work a few extra years in retirement to get by, and they're working primarily to supplement their income or build more of a nest egg. Because most haven't planned or saved enough to live comfortably in retirement, they are frustrated with the financial challenges they face in this stage of life.

Compared to Ageless Explorers and Comfortably Contents, Live for Todays are more worried about everyday expenses, health care costs, and outliving their money. They run greater risk of being derailed financially by health issues. The onset of retirement can be a shock, and they may continue to find retirement less fulfilling than they'd like because they have less flexibility than they'd like. They have regrets about their "be here now" lifestyle and wish they would have planned better for this stage in their lives.

Worried Strugglers

Worried Strugglers are, compared with the other segments, the least ready and able to enjoy retirement. They have fewer financial resources and fewer hopes and dreams for what they'd like to do. They report being more worried, less active, less healthy, and less happy.

Financially, they have done relatively little planning and preparation. If they've been saving, it's been at a lower rate and for fewer years. So they have greater reliance on employer pensions (if any) and Social Security for retirement income. They're more likely to have to work in retirement to make ends meet, but also more likely to have been forced into retirement by poor health. They don't travel spontaneously, but save for the annual getaway. Their physical sphere is generally close to home, and family, friends, and neighbors provide sources of enjoyment. Family support may be needed to sustain them personally and financially.

Many Worried Strugglers feel they've been dealt a bad hand late in life and they are frustrated that others seem to have it better. For this segment, retirement is not the "golden years," but instead a largely unpleasant experience. Yet they report that they're not giving up and most think of themselves as pragmatic, as survivors.

***

Over the years, as we have discussed these four different segments of retirees, for obvious reasons, nearly everyone says they hope they don't wind up as Live for Todays or Worried Strugglers in their later years. This is a segmentation of retirees overall. In Chapters 4 and 6, we'll discuss two more cuts based on retirees' attitudes toward work and health.

Retirement Is a Journey, Not a Destination

Not only are there different types of retirees, but the retirement lifescape is a moving target. People begin their retirement at different ages under different circumstances. Then they proceed through retirement in different ways at different paces. You can no longer tell where a retiree is in the journey simply based on age. We have seen far too many marketers treat 64-year-olds and 93-year-olds the same, just because they're both "retired." It turns out, though, that there are some common patterns. Inspired by the insightful analysis of the idea that there were distinct stages of grief and bereavement by Dr. Elizabeth Kubler Ross (with whom Ken collaborated occasionally in the 1970s), we have been examining the stages of retirement for years. We've learned that retirees' attitudes, needs, and priorities do evolve in five stages along the typical retirement journey.[13]

Stage 1: Imagination. Starting 15 or more years before their planned retirement, many people start to imagine how they might spend their retirement years. With other responsibilities and concerns front-and-center, starting with family and job, they don't dwell on retirement, but it appears that they do think about it quite positively. As their vision becomes clearer, especially about what they'd like to do and achieve in retirement, enthusiasm grows. In this imagination period, many realize that they should already be saving for retirement, including taking full advantage of employer and private retirement savings programs. Unfortunately, as we'll discuss later, most are not actually doing this.

Stage 2: Anticipation. Starting about 5 years before retirement, anticipation and preparation begin to percolate. Excitement builds as plans for recreation, hobbies, family, travel, and post-retirement careers begin to coalesce. Most people feel that their retirement ambitions may be in reach. At the same time, reality sets in, especially around financial preparation, and many people get financial advice and try to ramp up their savings. And as retirement draws closer, other anxieties increase around any health issues, how they will adapt to the absence of a regular paycheck, and how things will work out.

Stage 3: Liberation. "Retirement Day" arrives and retirees feel an immediate mix of freedom, empowerment, and relief that it's finally here. Most get busy with a planned backlog of activities and priorities – travel, hobbies, time to reconnect with spouses and families. They report that they are having fun and they enthusiastically enjoy their newfound free time, though they may have trouble structuring it. During the initial adjustment to retirement, they are most likely to be working with financial advisors and life coaches. How long does this honeymoon period of liberation last? Not long. Our research showed that, on average, it's less than two years.

Stage 4: Reorientation. Starting about two years into retirement, people have largely transitioned out of their work identities and have begun to figure out what retirement means for them. After the initial burst of excitement, many find they need to adjust their expectations and plans. For most, retirement offers even more new choices and opportunities than they had anticipated – and that's exciting. Those who relocate tend to do so a few years into retirement. As life's clock continues to tick, retirees in this phase may have growing worries about health and finances. However, most reinvent themselves, overcome obstacles, make adjustments in both lifestyles and expectations, and reorient themselves around what will make their retirement personally fulfilling. Our research shows that many enjoy a prolonged "sweet spot" of retirement where happiness, contentment, and fun are at all-time highs. This stage of reorientation and enjoyment typically lasts a dozen years or more.

Stage 5: Reconciliation. Starting around 15 years or more into retirement, as health problems and limitations increase, most people tend to slow down their pace of activities and enjoy more rest and relaxation. Our research has shown that while many retirees in this phase are still enjoying themselves and trying to remain hopeful and content, that's mixed with sadness due to their own illness or that of a loved one, loss of friends and loved ones, and worries about further loss. Many are widowed, often after a period of caregiving for the spouse. Family connections and activities become more central to their lives. In this later stage of retirement, people engage in more personal reflection and are coming to terms with their lives and the legacies they wish to leave.

Retirement is being transformed by demographic forces and by a very different generation of retirees. Retirement isn't just a major adjustment in work status and financial arrangements. It has reverberations across the most important facets of life: family relationships, leisure time, living arrangements, staying healthy, and giving back. For organizations that want to effectively engage and serve today's and tomorrow's retirees, the challenges are both multilayered and multidimensional. They need to appreciate those interconnections in people's lives – between family relationships and housing aspirations, for example. Or between wealth and health. Or even between loneliness and volunteerism. They need to recognize both the wide variety of retirees and the revealing patterns in their circumstances and needs. Organizations also need to view life in retirement in motion, as retirees progress through common stages but with quite variable timing. And they need to recognize how the Boomers continue to rewrite the rules as they go. It takes knowledge, anticipation, and innovation to keep pace.

What do retirees want? Interestingly, our research has taught us that the American dream of "life, liberty, and the pursuit of happiness" is morphing slightly for today's retirees. What they want is health for life, freedom to be one's authentic self, and a chance to pursue one's purpose and personal version of happiness.

2

Ageism Sucks

It's Bad for People and Bad for Business

Due to America's obsession with youth – ironically formulated and solidified when Boomers were young – most product and service developers and marketers direct most of their attention to Millennials and Gen Zers. But those cohorts are predominantly broke, time-constrained, and only marginally loyal to products and services. Focusing on the historically "sought-after youth market" is a costly mistake when today's older men and women now have considerable wealth, time, and interests to satisfy.

As we explored in Chapter 1, retirement is currently undergoing a dramatic transition. Due to increasing longevity – particularly of women – and the aging of the Boomers, the swelling ranks of retirees are forming an unprecedented social and market force. And since today's cohorts of older men and women are psychologically, culturally, and financially different from previous older generations, they have new and far more diverse aspirations and dreams for their retirement lifestyles. As a result, there's a far bigger upside to aging – and one that is largely untapped. The opportunity is hiding in plain sight. Seizing it is going to require a fresh appreciation for today's and tomorrow's retirees: who they are; what they'll want to feel, eat, drive, wear, and share; and how they'll want to enjoy and find purpose in their decades of newfound time affluence.

Disinterest in retirees – whether it's due to bias and prejudice, ignorance, or inexperience – may be causing you and your organization – whether you're General Motors or a Silicon Valley start-up – to miss out on the greatest business growth opportunities ever. The Boomers are like a 76-million-pound elephant moving across the lifeline, and the best way to catch it is to get in front and dig a big hole. That requires fresh ideas. Enough with the big button phones. The time has come for imaginative and innovative solutions to the challenges, needs, and aspirations of over one billion men and women worldwide. And that's where informed, attuned, and inspired marketing comes in.

When Old Was In

It might surprise you to know that it used to be "in" to be old – not just in Asia and Scandinavia – but right here in the United States as well. At the time of the signing of the U.S. Constitution, the average life expectancy was only 37, and the median age was a mere 16. All those men at the signing were wearing white wigs. They weren't old but they were trying to look old. Although it's hard to imagine, during that period of history, both men and women were inclined to exaggerate their age and even tried to appear older than they actually were, hence the white wigs. Men's clothing was cut in a way that emphasized the posture and build of the elderly: narrow and rounded shoulders, broad hips and waist, and coat backs designed to make the spine appear to be bent by the weight of many years. As for women's fashions, the dresses were designed to stress mature features. Heavy swirling skirts accentuated broad hips. Formal wear called for exposed shoulders and décolletage, features that worked to a mature woman's advantage.

Why? It was believed that long-lived men and women were the beneficiaries of divine will. There was no germ theory or scientific understanding of health and disease, so it was generally believed that if you were living into your later years, God wanted you around. As Increase Mather, an early president of Harvard College and pastor of the North Church in Boston, preached in 1716, "If a man is favored with long life . . . it is God that has lengthened his days."[1] The elderly were venerated and treated with great respect. The achievement of even modest longevity – 50 or 60 years – was admired, and the elderly came to be looked upon as advisers to their less-experienced younger fellows.

Since skills and technology evolved slowly at this time, the older you were, the more likely you had a little bit more wisdom. And let's not forget that elders owned everything. We were an agricultural-based society, and therefore social control lay in the ownership of land, which was almost always retained by elder parents or grandparents. People didn't work for "money" that could be spent as they liked. Instead they worked to complete chores, which were primarily farm-related and family based. If you hoped to one day have some acreage of your own, it would be smart to work hard and respect Grandpa.

Then, in the second half of the nineteenth century, there was a massive industrial, economic, and sociological flip, and America began its long obsession with youth. Suddenly young people could separate from their families, go to work, and live in cities. The industrial age introduced a whole new set of priorities; youthful energy and mobility came to be prized over stability, experience, and homespun wisdom. On the farm, older men and women could continue contributing to some aspect of work or family life, but in the factory, there was no sympathy for aging hands slowing down the assembly line. And since all the industrial technologies were new, the wisdom of the old offered no useful advantage over the enthusiasm, endurance, and raw strength of the young.

The status and privilege old people had enjoyed as property owners and family heads eroded in the emerging industrial era, in which they were coming to be seen as an obstacle to progress – a social burden. Bursting with energy and unencumbered by any prejudices about how to do their work, the young were most suited to the changing times. The new city-based occupations were now considered indispensable to the nation's progress, and the young workers who filled these positions were rewarded with higher pay and higher status. The jobs also allowed young men to break free from economic dependence on their elders. For the first time in history, knowledge of and commitment to the old ways of doing things could be seen as a distinct disadvantage.

This view was voiced by many prominent leaders of the time, including the highly respected physician-philosopher Dr. William Osler. In his now infamous 1905 valedictory at Johns Hopkins University,[2] Osler argued that men older than 40 had become useless cogs in modern society: "All the great advances have come from men under 40, so the history of the world shows that a very large proportion of the evils may be traced to the sexagenarians – nearly all of the great mistakes politically and socially, all of the worst poems, most of the bad pictures, a majority of the bad novels, not a few of the bad sermons and speeches. Take the sum of human achievement in action, in science, in art, in literature. Subtract the work of men above 40, and . . . we would practically be where we are today." Promoting the notion that older men and women were a drain on society, Osler repeatedly emphasized the "uselessness of men above 60 years of age, and the incalculable benefit it would be in commercial, political, and in professional life, if as a matter of course, men stopped work at this age." Modern times had begun, and by the roaring '20s, youth was worshipped along with young styles of dancing, sex, and fashion.

This "young is in, old is out" point of view got turbocharged after the end of the Depression and then the end of World War II, with the birth of the Boomers, the ensuing rise of middle-class affluence, and the emergence of modern media and marketing. Young people represented a growth sector – new people who hadn't yet decided what kind of shampoo, shoes, toothpaste, or cars they were going to prefer. Older people of the time had been brand loyal, frugal, and focused on winding down more than gearing up. In that era, it was smart for marketers of nearly everything to try to engage people between around 15 and 25 when they were forming their identities, coming into a little bit of spending money, and hadn't locked down their product and brand preferences.

People often comment to us about how hard it would be to fashion aspirational marketing geared to older men and women. After all, they tell us, they're over the hill, set in their ways, and not nearly as appealing as young people. It's worth noting that when the Boomers became teens in the 1960s, the teenage years were widely considered the most miserable stage of life. Teenagers were stuck at home, seeking identity, sexually frustrated, full of Holden Caufield-style anxiety and depression, pretty miserable overall. Then in the 1960s, in a bold move, Pepsi aligned its brand with young Boomers and "those who think young." Now teenagers were being portrayed as looking and feeling good, enjoying Pepsi with friends – all of whom appeared to be having the best time of their lives. The campaign was not limited to those who *are* young, but it got older people wanting to think and be young again. Ingenious marketing helped transform the teen years into a semi-make-believe desirable stage of life. In retrospect, reframing adolescence helped fuel the youth obsession and corresponding ageism that's with us today. Look at all the young people in the movies, look at all the young people in the ads, they look like they're having so much fun and they're so sexy and they're young. And that has stuck, even though times have changed dramatically.

Today most market research, marketing dollars, and advertising dollars are still funneled toward young people. Does this make good business sense? We don't think so. The ranks of today's retirees are growing, and perhaps more importantly, living in new ways and eager to try all sorts of new things. But ageism continues to blind organizations and prevent them from seeing the growth potential of the retiree market. And ageism takes many forms, some of which we are so accustomed to, they've become invisible.

For example, let's consider the long-popular TV show *American Idol*. This entertaining show claims to offer contestants a chance to express their talents and possibly achieve the American dream of a recording career. However, no one over 28 can apply. Why? Can't 64-year-olds sing? Can't 70-year-olds have a dream of becoming an American idol? If this kind of restriction were applied to African American or Jewish people, or short people or overweight people, it would never be tolerated. However, because ageism is so ingrained our culture, no one seems to mind.

Ageism Is Both Ignorant and Blinding

Ageism runs deep. It's in the design of products that require young, facile fingers and sharp eyesight, the length of time it takes traffic lights to change, and the auditory range on our cell phones. It's in the management systems and cultures of organizations and job markets that assume youth outperforms age (based on no evidence) and the fact that geriatrics remains the least popular specialty in medicine. One of the most glaring depictions of outright ageism can be found every day in the promoted analyses of last night's TV watching, which always emphasize not just viewership in general but viewership by what they refer to as the "sought-after youth demographic," which used to be 18–34 but is now usually 18–49. Imagine if all this coverage referred to the "sought-after Caucasian demographic," or the "sought-after overweight demographic." The core assumptions suck: Young is good and old isn't. We prefer young customers and find older ones undesirable.

Dr. Robert Butler was, without question, the leading twentieth-century pioneer and thought leader in the fields of aging, gerontology, and geriatrics. A kind and high-minded man, he was the Founding Director of the National Institutes of Aging, a deep thinker, a prolific writer, and he was Ken's dear friend and lifelong mentor. In 1976, in his Pulitzer Prize–winning book *Why Survive: Growing Old in America*, Butler introduced the phenomenon of ageism and defined it as "the discrimination, abuse, stereotyping, contempt for, and avoidance of older people." He even introduced a psychiatric disorder, "gerontophobia," which was characterized by a discomfort not only with older people, but with one's own aging process. He felt that gerontophobia, a Peter Pan-ish desire to not age, was becoming pervasive in our culture.

This kind of ageist bias is overt in some marketing campaigns and advertisements, including by companies and organizations from tech to finance that could and should be eagerly serving – and profiting from – the retiree market. A pair of 2018 campaigns received well-deserved backlash. "Don't Get Mad, Get E-Trade" ads depicted buffoonish people in their 80s having to work at jobs they were ill-suited for and make a hash of, including lifeguard and firefighter. They didn't save enough money for retirement. The campaign simultaneously mocked retirees who were struggling financially and alienated those who actually control the largest share of wealth and investable assets. Similarly, the Acronym organization's "Dear Young People, Don't Vote" campaign in 2018 was designed to

encourage – or scare – young people to vote. However, by depict-
ing older people as selfish and unconcerned about the issues of the
day – climate change, women's rights – and about the Millennials'
futures, ageism was the ugly underbelly of the campaign. There's
nothing like fomenting generational warfare!

Lori Bitter, author of *The Grandparent Economy: How Baby
Boomers Are Bridging the Generation Gap* and a leading expert on the
business of aging, pointed out another good example of bad form:
"The Tide detergent ad starts with a full house – a couple, their two
adult children, and the in-laws just moved in. The couple is fold-
ing clothes and talking about the need for one detergent that fits
the needs of everyone. The spot is trying to land a humorous point
about multigenerational living but ends with Grandpa entering in
his underwear, looking for his pants. Why make fun of him? There
are 100 other clever ways to write that spot."

Mike Hodin, PhD, CEO of the Global Coalition on Aging,
observes, "The regular depiction of an old person is a guy hunched
over with a cane. That's a classic sort of ageism – presuming that
people are going to be unhealthy. The focus is on disabilities, not
capabilities." Modern Elder Academy Founder Chip Conley points
out that "the large majority of older people see ads as patronizing
and stereotypical, and feel that advertisers only care about younger
people. The bottom line is that most advertisers, young or old, get a
big F for their efforts to understand the older population."

There are tons of bad examples. In Duracell's "Beach vs Bear,"
the beach (and long battery life) is represented by a weird-looking,
skinny old man with a metal detector. At ad's end, he is so weighed
down with oversized bling around his neck that he can't straighten
up. Trebbiano Handbags' "Seen enough old bags?" ad has four older
women in frumpy dresses and hats crammed on a couch drinking
tea. Many people recall an original in this sad genre, Wendy's 1984
"Where's the Beef?" campaign with addled old women examining
a competitor's burger and shouting like idiots the cranky question,
"Where's the beef?"

Such ads may be memorable in their ridiculousness, but how
do they get released? Their creators must think they're funny. But
what's funny about insensitivity, caricature, and ridicule? And how
smart is it to alienate a large and growing segment of the market?

Paul Irving, JD, author of *The Upside of Aging* and chairman of the Milken Institute Center for the Future of Aging, makes the case forcefully: "Take the E-Trade ad with the clownish, embarrassing images of older people. Some may think it's cute and harmless to make fun of older adults, to make light of their age and experience. I think that if you did that same ad with stereotyped images of women, people of color, or LGBTQ individuals, there would be outrage, and rightly so."

Most ageism is less explicit and more the product of ignorance and inexperience than bias and prejudice. It may be less mean spirited, but it's still off-putting to mature customers and bad for business. In much of modern marketing, far too often, older people are conspicuous in their absence from ads and marketing campaigns. It's ageism by omission. While people over 50 represent 56% of consumer spending, why are they only 20% of the people depicted in media and commercials? And they don't like that at all, because the message is clear: "This brand doesn't really value me."

For example, the Amazon Echo device and Alexa voice response technology offer a wide variety of functions for a safe, convenient, and enjoyable home, functions that matter to people of all ages. Last year in advance of flying to Seattle to give a keynote speech on the "Age Wave," Ken spent some time on the Alexa website watching all the wonderful videos about innovative ways that people could use this remarkable new technology to make their lives better. However, considering how smart the folks at Amazon are, he was stunned to discover that while there were dozens of compelling videos, everyone was young and there were no retirees to be found. The technology was targeted at younger and presumably more tech-adept consumers. Their disregard for older men and women was both blatant and costly, and Ken told the Amazon executives that in no uncertain terms. Similarly, driver-assist services and safety technologies have become standard fare in passenger vehicles. These, too, can be especially useful for older drivers (and the average new car buyer is 56). But how many ads do we see featuring older drivers? Hardly any.

When organizations don't take active interest in studying and understanding the market, don't have practice and experience doing so, the default is to depict older people with bland or negative stereotypes and outdated narratives about what it means to be older. When older people are in ads, they're seldom portrayed authentically. This lack of attunement with today's and tomorrow's retirement dreams translates into an absence of sensitivity, respect, and imagination. Most organizations remain willfully ignorant about retirees – the most massive growth market hiding in plain sight.

Ageism Blocks Authenticity

When businesses do try to target the older audience, the messages are often inauthentic, unrealistic, and out of touch. Experienced and discerning older consumers see the disconnect and it turns them off. People want to have their experience portrayed authentically, and they want to be engaged by real people, not just fantastic or horrific examples. This lack of authentic engagement is another outcome of the bias and ignorance about the retiree market that remains prevalent. Many of the experts we've consulted weighed in on this problem.

Lori Bitter told us, "The one thing I hear all the time from older people is they don't see themselves in anything that's being advertised on television. They don't see themselves in the world of marketing anymore. And older women are harder to market to because they have a kind of no-bullshit meter, a filter that says, 'Don't try to tell me who I am or what I should be. Show me people who are like me, and I'll decide whether it resonates.'"

Richard Eisenberg, Managing Editor of *Next Avenue*, couldn't agree more: "I'd like to see more advertising and marketing that shows how people are actually spending their days in retirement. It can be upbeat or not upbeat, but I'd like to see the reality of how people are actually living in their late sixties, seventies, or eighties." Dr. Charlotte Yeh, Chief Medical Officer of AARP Services, Inc., points out that businesses have to keep up with their customers, but most fail to do so: "An *Allure Magazine*/AARP survey found that four in five people 55 and older say that their favorite retail brand no longer understands them or what they need, and seven in ten women said their loyalty to a brand can change and they're much more likely to purchase when ads feature 'somebody like me.'"

As finances expert and author of *Never Too Old to Get Rich: The Entrepreneur's Guide to Starting a Business Mid-Life* Kerry Hannon observes, "Old people are portrayed at two extremes. They're vulnerable. They're frail. They fell down, and they can't get up. Or they're 70, attractive and fit, and still going strong with all those dollars to spend on a fancy new car." Marc Freedman, author of *How to Live Forever: The Enduring Power of Connecting the Generations* and founder and CEO of Encore.org, totally agrees, "You see one after another of these ads targeting older people, and they all have the same clichéd ideas about what a good life looks like. It's like a video stream of stock photos, with people who feel like cardboard characters. People have opened a vineyard, or a bed-and-breakfast, a kind of reinvention story that seems effortless, and the clouds part, and the birds sing."

Fernando Torres-Gil, PhD, a leading spokesperson on aging and public policy and the first Assistant Secretary for Aging in the Department of Health and Human Services, told us: "I get really tired of commercials that portray all of us as growing old in the absolute best circumstances. The worst culprits are the pharmaceutical industry, with ads promoting drugs that are going to cost a small fortune and showing these couples and older adults in the absolute perfect nirvana. 'Buy our drugs, and life will be happily ever after.' The bottom line is that such stereotypes convey the wrong impression of what it means to be an older adult. It would certainly be nice if we could have the variety of portraits of the ways that we're all going to grow old with different kinds of conditions, but of course do it in a tasteful way."

Ageism is often in combination with other forms of bias and discrimination, compounding the market damage. An extreme example is Virgin America's "Fool around with a younger, hotter airline" billboards. In addition to exploiting images of young women, the ads basically proclaim that "being old is bad." A petition to end the campaign declared, "It's time for Virgin America to find a way to sell plane tickets that doesn't exploit and disparage 50% of their target market." If you count those offended by the ageist stance, it's a lot more than 50% who stand to be offended.

The experts we have spoken with also offered unsettling perspectives and advice on what happens when ageism coincides with other forms of discrimination. Karyne Jones, CEO of the National Caucus and Center on Black Aging, reflected, "There aren't many companies reaching out and marketing to the older black community. Sure, there are black people in commercials. But with older black women, they're going to a pharmacy for a flu shot. Or they're depicted in caregiving situations, which is a positive light but still stereotyped. They're not driving a great car or exercising or shopping at the best stores. Maybe a young woman of color is shown in that light, but not older women."

Fernando Torres-Gil, who himself was stricken with polio as a child, speaks for people with disabilities: "Advertising has traditionally assumed that everyone was young and beautiful and physically healthy and mobile. Now you are seeing, for example, some portraits of individuals in wheelchairs, which is good as acknowledgment that not all of us are similarly physically able. But what you're also seeing is that they make the individuals look as young, as vibrant, and as appealing as possible, and they're nearly all white. It's still stereotyping."

Michael Adams, JD, CEO of SAGE, the oldest and largest organization in the country dedicated to improving the lives of LGBTQ older adults, describes explicit and tacit ageism affecting his community: "There's a level of ageism in the gay male community that is probably greater than in older communities in general. Some of that probably has to do with the biased historical notion that gay men are sissies. The response for some has been a kind of hyper-virility – working out, having great bodies, and showing them off. Now that companies are marketing to the community, ageism gets reinforced because the images that they tend to show are very oriented toward young people, much less likely to show older folks. As a result, older LGBTQ people don't see themselves and their interests being represented in advertising and marketing. However, marketing campaigns that are specifically geared toward this community tend to be really well received. LGBTQ customers are highly loyal to companies that demonstrate a commitment to the community."

Percil Stanford, PhD, renowned gerontologist, author, professor, and former Chief of Diversity and Inclusion at AARP, offers a summary recommendation: "Marketing teams need to have more people of color, more people of different ages and backgrounds. Take the time to understand what it is to walk in their shoes, and thus how to get people in those shoes interested in your products and services."

Advertising: Hardly Any Older People in the Room

What's behind the ageism in advertising and marketing campaigns? Behind the lack of interest in the older market? Behind the lack of imagination about life in retirement? Behind the reliance on bad jokes and tired stereotypes? Behind the lack of authenticity? We think there's a generation gap – maybe intentional, maybe not. However, the advertising industry is disproportionately populated by young people, with the average age of agency employees at 34.[3] Not surprisingly, they tend to be transfixed by their own age cohort and stage of life, by what's new and modern and interesting in their – and their friends' – eyes. Because they have never been older themselves, they often lack perspective and experience in knowing what to make of older customers. And their default for thinking about older people may be their grandparents, who grew older with yesterday's fashions and yesterday's mindset about who you could be in your sixties, seventies, and beyond. Unfortunately, in this image-shaping industry, ageism is rampant.

So life in retirement today is not on the radar screen, and people with older experience and perspective are not in the room. Those in the room may assume, often mistakenly, that appealing to older customers will turn off younger ones. In short, advertising and marketing is among the most youth-obsessed industries, chasing the young market even when that's not where the money is.

Mike Hodin, who before he created the Global Coalition on Aging was global head of communications for Pfizer, knows what he's talking about: "There's ignorance leading to confusion over what it means to be getting older. Marketers are making assumptions about how older people think, behave, what they want. And the confusion is exacerbated by the fact that those who are making the assumptions are probably in their thirties. I have to assume that none of these companies are doing market research on older consumers the way they do on Millennials. If you're marketing to women, you might have a couple women on the marketing team. If you're marketing to older people, put a 70-year-old on your marketing team, not just for diversity but because it's going to help you make money. This isn't charity, it's smart business."

In 2019, AARP conducted a study of the portrayal in online media images of people age 50 and up, who represent 46% of the adult population but only 15% of the people pictured. They found that older adults are seven times as likely to be portrayed negatively as younger ones, and the portrayals are heavily stereotyped. Everyone seems to have gray hair and be alone. People are very seldom pictured at work, using technology, or as well-off. As a counterforce and example to the media industry, AARP partnered with Getty Images to publish a collection of 1,400 images that challenge the stereotypes of aging. The images portray a variety of active lifestyles and depict more authentically how people 50+ live and age.[4]

Leading the Way

Some companies have begun to take large steps toward more deeply understanding the hopes, needs, and challenges of retirees and specifically aging Boomers. Perhaps the most forward-thinking is Bank of America Merrill Lynch, with whom Age Wave has partnered on numerous cutting-edge studies. When we recently asked Merrill Lynch Wealth Management's President Andy Sieg why they were so interested in this phenomenon, he reflected:

There's no trend that's reshaping the investment landscape or the broad financial services landscape or all of our lives more so than aging and longevity. When you think about the clients that we serve, which are more than 60 million Americans ranging from families just starting out, to people in the prime of their career, to those who are later in life and thinking about second acts and the like, every client segment is seeing their life changed by longevity. In all likelihood, they will need to be providing income streams for a later life that's going to be much longer than they anticipated. We see many clients who are decades away from retirement, but they are experiencing issues of later life in a very palpable way because they find themselves as caregivers today for their parents or their in-laws or others. If we want to really meet their needs, everyone on our team must have a deep understanding and respect for the future of retirement and how we can best help individuals and their families live their best lives.

We probed further and asked Sieg how the orientation of the firm has shifted. He explained, "Our research has taught us that these changes are affecting a lot more than clients' balance sheets. What we've learned has caused us to bring a much broader lens to the way we think about serving clients. By that, I mean the business of Merrill today as part of Bank of America goes well beyond simple asset allocation. We need to be attentive to all the facets of our client's and their family's life."

We then asked, "Given your deep exploration of these issues, what advice would you give to companies or marketers or entrepreneurs who want to try to pursue the new generation of retirees?" He replied:

> Commit yourself to cross training. I think almost everyone who is out there is a specialist in a fairly narrow slice of what this new world of longevity is all about, and very few have traversed the whole landscape – what you call "lifescape" – in order both to understand breakthrough opportunities for their businesses and how to better deliver the services that they're offering today. I've been struck that the experts we've talked with in different disciplines have been relatively slow to connect with people in other categories of business, products, and services on these issues. Similarly, many academics would do well to try to broaden their perspective on later life, and I think there's an opportunity for innovative business leaders and academic institutions to help make that holistic perspective more front and center.

The New Metric of Maturity

With the rising of the age wave, this is all about to change. Betty Friedan wrote *The Feminine Mystique* in 1963, and 30 years later a best-selling book called *The Fountain of Age*. Ken was a friend and colleague, and he recounts some of what he learned from her:

> Betty and I gave a lot of presentations together, and for a while I became her sidekick. One morning, before we gave a talk about older women for the senior executives of CBS television, we were having breakfast. I asked what she was thinking about when she wrote *The Feminine Mystique*. She said, "I felt at the time that women had historically been measured by the metric of men, how they could please a man or how they can measure up to a man. I felt the time had come that women be not measured by the metric of men anymore, ever again, that they be measured by their own metric, who they are, what their potential was, what they could make of their lives."
>
> I then asked her what she was thinking about when she wrote *The Fountain of Age*. She said that we had come to a place in history where we measure everybody by the metric of youth and, guess what, when you're 50 or 60 or 70, you're not going to feel very good about yourself because you're not going to look as good as you did when you were young. You're not going to be as quick, or your body's not going to be the same. Maybe it's time we began to measure the world by the metric of age and maturity: How wise are you? How thoughtful are you? How experienced are you?

It's time to put an end to the bias, prejudice, and ignorance of ageism and reframe the meaning, importance, and value of maturity.

3

Reframing Aging

There's a New Story to Tell

WE ARE IN A NEW ERA of aging, and it's time to tell a new story. People are taking longer to grow "old" and taking even longer to think of themselves as "old." Boomer retirees are more active than previous generations and more interested in being activated by new experiences. Advanced age may bring physical decline and chronic health conditions, but that's not the main storyline of retirement. Through most of the retirement journey, people are happier, more content, and having more fun than at any time in their lives. With age comes perspective, self-knowledge, emotional intelligence, more enjoyment of freedom and of family and friends. People have more awareness of the ticking of the clock, which imparts an urgency to life, but also to give back, teach, and learn more. People reinvent. Many become stronger and grander versions of themselves.

Aspiration, Not Desperation

The dominant arc through most people's retirement years is now an ascent, not a descent. Chip Conley, author of *Wisdom@Work: The*

Making of a Modern Elder and founder of the Modern Elder Academy, explains the "U-curve" phenomenon: "Older people have more hope and excitement for the future than they do for the past, which is a big surprise to many. Businesses and advertisers need to recognize and tap into the 'U-curve of happiness.' Social science studies show that, pretty much across all cultures, people's level of happiness diminishes starting about age 25. Around 50, they may hit bottom, but then happiness goes up. With each passing decade, you feel better and more content about life. So new research is showing that today, people in their seventies are happier than people in their fifties."

Dr. Charlotte Yeh, Chief Medical Officer of AARP Services, Inc., makes an important point: "We need to reframe aging in both our language and our imagery. The City of Boston renamed its 'Commission on Affairs of the Elderly' to the 'Age Strong Commission.' Too many people believe that at 64 you are a productive, contributing member of society. And then at 65 you're supposed to retire, go on Social Security and Medicare, and overnight you become irrelevant and become dependent. What we really need to say is that at 65 keep it moving. I like to say it's not aging in place. It's thriving in motion."

The Age Strong Commission's public awareness campaign features eight Bostonians who "disrupt the negative messaging about aging by being themselves." Each is profiled to refute a specific ageist stereotype – inactive, cranky, frail, frumpy, childish, helpless, senile, over the hill. For example, Vinny, 83, has the rebuttal to frail: "I'm a longtime boxer, and I can still pack a punch. I hit the heavy bag at the gym and swim laps every day. I am a lot of things, and frail isn't one of them." Irene, 103, has the rebuttal to senile: "You think I'm out of touch? Whatevah! I use a smartphone, paint every day, play Sudoku on my tablet, and spend time with my boyfriend. I am a lot of things, and senile isn't one of them."

The End of "Seniors" and the Rise of "Modern Elders"

Maggie Kuhn was a woman far ahead of her time. She was both a visionary and a role model for young and old, attesting to our potential for strength, worth, and beauty in life's later years. She was also

Ken's dear friend and mentor. Way back in 1970, she co-founded the Gray Panthers after long, productive stints on the staffs of the YWCA and the national office of the United Presbyterian Church. Finding herself forcibly retired, bereft of her accustomed role and a sense of meaningful involvement, she transformed into an outspoken and influential activist. Banding together with a small group of like-minded friends, she launched the Gray Panthers, which in a decade became a coalition of more than 10,000 people of all ages who were committed to an activist approach to social change around aging. She and her fellow Gray Panthers (Ken was an active member back in that era) took a stand against any people and groups who demonstrated ageism, especially among those organizations that are supposed to serve the elderly.

Nicknamed "America's wrinkled radical" in her seventies, she unflinchingly challenged the "powers that be," from the U.S. Senate to the American Medical Association to the National Gerontological Society, and countless other groups who displayed varying forms of ageism and age-related prejudice. She was slight (she couldn't have weighed more than 95 pounds) and a bit frail with hands gnarled from arthritis – yet when she went after anything, whether it be a topic or a person, she was relentless. She could be found espousing her views about the liberation of aging on everything from *The Evening News* to *Saturday Night Live* until she passed away at the ripe age of 89 in 1995. Maggie wrote several books, *Get Out of There and Do Something About Injustice, Maggie Kuhn on Aging,* and *No Stone Unturned,* as well as numerous monographs on various aspects of aging, health care, work, older women, and religion.

One night before a big health care conference in Berkeley, California, in which Ken and Maggie were speakers, they got to talking over dinner about words and language and how they didn't always make the point in the way they should. "For example," Maggie said over dessert, "we need a better word or phrase to describe long-term care and how we should be caring for our elders with greater respect and honor." Maggie hated the word "seniors," and she also disliked being referred to as "elderly," though she liked the tone and dignity of being thought of as an "elder." "So," she challenged Ken, "before you pick me up tomorrow morning to drive me to the conference, make up a new, better word to replace long-term care or geriatric care."

Ken was up all night thinking about this and playing with all sorts of words, phrases, and sentences. When Maggie got in his car the next morning, he said, "How about 'eldercare'?" She smiled and told him she liked it a lot, as did he. It stuck.

Maggie Kuhn's gravitas and preference notwithstanding, for the past four to five decades, "senior" has been the widespread term for older adults. But it is losing popularity. Although it carries some positive connotations around knowledge and experience, it is usually paired with "citizen," especially by government and social service agencies, where the emphasis has traditionally been on decline and disability. Many, like Maggie Kuhn, now find "senior citizen" to be patronizing and ready to be "retired."

Meanwhile, "elder" has very positive meaning in religious organizations and many cultures around the world. Ken was in Kenya recently where older Masai men and women are respectfully referred to as "elders," and younger Masai are referred to as "junior elders." Chip Conley embraces the idea of "modern elder," which we like, too. For many people, it's okay to be an "elder," but they don't want to be described as "elderly." Another contender, the word "mature" has positive meaning but can seem euphemistic or even evasive.

The most generally acceptable terms today seem to be "older adult" and "older person," and simply saying "older" and "younger" are useful to distinguish age cohorts. All the candidate terms have their advocates and their foes. In this book, we go with the flow and use *older*, *mature*, *senior*, or *elder* as the context suggests.

It Isn't About a Number

Age has long been a convenient if simplistic way to characterize citizens and customers. And it's still a trigger, as anyone who has reached the Medicare eligibility age of 65 and felt the onslaught of insurance industry promotions can testify. But today, age says less and less about the individual. If we gathered a group of 65-year-olds, their circumstances and experiences would be all over the map. One could be newly married, another recently widowed. One might be going back to college, another is starting an encore career as a teacher. One is happily empty nesting, another is moving in with their grandkids. One is scraping to get by, another is a multi-millionaire and starting a foundation.

Most retirees simply don't want to be characterized by their age. Research has consistently shown that they typically view themselves as feeling a decade or more younger than their chronological age. So making assumptions based on their age is off-putting, and sometimes even insulting. We realize that this is a far cry from the Colonial era when people lied about their age by adding years. Most people today would either rather be a few years younger than what they are – or not be tied to any specific age at all. However, we are witnessing a growing number of self-confident Boomers who are proud of their age. Karyne Jones, CEO of the National Caucus and Center on Black Aging, says, "I own my age. I have never gone for this '70 is the new 50' stuff because it says that you shouldn't be proud of where you are in your lifespan."

As we mentioned in Chapter 2, we have learned that older men and women often feel that youth-oriented marketers just don't get them. So much of the marketing and media they encounter seems disrespectful or just plain ignorant. We've repeatedly heard that they are not looking for sympathy, but empathy: they want the people designing products, services, programs, and even communications to learn how to see and feel the world from the modern elders' perspectives. This can sometimes be tricky, because young people may have limited experience with older adults, and they will often generalize based on their cool grandma or their cranky old uncle. Hence the need for organizations to go beyond their comfort zones and really listen to what the new generation of retirees is saying about their hopes, fears, and dreams.

New Freedom, Less Worry, More Fun

Our research confirms that people are happier, more content, having more fun, and feeling a greater overall sense of well-being after the age of 65 than at any stage of their lives. Many retirees enter what we've named the "freedom zone." Nearly all retirees (92%) say they enjoy the freedom and flexibility of a less structured life in retirement.[1] They tell us that they have *freedom from* old constraints, starting with most of the daily pressures of juggling work and family responsibilities. And they have more *freedom to* do what they want and on their own terms – sleep in or get up and exercise, take a drive or read a book, volunteer or learn a skill, hang out with the grandchildren or fall in love.

More freedom translates into more opportunity to have fun. Popular perception (and the media) may tend to associate fun with the carefree days of youth. Our own surveys show that U-curve, originally researched by Dr. Laura Carstensen at the Stanford Center on Longevity. The experience of fun dips in mid-life and then rises to peak in retirement (Figure 3.1).

What makes life more fun? Less stress from work. More free time, including for family. Greater freedom to do what you enjoy, rather than what others expect of you. And growing self-knowledge and awareness of what you truly enjoy doing (Figure 3.2). Lori Bitter, author of *The Grandparent Economy*, told us, "We become more of ourselves as we get older. We just let stuff that seems frivolous and not really authentic to who we are fall away. I think that's true of friendships, and true of activities that we may have taken part in but that no longer really interest us or meet our needs."

It's not just fun that is on the rise. With today's longevity and new post-career lifestyle options, overall emotional well-being peaks in the retirement years, where more people report being happy, confident, content, and relaxed. And contrary to ageist

Figure 3.1   How Much Fun Are You Having at This Stage of Life? (Scale 1–10)

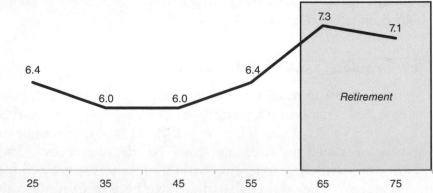

Source: Age Wave / Merrill Lynch, *Leisure in Retirement: Beyond the Bucket List*

Figure 3.2 Why Is Retirement *More* Fun?

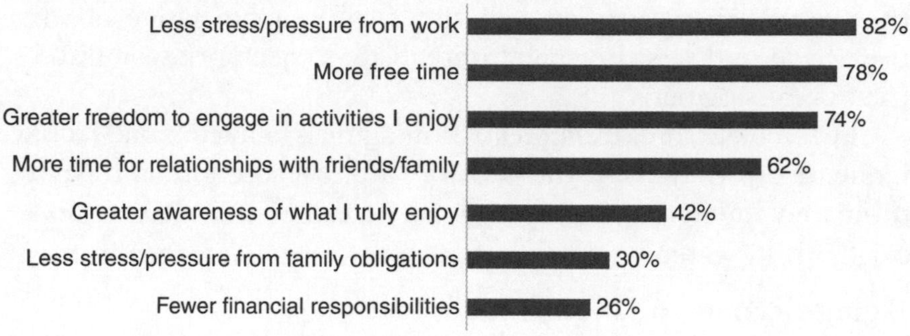

Less stress/pressure from work 82%
More free time 78%
Greater freedom to engage in activities I enjoy 74%
More time for relationships with friends/family 62%
Greater awareness of what I truly enjoy 42%
Less stress/pressure from family obligations 30%
Fewer financial responsibilities 26%

Source: Age Wave / Merrill Lynch, *Leisure in Retirement: Beyond the Bucket List*

stereotypes, they are the least likely to report being worn out, anxious, lonely, or bored (Figure 3.3). Put those trends together, and people between the ages of about 60 and 75 reach the pinnacle of the freedom zone, where they report high levels and great balance of free time, fun, and emotional well-being. Life in retirement is theirs to enjoy.

A note of caution is warranted here. Not all older people are healthy, happy, or having fun. Many are miserable, some of whom have been miserable their whole lives. Yet, in study after study, the majority – not all, but most – of retirees are turning out to be

Figure 3.3 The Retirement Freedom Zone

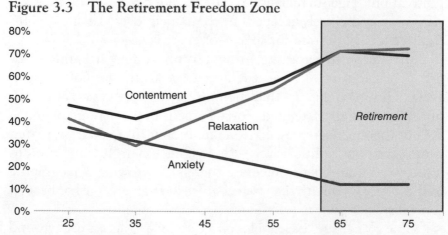

80%
70%
60%
50%
40%
30%
20%
10%
0%
Contentment
Relaxation
Anxiety
Retirement
25
35
45
55
65
75

Source: Age Wave / Merrill Lynch, *Leisure in Retirement: Beyond the Bucket List*

living their best years. Not only are they enjoying themselves, but they've circled the sun enough times to be appreciative of what they have and less driven by unrealistic expectations or FOMO (fear of missing out).

Let's look at three examples of how aging is being reframed today. Collectively, they point the way forward, because reframing aging ultimately involves what we say, how we think, and what we do.

Aging Becomes a "Non-Issue"

Readers of the May 2019 issue of *British Vogue* got a bonus: an 80-page supplement in which all of the models, designers, photographers, and make-up artists were over 50. The cover model and lead interview was a fit and beautiful 81-year-old Jane Fonda. Featured inside were 74-year-old Helen Mirren, 64-year-old Isabelle Adjani, and 60-year-old make-up artist Val Garland. They called the publication "The Non-Issue."

Sponsored by L'Oréal Paris and created by McCann London and McCann Paris, the supplement drew widespread attention to the issue of aging and seized the chance to declare that it should be a non-issue. A companion video opens with the declaration: "Women over 50 remain invisible in the fashion and beauty industries. We at L'Oréal Paris believe that age is a non-issue." Charlotte Franceries, beauty team president at McCann Paris, explains the motivation: "Ageism remains an often-overlooked form of discrimination, unconsciously accepted by so many in everyday life. . . . It's time we all awoke from the inertia of everyday ageism."

In addition to surprising, enlightening, and entertaining readers, "The Non-Issue" issue sent a message to the fashion, beauty, and publishing industries that their unvarying celebration of youthful beauty was short-sighted. Forty percent of women are over age 50, but their media representation rate is only 15%.[2] Actress, writer, fitness guru, and political activist Jane Fonda said: "It's important to understand that older women are the fastest growing demographic in the whole world. It's time to recognize our value." Age has beauty, too, often alongside extraordinary accomplishment.

"The Non-Issue" issue included a QR code to access background information and video on how the publication came together.

On newsstands it actually outsold September, traditionally the best-selling month, and it drew over 40,000 new readers to *British Vogue*.

A catalyst behind "The Non-Issue" was McCann Worldgroup's 2017 global study, "The Truth About Age." It found that, in all regions of the world, people of all ages were defying the traditional expectations associated with their lifestages – in other words, they're not acting their age. Two-thirds of people in their seventies believe that "you're never too old to casually date." The age group that fears death least is in their seventies; those who fear it most are in their twenties.

Nadia Tuma-Weldon is a global director of McCann Worldgroup Truth Central, where she digs deep to unearth people's underlying beliefs behind today's major trends, and she led the "Truth about Age" study. We called her to better understand what she had learned. "In the aging study," she told us, "we found that age is no longer a reliable predictor of just about anything. Age doesn't predict your style, health, aspirations, how you date, or how you behave." She sees opportunities for brands to speak to retirees in ways that don't make them feel old. After all, "You only feel as old as the culture around you."

Others already frame aging in consistently positive ways. Targeted media like *AARP Magazine* and other publications have been doing so effectively for years. But general audience publications tend to be behind the curve. Leaders at McCann, L'Oréal, and *Vogue* would no doubt agree that "The Non-Issue" was only a step. The fashion, beauty, advertising, and media industries are among those most in need of lessons on reframing aging.

Modern Elders Are Reinventing, Not Retiring

In addition to being a visionary spokesperson for modern elderhood, Chip Conley is walking the walk and talking the talk in his own life. In his late fifties, he has already had multiple careers and evolving roles as leader, mentor, and lifelong learner. At age 26, after receiving his undergraduate and master's degrees in business from Stanford, he founded the boutique hotel and restaurant company Joie de Vivre Hospitality. After running and growing the company for over two decades, he successfully sold it in 2010. Then, after this "retirement" in 2013, he was recruited by the co-founders of Airbnb as Head of Global Hospitality and Strategy, where he helped grow the brand dramatically.

His experience there, where he was twice the age of the average employee, led him to coin the term "modern elder" to describe his role: "someone who marries wisdom and experience with curiosity, a beginner's mind, and a willingness to learn from those younger." His book *Wisdom@Work* recounts how he learned to "intern publicly and mentor privately," becoming a modern elder, "both student and sage." More recently, he believes that we would all do well to become what he calls "menterns," reflecting the dual roles of teacher and student.

In 2018, Chip married his interests in hospitality and personal reinvention and founded the Modern Elder Academy (MEA) in Baja California Sur, with the mission to help people navigate midlife and prepare for their roles as modern elders. Inspired by lessons learned from serving on the boards of both Burning Man and Esalen Institute, Conley's new academy describes itself as:

> The world's first midlife wisdom school. Our unique curriculum includes classroom learning as well as bread baking and breaking, impromptu dance parties, cultural experiences, morning meditations, and surreal sunsets. The experience supports our attendees ("compadres," whose average age is 52) as they navigate this midlife journey and reframe a lifetime of experience. They receive a Certificate in Mindset Management, and emerge feeling more relevant, resilient, adaptable, and empowered to create what's next.

Modern Elder Academy is an educational experience in a luxury resort. Situated on Pacific Ocean beachfront, the amenities include a pool, a massage studio, and a silent contemplation park on a preserved dune. The curriculum is unique, with workshops titled "The Making of a Modern Elder," "Enhancing Your Emotional Aliveness," and "Crafting Your Encore Career." The Modern Elder Academy library has sections on "What can death teach me about life?" and "What are the unexpected pleasures of aging?"

Journalist Tina Seelig wrote about taking a Modern Elder Academy course for *Medium*: "We carefully considered what 'business' each of us are in. . . . We drilled down to explore what we really want to contribute to the world. It was fascinating to see people light up when they realized what they really wanted to contribute. Essentially, it felt as though we were all slowly moving into our hearts from our heads."[3]

Conley explains the story that Modern Elder Academy helps people retell: "The social narrative is basically that midlife is a crisis and after a crisis you have decrepitude. But you actually are much happier in your 60s and 70s, so why aren't we preparing for that?"[4] On Conley's drawing board are small, intergenerational communities around the world. "Instead of creating a seniors' community with a golf course, we'd be creating 12 acres with a Wisdom Center in the middle, with workshops and programs to develop wisdom at any age," says Conley.[5]

A growing number of major universities – Harvard, Stanford, University of Minnesota, University of Texas, Notre Dame – have programs for mid-to-late-career professionals who want to reset. We wonder why every educational institution isn't in the business not only of encouraging retirees and other elders to take or audit regular courses, but also of offering courses that help them navigate and even reinvent their careers and lives.

Why are these needed? When our children near the end of their high school years, there's a great deal of support and activity available to help them consider how to get into and make the most of college. There are college representatives who visit high schools to talk about their programs and communities. Parents take the kids on tours to get a feel for the kind of facilities, programs, and culture each school offers. Websites and social media connect the kids with candidate schools and their current students to get a flavor of life at each college. All of this to prepare for a four- or five-year segment of life.

Yet when it comes to retirement, which for most people is a multi-decade adventure, there's almost nothing by way of onramps, orientation programs, or tryouts. We are sure that this will change in the years ahead, as life coaches, retirement advisors, travel guides, and even summer camps begin to cater to the retiree-to-be.

The Power of Universal Design

It began with a peeler and a problem: Why aren't kitchen utensils easier for people with arthritis, who were generally older, to use?

After four decades in the kitchenware business and selling the company he founded, Sam Farber retired in 1988 at age 66. Kitchenware was in his blood – an uncle had founded Farberware in 1900. Shortly after retiring, Sam and his wife, Betsey, rented a home in Provence, France, for an extended vacation. Betsey had developed mild arthritis and the peeler and kitchen tools in the rented home were difficult for her to use. Sam saw a need and an opportunity to create kitchen tools to help people with reduced dexterity and be more comfortable for everyone.

He started experimenting using modeling clay to try to devise more comfortable tool handles. Then he joined forces with Davin Stowell, founder of Smart Design, a New York industrial design firm. They researched a variety of designs and held workshops and focus groups to understand the difficulties of older people and those with arthritis. Then they developed alternatives and tested them with a wide range of users – people of different ages with different hand types and sizes, different hand problems and no hand problems, and different degrees of manual strength and dexterity. They consulted chefs and ergonomics experts.

They also paid a lot of attention to the appearance of the peeler and other tools. They wanted the products to be useful and attractive to the mainstream market, not just those who needed help. They were committed to "universal design" – producing things that were easier to use for as many people as possible, in other words, "designing products for young and old, male and female, lefties and righties and many with special needs."[6]

The OXO product line of 15 "Good Grips" kitchen tools was launched at the 1990 San Francisco Gourmet Products Show. At $6, the swivel peeler retailed for three times the average barebones peeler. But the larger, easy-to-hold handle and angle of approach made the peeler an instant sensation. The next year, OXO had $3 million in sales and by 2000 it was $60 million. The company spent little on advertising because the products were so often featured in the media for their quality and design.[7]

Today the company makes over 1,000 products under a variety of brands, having covered the range of kitchen tools and expanding into hardware, gardening tools, office supplies, and products for young families – the OXO Tot collection. The most popular product is the salad spinner, operated by pressing down on the large, black button (rather than gripping and turning handles).

Sam Farber sold OXO to General Housewares in 1992 for $6.2 million (today it is part of Helen of Troy Limited) and re-retired, but he had started a revolution. OXO has become an iconic international brand, winning more than 100 design awards, and the company continues to maintain its position as a market leader with a commitment to universal design. It's worth noting that even the name OXO reflects the commitment to universal design. It can be flipped and read in any direction – horizontal, vertical, upside down, or backwards.

Many of the conveniences that we all take for granted are instances of universal design: automatic doors and electric toothbrushes, audio books and noise-canceling headphones, and more recently Toto "Washlet" automatic toilets and Nike FlyEase shoes without laces. These products that are convenient and useful for older consumers are convenient and useful for *everyone*. Product makers can reframe their attitude toward aging by designing products that appeal to and serve broader markets. Even in an age of customization, personalization, and product variety, the baseline product or platform can follow the principles of universal design.

Back in the 1980s, Ken and Maggie Kuhn were asked to speak at a Western Gerontological Society annual conference about universal design. They decided to focus on common items in need of improvement: doorknobs. The two troublemakers talked about how building designers weren't being very kind to older men and women by having traditional doorknobs in all their buildings, whether they be private homes or public buildings like hospitals and libraries. Structurally, doorknobs are hard to grasp, difficult to turn, and can be challenging to operate if you have arthritis in your hands, as many older people do. Maggie and Ken also argued that doorknobs don't work that well for a young mom with a baby in her arms or someone carrying bags of groceries. They proposed that all doorknobs be replaced by door levers. The people in the room laughed at their audacity, but many left that session and wrote and talked about the need for more universal design. Within a decade, knobs in public buildings were replaced by door levers everywhere, and levers were the default for new construction and renovation.

Currently, only 2% of all the housing stock in America is "aging-friendly." There's still much work to be done.

The New Story Can Be Fun to Tell

Too many portrayals treat aging as a serious condition, to be approached cautiously and somberly. In fact, older consumers have the experience to recognize how they're portrayed and the self-knowledge to poke fun at themselves. Retirees are having fun, and marketers would do well to join in the fun. We're fond of the role reversal in BMO Harris Bank's "New Wallet" advertisement developed by Young & Rubicam Group. A teen presents his grandmother a birthday gift. Her response: "A wallet! Um, what's this for?" She then demos for the grandson how she uses the bank's smartphone app to make purchases with cash or credit cards, transfer money, and so on. The voiceover defines the "BMO Effect" – "the feeling you get when your phone becomes your wallet."

Portrayals can be funny without caricature. The popular and award-winning Netflix sitcom *The Kominsky Method* features two older guys, played by Michael Douglas and Alan Arkin. There's lots going on in their lives – one recently widowed, the other with a new girlfriend and prostate problems, both dealing with adult children – but there's comedy at every turn. Likewise, *Grace and Frankie* is a refreshing spin on *Golden Girls*, with two older women living together after their husbands left the women for each other. These shows, by the way, are hits with people of all ages.

Dr. Bill Thomas is one of the world's most impassioned and knowledgeable leaders in the field of aging. A geriatrician by training, he was recognized by *The Wall Street Journal* as one of a dozen innovators changing the future of retirement in America.[8] In 2007, he and journalist Kavan Peterson co-founded ChangingAging.org, a live/digital platform designed to address the endemic ageism within American culture. In 2014 they collaborated to create and star in the ChangingAging Tour, live theatrical performances since held in over 130 cities across North America. How to make a program about aging fun? In the first tour, Thomas performed on stilts: "I wanted to demonstrate that if Elders kept growing on the outside like they do on the inside, they would be 12 feet tall and tower over all of us. I wanted to challenge the perception that because our bodies don't continue growing, the person doesn't continue growing." Audiences may expect a doctor in a lab coat giving a presentation. "I show up with a guitar, a faculty of musicians and performers, a theater set with costumes, music, art, mythology, storytelling, and neuroscience all mixed up. It's kind of like a TED Talk on steroids."[9]

True to its commitment to enable the athlete in everyone, Nike takes aspirational to the extreme – and generally we like what they've done. Decades ago, they broke through the age barrier with a fun and funny commercial that featured the 80-year-old retiree, marathoner, and former hod carrier Walt Stack. As we watch him engaged in his daily ritual of running across the Golden Gate Bridge, his voice overlay tells us, "I run 17 miles every morning." Then as the camera zooms in to capture his mischievous grin he says, "People ask me how I keep my teeth from chattering in the wintertime. . . . I leave them in my locker." Then the NIKE swoosh appears with the tagline "Just Do It."

One of Nike's more recent "Unlimited" campaign ads portrays Sister Madonna Buder, aka, "The Iron Nun." At age 82, she became the oldest person to ever finish an Ironman triathlon competition. Buder began training at 47, completed her first Ironman at 55, and now at 89 has completed 389 triathlons, including 45 Ironmans. The ad focuses on her working out and then right in the middle of a race. It closes with the narrator speculating whether the Ironman is too much for her. Her response, "The first 45 didn't kill me." Viewers of the ad don't need to aspire to become triathletes to gain inspiration from Sister Buder. They can aspire to be more active and be better versions of themselves.

"You carry your attitude with you," Sister Buder says in an interview. "You either achieve or you self-destruct. If you think positively, you can even turn a negative into a positive." In an article she wrote at age 88 called "What running taught the 'Iron Nun' about aging," she shares her unique advice: "First, remember yourself as a child. Imagine yourself as that little person skipping along without a care in the world. Second, never stop being that child. It will help you be pure, creative, and authentic."

Staying in the Game with a New Sense of Urgency

On the occasion of the Esalen Institute celebrating its 50th birthday in 2012, Ken had the honor of conducting an intimate interview with one of the most interesting women of our time. Living a full life of 99 years (currently, and still counting), 68 of them married to the famous architect and urban designer Lawrence Halprin, Anna Halprin has been a teacher and role model to tens of thousands of women and men in search of their authentic selves. Blending classic dance with the movements and practices of psychodrama and Gestalt, Halprin has almost singlehandedly transformed the fields of movement and postmodern dance. During the interview, Ken asked, "Do you think of yourself as an old woman?" After taking a few moments to gather her thoughts, Anna said:

> Yes, I do. I'm aware of that every day of my life. But I'm not an "old woman" in the sense that I'm kind of a cartoon character of an old woman. I am not that. I will never allow myself to be that. Rather, I think of being an old woman in terms of what am I doing with my life. There's an *urgency* I increasingly feel that every day has got to count. What's the right thing for me to be doing right now? Becoming old for me is a way of being urgent about life.
>
> For example, last year I tripped on something and fractured my pelvis. I was furious. I went to bed and thought I'd be all right in the morning. But in the middle of the night, I was in excruciating pain, so I called 911 and was taken to the hospital. The doctor there said, "Mrs. Halprin, you've got a fracture. It's going to take six to eight weeks to heal." So I said, "Well, too bad," and he said, "What do you mean? Aren't you going

to check into the hospital?" I said, "No, I've got to leave now because I have a movement class to teach at 10 am."

Increasingly, today's retirees are exploring, not retreating. More and more have renewed purpose and new, often higher ambitions in retirement. Even when they encounter health or other difficulties, Boomer retirees aren't resigned to a slow decline. Rather, they want to continue to become better versions of themselves. That's the new story of aging and retirement.

4

Putting Wisdom to Work

The New Role, Timing, and Purpose of Post-Retirement Employment

THE AEROSPACE CORPORATION has provided independent technical and scientific research, development, and advisory services to national security space (NSS) programs since 1960. Its workforce consists largely of highly qualified and experienced engineers, and its staffing needs vary significantly with the current contracts. The company's "Retiree Casual" program, established in 1985, brings retirees back to work part time. Employees can retire with full benefits as early as age 55, and after a gap of six months or more, return to work on a project basis for up to 500 hours per year. Most participants are engineers, but the program is open to all employees and includes contract managers and administrative assistants. In addition to their main roles, retiree casuals often serve as mentors, training program instructors, and recruiters.

For Aerospace retirees, the Retiree Casual program keeps former employees connected to their professions and their colleagues. For the company, the benefits are many. Phil Mathews, Principal Director for Talent Acquisition, states, "We are rehiring technical experts who understand our mission and are passionate to be able to continue to support it. The program also affords great mentor and knowledge sharing opportunities. We are proud to support this wonderful program."

Scripps Health, founded in 1924, is a not-for-profit, integrated health care system in San Diego, California. Scripps offers employees a program to help them "downshift" into retirement by varying the cadence of their work. Employees with 20+ years of service can phase into retirement over a period of up to one year with full benefits. The program is available for all job categories, including nursing, hospitality, and leadership. Eric Cole, Vice President of Human Resources, explains the intent: "We value the diversity of our workforce, and for those who want to phase into retirement, we offer the structure to accomplish that. For Scripps, it's a win-win arrangement – we have the opportunity to facilitate knowledge transfer while assisting the participant with a gradual transition." Workforce diversity is reflected in the fact that a significant percentage of new hires – 13.5% over the past two years – are over the age of 50. And the organization recaptures talent by hiring former employees who have stayed in touch through the Scripps Alumni Network.

CVS Health has long recognized the value of older employees, who comprise over 20% of their workforce. Customer demographics are changing and mature workers can respond and relate more effectively to older customers. Their "talent is ageless" initiative focuses on mature job candidates who are either reentering the workforce or changing careers. The company partners with federal, state, and local agencies and organizations to recruit, train, and place candidates who fit the needs of specific stores. New hires are often paired with mentors and have access to a variety of additional development and support programs for mature workers. Their innovative "snowbird" program has several hundred employees, including many pharmacists, relocating seasonally, just as their customers do, often from the Northeast to Florida for the winter.

Aerospace Corporation, Scripps Health, and CVS Health are just three of the growing number of organizations that have robust hiring and retention practices focused on utilizing the talent of older adults. Michelin North America, Mitre Corporation, and the U.K. National Institutes of Health also have longstanding phased retirement and retiree return programs. Pfizer's "Mentor Match" program connects employees of different ages and professional experience, and the senior leaders of the company mentor its fast-rising talent. Sodexo USA and Deutsche Bank have intergenerational employee networks that promote both cross-generational understanding and professional development. Deutsche Bank also forms intergenerational project teams.

What are these organizations up to? On one hand, they are protecting their talent supply in the face of both industry-specific labor shortages and the Boomer retirement wave. They are keeping experienced people longer, hiring them back as working retirees, and sharing knowledge and experience that would otherwise be lost to retirement. On the other hand, they are pioneering a future where a growing portion of the workforce will be older employees. They are developing programs and cultures that make them employers of choice for tomorrow's older and more multigenerational workforce.

Organizations that would follow suit may first need to escape some of the common myths and misunderstandings about work retirement (Table 4.1).

The Older Worker Payoff

Working in retirement is becoming the new normal. Today's retirees are working in record numbers. Seven in ten Baby Boomer workers expect to work past age 65, are already doing so, or do not plan to retire.[1] If "retirement" used to mean the end of work, now we're at a tipping point: a *majority* of people will be continuing to work for a while after they retire, and it will become increasingly unusual for retirees *not* to work. However, retirees want to work *differently* – part time, in less stressful and more engaging roles, often in new occupations, often for themselves, and for a few years or as long as they like.

This trend carries profound implications for the workforce. The labor force participation rate of workers 65+ has risen to levels not seen since the 1950s (Figure 4.1). In prior decades, workforce growth was driven by the influx of young workers. In the last decade, however, older workers have accounted for virtually all workforce growth, and those age 65+ continue to be the fastest-growing

Table 4.1 Busting Some Myths About Work in Retirement

Myth	Reality
Retirement means the end of work. People can't wait to retire, and they don't miss work when they do.	Pre-retirees say that retirement ideally includes some work, and the fully retired miss many things about work – most of all the social connections.
People work past retirement age only when they need the money.	Work satisfies many needs – psychological, social, and professional as well as financial. More people work in retirement because they want to than because they have to.
Retirement is a one-way street out of the workforce.	Retirees are working part time or cycling between work and leisure, and many return to the workforce after career intermissions.
Retirement work means more of the same.	Many retirees seek different lines of work and new employers – often themselves.
At retirement age, it's too late to launch a new career.	Retirees get additional education, reinvent their professional lives, return to early-career passions, and start new businesses.
Work in later life is hard and unappealing.	Working in later years is good for physical and mental health, and older workers are more satisfied with work and life than their younger counterparts.
Older workers can be liabilities.	Older workers are more experienced, committed, and engaged – productive and valuable in new ways.

segment of the labor force. This resurgence can prove a boon to employers across industries and government agencies that are facing shortages of skills and experience, as well as having difficulty hiring and retaining staff. It will not offset all the talent lost in the Boomer retirement wave, but it can mitigate the effects.

Figure 4.1   Age 65+ U.S. Labor Force Participation Rate

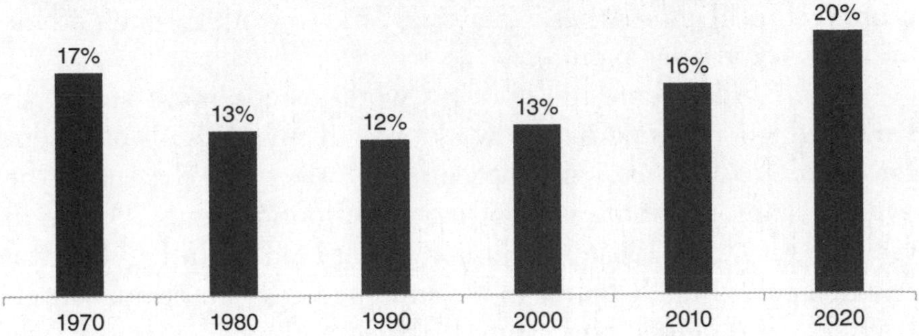

Source: U.S. Bureau of Labor Statistics

Around the world, the labor force participation rates of people 65 and older vary enormously. In most of Europe, the rate is in the (often low) single digits. But in South Korea, Japan, and New Zealand, it's 25% or more.[2] Countries that are facing age waves and labor shortages are changing the incentives. In Japan, age 65+ people comprise a record 12% of the workforce, and three-fourths of Japanese age 60-64 are still working. Prime Minister Shinzō Abe's reforms to bolster the economy include raising the eligibility age for receiving pensions from the government and requiring employers to permit employees to keep working to age 65 if they want (however, workers still officially "retire" at 60 and return at lower salaries). In Germany, the age 65+ participation rate is about 8%, but the working-age population is projected to shrink over the next 20 years. The country is also gradually raising the federal retirement age, and its "Initiative 50 Plus" provides training to older people, pairs them with unemployed young people as a mutual learning opportunity, and temporarily subsidizes the salaries of older people who take new jobs at lower pay.[3]

Working retirees (and older workers generally) bring experience and often need less training. They bring social awareness and skills for engaging with customers, including older ones. They have higher engagement levels, which translates into productivity and customer satisfaction. They tend to be loyal rather than job hop. Many are motivated to share their experience and give back to an organization, including by mentoring younger colleagues. And they bring special management skills, as a recent *MIT Sloan Management*

Review article points out: "While younger managers prefer narrower, more technical approaches, older ones tend to work through others and focus on the big picture."[4]

Chip Conley shares more of his work-in-retirement story: "In early 2013, I returned to the workforce in my mid-50s as a senior executive with tech start-up Airbnb. I was twice the age of the average employee and was reporting to co-founder and CEO Brian Chesky, who was 21 years my junior. What I lacked in DQ (Digital Intelligence), I made up for in accumulated EQ (Emotional Intelligence). The mutual mentoring I offered and received turned me into what I call a 'Modern Elder,' someone who marries wisdom and experience with curiosity, a beginner's mind, and a willingness to learn from those younger."

These "elder" cognitive skills are valuable in the workplace. Dr. Charlotte Yeh, Chief Medical Officer at AARP Services, Inc., explains: "As you age your brain doesn't process information as fast. You might not remember everything and you're not as quick as you once were. But on the other hand, you're a better problem solver. You have better vocabulary, better pattern recognition, better executive function. You get wiser and have more of the creativity that comes from experience." Chip Conley adds, "There's growing data showing the value of cognitive diversity on teams, and the best cognitive diversity comes from age diversity, more than diversity of gender, ethnicity, or background."

Encore.org founder and CEO Marc Freedman makes a similar and timely case for the value of older workers: "We keep hearing that technology is going to render older people obsolete. But the more that artificial intelligence encroaches on traditional roles, the more it brings to the fore a truism: Qualities from the heart, like empathy and the ability to connect, are essential to nearly every role in society. And those are the qualities that peak as we get older."

To tap into this growing and valuable workforce segment, employers must adjust practices ranging from work arrangements (e.g., to offer the part-time or project work most retirees prefer) to compensation and benefits (e.g., to mesh with health benefits retirees may already have). They must avoid the pitfall of taking older workers for granted, instead offering them opportunities to learn and do new work. They should offer employees options for phasing into retirement (thus retaining talent longer), stay in touch with their retirees (as a source of labor and referrals), and welcome retirees with engaging work and flexible arrangements. We find that many organizations are aware of the demographic shifts and feel the pressure of staff and skill shortfalls. Yet they have not made the needed adjustments to be employers of choice for working retirees.

Why People Work in Retirement

Four powerful forces are behind the rise in older workers:

- **Longevity.** Increasing life expectancy has produced retirements that can last 20 or 30 years or more. That's a long time to fill, and retirees are filling more of it (especially the early portion) with the stimulation of work, and in the process keeping their retirement savings topped up.
- **Pensions.** That topping up is increasingly necessary since most employers have eliminated guaranteed lifelong defined-benefit pensions. The burden of funding retirement has shifted from employers more to employees, and the relative role of Social Security is declining, so more retirees rely primarily on their 401(k) and personal savings accounts.
- **Economic uncertainty.** The 2007–2009 recession and its aftermath depressed employment and ate into the assets (especially in housing) and retirement savings of many. It served as a wake-up call for those who had insufficient savings and would find it financially unsustainable to retire without some employment income.
- **Revisioning later life.** It's not just about the money. The Boomer generation has looked at things differently and changed the norms throughout their lives. As they retire, they see their later lives as active on many fronts, full of purpose, stimulation, social interaction, and fulfillment, including from work. As more of them work in later life, retirement itself is transforming.

Longer lives mean lengthier retirements and potential difficulty funding them. So more people are questioning whether a 20+ year retirement without work is practical, affordable, or desirable. They are giving work an important place on their retirement agendas and reaping a variety of rewards – financial, social, physical, and psychological. As one retiree put it, "Not working, that was for my parents' generation. I can't imagine not doing anything for 30 years. Nor could I afford to."

This trend will likely not reverse any time soon. While many current retirees feel secure in their Social Security payments and may have employer pensions to fund their retirement, younger generations anticipate the need to rely primarily on personal savings and employment income in retirement.[5]

Chip Conley makes the case for working in retirement: "We survey our Modern Elder Academy alums, and people say it's foolish to retire, for three reasons. One, it accelerates your mortality rate. Two, there's the financial wisdom of working longer. As Stanford economist John Shoven noted, it's hard to finance a 30-year retirement on a 40-year career. Three, people doing hard physical labor are usually enthusiastic to get into retirement, but in a knowledge-worker world people can use their skills much longer, and therefore stay vital and engage with life longer."

Of course, people who reach their sixties with insufficient retirement funding will need to work in retirement out of financial necessity. For the majority of retirees, however, the nonfinancial benefits are just as important. Many retirees are shifting from full-time, often workaholic careers to part-time work on their own terms in roles they enjoy. Compared to their earlier careers, people describe their retirement work as far more flexible and fun, and far less boring and stressful.

In surveys of the general public, and even of pre-retirees in their fifties, respondents anticipate that they'd work in retirement primarily because they need the money.[6] However, when actual working retirees are asked about their reasons for working, they paint a different picture. Money counts a lot, but not as much as staying mentally sharp. Other common motivators include maintaining social connections, staying physically active, challenging oneself, and avoiding boredom. Four in ten working retirees say they can't imagine not working.[7] Retirees who work feel more stimulated, connected to others, and proud of their accomplishments. They can achieve satisfying work–leisure balance, pursue personal and entrepreneurial ambitions, and use work in retirement as the chance to give back. Most telling, more people say they work in retirement because they *want* to than because they *have* to. Those who choose to work in retirement can significantly improve their finances, but work has great value beyond the paycheck.

Retirees know that staying active and engaged is healthy. Eight in ten agree that work helps people stay more youthful, and two-thirds feel that, when people don't work, their physical and mental abilities decline faster. A study of 83,000 older adults across 15 years found that people who worked past age 65 were about three times more likely to report being in good health and about half as likely to have serious health problems, such as cancer or heart disease.[8] As one retiree put it: "If you don't work, you shorten your lifespan. You get old faster."

Social connections also prove very important. When we asked non-working retirees what they miss most about work, they said it's the social connections in the workplace. Dr. Charlotte Yeh underscores the point: "We did some focus groups on loneliness among retirees. In one group of men, they all said when they were working they had colleagues, friends, and were very active. When they retired they expected to continue to have the same network of friends. But the door came down and it wasn't the same anymore."

For many, work in retirement kindles a new or renewed sense of purpose through doing good and mentoring others. There are matchmakers to help. Encore.org taps the talent of people 50+ who want to contribute the experience they've accumulated over the years to do good. The Encore Fellows program gives participants paid positions – usually half-time for a year – using the skills from their working lives on behalf of non-profits and social enterprises. Major organizations embrace the program; a few even offer every retirement-eligible employee the chance to serve in a company-funded fellowship. The Encore Physicians program, supported by Kaiser Permanente Northern California Community Benefits, places retired physicians in part-time, paid roles in community health clinics.

Those who are especially happy working in retirement often cite one of four reasons:

- They returned to early-career roles or passions – "I get to be an engineer again."
- They returned to being individual contributors without the stress of managing others – "No more Monday meetings and weekly reports."
- They can give back to their organizations or professions – "I enjoy sharing what I know with the next generations."
- They can start their own business – "I'm working for myself and building something new."

Another retiree we spoke with offered the best scenario for working in retirement: "When you look at people inspired in their later life work, you realize it is because it's their passion. They don't consider what they do a job – they consider it their life." Mike Hodin, PhD, CEO of the Global Coalition on Aging, put it in a nutshell: "What do retirees want? There are lots of answers, but many simply want a job. They want to stay in the game."

How People Work in Retirement

Retirees want to be able to mix work with other pursuits. So most working retirees put in the equivalent of about half time. In terms of preferred work patterns, they fall into two almost equally divided camps. A little over half prefer working part time on a regular basis, which has the advantages of predictability and regular income. But nearly as popular is cycling back and forth between work and leisure. That can be on a seasonal basis, leaving time for special pursuits (camping in summer or skiing in winter). Or it can involve project-based work, which is a good fit for many kinds of organizations.

Some find ways to do project work mainly from home. Work at Home Vintage Experts (WAHVE) is a staffing agency for companies seeking experienced contractors for projects in accounting, human resources, and insurance. They seek to place "vintage professionals who have left the traditional workforce to phase into retirement." A variety of websites, including Upwork.com, Freelancer.com, and

Guru.com, match companies with project-based workers of all ages. AARP does regular research on what jobs are available where for those over age 50, and they provide online resources, including a job board, for employers and employees alike.

Many see retirement as a chance to try something new or even pursue careers they were unable to explore when working full time. Carol Thomas told *Next Avenue* how her lifelong love of photography turned into more than a hobby in retirement. After retiring as CEO of Education Northwest in Portland, Oregon, she began taking photography classes. Now photography has become her "second act," and she volunteers for Pro Bono Photo, a group that provides nonprofit environmental groups with free professional photography.

The majority (60%) of working retirees we surveyed said they stayed in the same or a similar line of work, but that leaves plenty who switch. When retirees choose to stay in the same line of work, they say it's because they're good at it and they know how to balance it with the rest of their lives. Few feel confined to their careers for financial reasons. The top reasons retirees move to a new line of work are all about flexibility and fulfillment: work schedule, enjoyment, and the opportunity to learn new things or pursue a passion or interest. Making more money is seldom the motivation for a switch. Those who take breaks from work at the start of retirement are more likely to change line of work, perhaps because they had the time to explore new options.

Retirees often welcome the chance to work for their pre-retirement employers on a part-time or project basis – providing the employer with experience, continuity, and opportunities for knowledge exchange. Many are motivated to give back to their employers, sometimes by lending their experience to business improvement projects, sometimes by training or mentoring younger coworkers. Others seek ways to advance their professions more generally. Law enforcement executives such as chiefs of police tend to retire at relatively young ages, and it's common for them to then join advisory or technology firms devoted to improving law enforcement work.

About one-quarter of workers over the age of 65 are self-employed as independent contractors or business owners. They're three times more likely to be working independently than younger workers are, and their overwhelming reason is the ultimate flexibility of working on one's own terms. Only 14% said they're on their own because they couldn't find employment (Figure 4.2).

When we say "entrepreneur," many may think of a Silicon Valley 20-something. The reality is that older people – with greater experience, business connections, and financial resources – consistently outpace younger ones in entrepreneurial activity. One-fourth of the new business owners (defined as those who have paid employees) in 2018 were 55 or over. That's up from 15% two decades earlier (Figure 4.3). And a 60-year-old startup founder is three times more likely to succeed than a 30-year-old founder.[9] Lori Bitter, author of *The Grandparent Economy*, points out that financial services firms are recognizing this trend: "American Express, for example, has a small business group that works with entrepreneurs, and it's very age inclusive. Their newsletters and ads and services all support people who are starting a business later in life."

Universities have recognized the need and opportunity to help experienced professionals prepare for and launch their "second act" careers. Stanford and Harvard have year-long programs. Notre Dame and the Universities of Texas and Minnesota have followed suit. Harvard's Advanced Leadership Initiative calls itself "a third stage in higher education designed to prepare experienced leaders to take on new challenges in the social sector where they have the potential to make an even greater societal impact than they did in their careers." These are year-long programs in conventional academic

Figure 4.2   Why People Start Businesses in Retirement

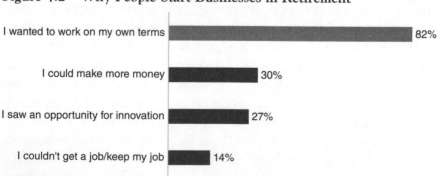

Source: Age Wave / Merrill Lynch, *Work in Retirement: Myths and Motivations*

Figure 4.3 Entrepreneurs by Age

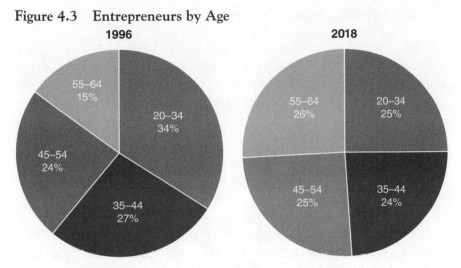

Source: Kauffman Indicators of Entrepreneurship, *2018 National Report on Early-Stage Entrepreneurship*

format. Shorter and much less expensive programs focused on social purpose and nonprofit roles are offered at Union Theological Seminary in New York City and University of Connecticut. Through Encore!Connecticut, professionals transition their skills and experience into managerial and professional roles – paid or volunteer – in the nonprofit sector. The program combines coursework with a two-month practicum in a nonprofit organization.[10]

Employers are also playing educator. Goldman Sachs, Deloitte, Credit Suisse, and HP Enterprise offer "returnship" or "career reboot" programs that help people who have been out of the workforce for a while get back up to speed. Cedars-Sinai Medical Center in Los Angeles has a physician reentry program. CloudFlare has 4-month paid internships for professionals returning to the workforce after taking time off for caregiving. Paul Irving, JD, chairman of the Milken Institute Center for the Future of Aging (as his encore career), has a recommendation: "Training for an encore career is an experience that we should provide to as many people as possible in very different ways. This is something that should be available on high school campuses at night and certainly in community colleges throughout America."

The Life Cycle of Work-in-Retirement

For some, the essence of retirement is to be free of work. They may have accomplished their career goals, be financially secure, have a slate of retirement activities planned, or want to be rid of the responsibility and stress of holding a job. Others may not have enjoyed their work and have been counting the days until retirement. Those at the opposite end of the spectrum can't imagine not working. They enjoy their work, have gotten good at it, and are passionate about it. This category includes high proportions of artists, entertainers, writers, educators, craftspeople, and those who build things, including family businesses.

For the large portion of retirees in between, part-time work can be an attractive option, especially early in retirement, and they commonly take a break from work before returning to it. Employers who understand this common life cycle of work in retirement are able to engage retirees in the right ways at the right times, including helping them phase into retirement and then back into the workplace.

Many people who know they want to work in retirement give themselves a head start beginning several years in advance, and their preparation naturally intensifies as retirement approaches. They talk with friends who are working in retirement, network with professional colleagues, consult with their employers about opportunities to continue working in retirement (or phasing into it), perhaps get some additional education or skills training, and put together a personal "business plan." Some engage career planners when approaching retirement. The Retirement Coaches Association and the National Career Development Association help them find certified career counselors, and companies like The Muse offer quick access to profiles of coaches.

About half of working retirees told us they took a significant break from work when they first retired. They wanted to take time to relax, recharge, give "not working" a try, take extended vacations, get some projects done, and perhaps do some of the work-in-retirement preparation that they'd postponed. The length of these "career intermissions" varies widely, but most are more than six months, and the average intermission is over two years. Those who take intermissions tend to enjoy them as sabbaticals – chances to escape the responsibilities and stresses of busy careers – more than filling them with new responsibilities.

As the standing joke has it, "I failed retirement and went back to work." One working retiree gave us a different spin: "It took just three years of retirement before the bucket list started getting empty." Returning to work after an intermission may require some catching up with industry changes, technologies, or everyday methods and skills. But the intermission has probably clarified what work retirees want to pursue and how much they want to work. Some will job hunt, some move into jobs that have been waiting in the wings, and some take the plunge to work for themselves or start businesses. Retirees tend to have the flexibility and perspective to reengage with work on their own terms.

Almost all working retirees decide at some point to "finally retire." They may have met career goals, solidified their financial security, encountered health problems, or simply decided that they were ready for more leisure and other activities. When they do finally fully retire, they may experience a reduced version of the culture shock people feel when retirement means quitting full-time work "cold turkey."

Workforce Ageism, Skills Obsolescence, and Other Barriers

There are, of course, challenges to reentering the workforce, especially following a lengthy career intermission. When older workers seek employment, it can take nearly twice as long to find a job as younger workers take.[11] Perceptive employers can recognize the hurdles and help working retirees over them.

Retirees find the biggest issue to be skills slippage (Figure 4.4), and 40% of Boomers say they are keeping their skills up to date to ensure they'll be able to continue working in retirement if needed.[12] Other barriers include employer assumptions regarding role and pay, losing touch with business trends, and lost relationships with key contacts.

We asked working retirees for their advice to pre-retirees who are considering employment in retirement. Three-fourths recommend being open to trying something new and being willing to earn

Figure 4.4   Challenges Reentering the Workforce

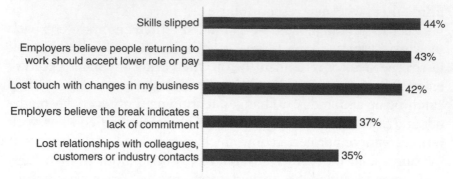

Source: Age Wave / Merrill Lynch, *Work in Retirement: Myths and Motivations*

less in order to do something you truly enjoy. We also asked what they would do to make themselves more employable (Figure 4.5). Keeping up with technology tops the list, followed by physical and mental exercise and taking relevant classes. Those are all deemed more important than cosmetic changes to oneself or one's resume.

The biggest barrier retirees face, however, is more systemic. Ageism in the workforce has been illegal since the Age Discrimination Employment Act of 1967, yet it remains prevalent. A 2018 AARP study found that nearly two in three workers aged 45 and older have seen or experienced age discrimination on the job.

Figure 4.5   What Working Retirees Would Consider to Remain Employable

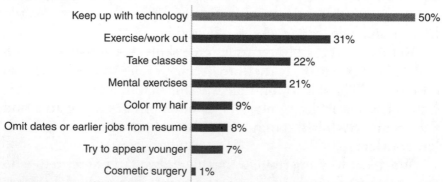

Source: Age Wave / Merrill Lynch, *Work in Retirement: Myths and Motivations*

And a study from ProPublica and the Urban Institute found that about 56% of Americans over age 50 have faced or could face "employer-driven" job loss.

Sometimes the problem goes public. Until 2018, Facebook was enabling companies to post job advertisements based on the user's age. ProPublica published an investigative piece on how IBM had pushed out upwards of 20,000 older workers. But more often ageism happens behind the scenes. And there's a fuzzy line between outright discrimination and subtle bias, as Chip Conley writes in *MarketWatch*: "One paradox of our time is that baby boomers enjoy better health than ever, remain vibrant and stay in the workplace longer, but feel less and less relevant. They worry, justifiably, that bosses or potential employers may see their experience and the clocked years that come with it as more of a liability than an asset." For all the reasons we've discussed, such attitudes toward older employees are extremely short-sighted.

Four Types of Working Retirees

We've described how people work in retirement for a variety of reasons and in a variety of patterns. Looking across them, our research has revealed four distinct types of working retirees, each with different attitudes, priorities, and ambitions for work and its place in life (Figure 4.6). Recognizing and appreciating these segments can help organizations be realistic about the variety of older employees and how to attract and retain them.

Builders

Builders keep right on working and achieving in retirement. Work is an important part of their identity, and they feel at the top of their game. Working in retirement provides the opportunity to use their expertise, try new things, and accomplish more. Builders have the highest levels of engagement and satisfaction (84%) with work. They are energized by work, see it as a way to stay mentally and physically healthy, and feel they would be bored if they didn't work in retirement. They are proud of their accomplishments and most likely to consider themselves workaholics, even in retirement.

Figure 4.6   Segmentation of Working Retirees

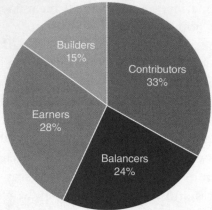

Source: Age Wave / Merrill Lynch, *Work in Retirement: Myths and Motivations*

Builders are also the most likely of the segments (39%) to be self-employed and to have started their own businesses in retirement. They tend to stay in the same line of work because they're good at what they do. They do the most planning for working in retirement and are least likely to take a significant career intermission. Demographically, Builders are more likely to be men (61%) and highly educated. They have the highest levels of income and assets, and they are most likely (54%) to feel financially prepared for retirement. Their soundtrack for working in retirement is Rod Stewart's "Forever Young."

Contributors

Contributors find ways to give back, often by working for nonprofits. Retirement is a whole new chapter of working life and an opportunity to do good. Work is a means to the end of helping others, the community, or worthy causes, and those results constitute much of the reward of working. Contributors are very engaged at work and have a high satisfaction level (75%). They also tend to feel happy, connected to others, and content in their lives. They feel that giving back in retirement should be the norm.

Most Contributors change jobs in retirement to pursue a passion or interest. Four in ten work for nonprofit organizations, and they are also most likely to volunteer significant amounts of their time. Many have prepared for working in retirement by volunteering in a relevant field, taking classes, and networking with colleagues or friends. If they take a career intermission, they return to work because they want to be making a meaningful contribution. Demographically, the majority (53%) of Contributors are women. They tend to be well educated and comfortable financially. Their soundtrack for working in retirement is Frank Sinatra's "The Best Is Yet to Come."

Balancers

Balancers work in retirement largely for the activity and social connections, and without letting work dominate their lives. They may need the extra money, but work–life balance is the top priority. They feel that they have paid their dues and that retirement is their time. They want enjoyable work, flexible schedules, and likeable colleagues. They are relatively satisfied (67%) with work, but not highly motivated to put in extra effort, and they don't feel a strong need to give back. They tend to feel happy, content, and relaxed about life in general.

Balancers are most likely to work part time without changing lines of work. They did little to prepare for working in retirement, and if they take career intermissions, they return to work because they missed their work friends and relationships, or because they simply found a good opportunity. Demographically, Balancers' gender split is 50–50, and they are most likely to be married. They are somewhat less educated than average but have above average income and assets. Less than half (42%) feel financially prepared for retirement. Their soundtrack for working in retirement is the Eagles' "Take It Easy."

Earners

Earners keep working primarily to pay the bills, and with less satisfaction than the other segments. They're the least likely to say they'd keep working if they won the lottery, or that they'd be bored if they didn't work. Earners express more frustration than other working retirees do, including over ageism, lack of training, and feeling irrelevant or unmotivated. They may feel like they got a raw deal – that retirement was supposed to be leisure time. They have poorer general health and miss more days of work due to personal illness than other retiree workers.

Earners most often work for an organization other than they retired from. Whether they pursue a different or similar line of work, their priority is the income. They did little preparation for working in retirement and often regret that they didn't plan better. Those who take a career intermission return to work when they need the additional income. Demographically, they are slightly more likely to be female (53%), most likely to be unmarried, and have less than average education. They have the lowest assets and income, and are least likely to have guaranteed pensions. Almost none feel financially prepared for retirement. Their soundtrack for working in retirement is Simon and Garfunkel's "Bridge over Troubled Water."

Employers are not likely to attract a lot of Builders because they are fewer in number and tend to work on their own, but their expertise and ambition can both be very valuable. Contributors will gravitate toward roles that involve serving customers or colleagues and sharing their experience. With Balancers, the employer should keep working arrangements clear and respect how these employees separate work from the rest of their lives. Organizations employ a lot of Earners (of all ages). Their productivity can best be maintained by keeping the work engaging and by regularly recognizing their contributions.

How Employers Can Engage Working Retirees

Businesses, nonprofits, and other organizations that want to make the most of the retirement-age workforce – to alleviate labor and skills shortages, improve business performance, and promote knowledge and experience sharing – must be programmatic in their approach. It will make little difference to hire individual retirees here and there. You need to engage them at scale. The process begins with getting in touch with the demographics of an organization's workforce. What is the age distribution? Is a retirement wave under way or impending? What key roles and skills may be in short supply? And what are the options for retaining and replenishing the supply of talent?

We started this chapter with examples of programs at progressive organizations. Here we briefly review five key programs for engaging, retaining, and leveraging the experience of older employees and working retirees. You may devise local variations that fit your employees, culture, and need for experienced labor.

Phased Retirement programs, like that at Scripps Health, offer reduced responsibilities and flexible role and work arrangements as employees approach retirement. Forty-two percent of pre-retirement Boomers envision phasing into retirement, yet only 29% say their employer offers any sort of phased retirement arrangements.[13] Phased retirement enables the organization to keep talent longer, and the individual to give partial retirement a try instead of quitting "cold turkey." The most effective programs also incorporate knowledge exchange to understudies or teams of colleagues.

Retiree Return programs, like Aerospace Corporation's, tap into the large talent pool of qualified retirees to meet staffing and skills needs cost-effectively, as well as promote knowledge and experience exchange. Retirees can be hired or rehired efficiently. And when they are deployed in customer-facing roles and reflect the customer demographics, they can engage customers effectively. So the business case serves retirees (who want to keep their hands in), the organization (that can hire and onboard people efficiently), and often the customers (who can better relate to the employees serving them).

Retiree Networks are communities of retirees that can serve as a channel for a variety of activities, including rehiring retirees, collecting business and employee referrals, enlisting retirees to participate in community programs, and, depending on the business, serving retirees as customers. Retiree networks may be organized and managed by the company or the retirees themselves, and they are typically supported by a website, regular communications, and local events.

Career Reinvention programs serve employees of all ages by facilitating in-company role, location, or career changes. But these "second acts" can be especially valuable for rejuvenating and reengaging older employees, many of whom may not be getting all the career development opportunities that younger colleagues have. Reinventors gain new skills and experience while sharing what they already know. The company can use career reinvention to fill talent gaps, expand skills and experience, and enable mobility and cross-pollination across departments or lines of business.

Knowledge Exchange happens through a variety of means – from ongoing mentoring, to occasional events, to intergenerational team structures, to online repositories of information. The objectives are both to capture and retain knowledge and experience before it walks out the retirement door, and to accelerate the development and productivity of other employees. Many retirees and pre-retirees are happy to give back to their employers by playing teaching and mentoring roles.

These five programs can work together and reinforce each other, and a comprehensive approach to an older workforce will incorporate several. Programs must recognize what working retirees want – starting with engaging work, enjoyable workplaces, and flexible work arrangements. They must also manage an ongoing tension. On one hand, though typically part-time, retirees want to fit in and be treated like regular employees, including when it comes to learning opportunities and on-the-job variety. On the other hand, they need adjustments appropriate to their lifestage, including to scheduling and compensation and benefits. The special ingredient in many successful programs is how organizations mix the generations, enabling knowledge and experience exchange in both directions. Everyone enjoys that process.

Actions and Opportunities for Employers

1. Conduct an ageism audit to make sure that hiring and management practices, and the tacit assumptions of managers, do not treat older employees or prospects unfairly.
2. Develop an older workforce strategy, starting with talent needs and risks, to determine the programs necessary to maintain talent supply.
3. Offer flexible work schedules, part-time work, and project-based roles to working retirees and employees phasing into retirement. Recognize that the role of work in their lives is changing.
4. Adjust compensation and benefits for working retirees to dovetail with the pensions and health coverages they already have.
5. Adjust and accelerate the onboarding process for working retirees, and celebrate their return to the workplace.
6. Engage working retirees with variety on the job and opportunities to learn and grow, just as with employees of all ages.
7. Leverage the special experience of older workers, including as mentors to younger colleagues, and make giving back part of their roles.
8. If you are in a recruiting firm or job placement service, grow your business by educating your clients about the advantages of hiring older employees and working retirees.
9. If you are in financial or business services, devise offerings to serve older entrepreneurs and marketing approaches to reach them.
10. If you are in a nonprofit or public service, work with organizations like Encore.org to gain access to experience and expertise at reasonable rates.
11. If yours is a large enterprise, and it does not have a retiree or all-alumni network, form one. It will serve you in many ways.

5

The Time Affluence Explosion

Fifty Trillion Hours of Leisure to Fill

JIM BENDT IS a former advertising executive turned travel advisor. He opened a travel agency at the same time the industry was shrinking from 30,000 to 15,000 firms, due to the rise in online self-booking. In his industry research, he found that transactional agencies were being supplanted by Expedia or Travelocity, but others that were more relationship-based were doing well: "The agencies that were actually thriving and growing were the ones that took on more of an advisory role to their clients, like how a financial advisor or an attorney would serve their clients." He and his wife Linda founded Pique Travel Design and joined forces with Virtuoso in developing the Wanderlist travel tools and portfolio. That's right, not "bucket list," but "Wanderlist."

Virtuoso, the organization behind the Wanderlist, is the world's largest travel network focused on crafting bespoke, once-in-a-lifetime experiences. Under the visionary leadership of Chairman/CEO Matthew Upchurch, Virtuoso's 20,000 travel advisors recognize that the special trip to explore one's family's past in Italy or that cruise up the Amazon with grandchildren is so important and valuable that the planning and on-the-ground execution are best not left to chance. The Virtuoso website proclaims: "When you work with a Virtuoso travel advisor, not only will you gain access to deep travel expertise, you'll also discover a specialist in *you*. Someone who knows *your* passions. *Your* unique style. And *your* dreams." Upchurch believes that do-it-yourself travel planning can only go so far, even with the proliferation of internet offerings. Since their clients have been, in some cases, waiting a lifetime for this special trip or don't want things to go awry once it begins, having an experienced and dedicated "travel advisor" (not an "agent," as he's quick to point out), can make all the difference in the world.

For many years, Upchurch and his team were working on a new approach to travel planning which they lovingly called "Return on Life," playing off of the "Return on Equity" (ROE) focus of the financial planning industry. When he learned of Bendt's ideas, he provided the resources, platform, and partnerships necessary to bring their joint vision to life.

When creating their Wanderlist, prospective travelers fill out a fun online questionnaire rating their interests, hopes, preferences, dream destinations, and both positive and negative travel experiences. The results are analyzed with proprietary algorithms, and then a Virtuoso travel advisor thoughtfully helps them discover the destinations and activities that will best match their aspirations, and even recommend ones they may never have considered or even heard of. Advisors then work with the travelers to create customized travel portfolios that map out their present and future travel plans. Although people fill out the questionnaires individually, the entire family is encouraged to participate, and the recommendations are then shaped for couples or entire families. Upchurch told us that the "gamification" around Wanderlist and the ability of each individual – spouse, grandchild, and so on – to "play" with this resource on their own creates insights that otherwise would never be brought to the light of day.

The results are often surprising, and some clients discover what should have been obvious. As one Wanderlist client reflected: "My wife and I were intrigued by the idea of comparing our travel interests. After 24 years of marriage we should have had a pretty good idea of what each of us was hoping for, right? Well, there were surprises. While we were talking with our advisor, my wife was reminiscing about the time she spent in France during college. I had been dreaming of a golf and beach getaway, and I had no idea that Paris still held such special meaning for her. So, guess what we did for our 25th anniversary?"

Bendt observes that while part of Wanderlist's magic is Netflix-esque technology and design, the platform is really about offering a truly personal experience-focused consulting service: "We know that one of our clients' most important assets is their leisure time, and when it's treated haphazardly, they can regret the opportunities they missed. And they've lived long enough to know that, especially with families, some of those experiences simply can't be repeated." He adds, "I would say the number-one client for Wanderlist is the Boomer generation. Not that this doesn't have appeal to other age groups, but it's really the Boomers who are recognizing the importance of managing and truly making the most of their leisure time."

The Baby Boom Leisure Boom

The age wave is creating a truly unprecedented leisure wave. The nearly 10,000 Boomers retiring each day find themselves shifting from *time constrained* to *time affluent* for the first time in their adult lives. The average American age 65+ now has 7.4 hours of leisure time per day, while those aged 35 to 44 are the most time constrained (Figure 5.1)

Figure 5.1   Average Hours of Leisure per Person per Day

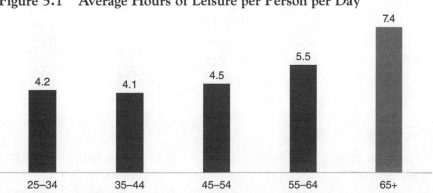

Source: U.S. Bureau of Labor Statistics, American Time Use Survey, 2018

Collectively, that's 195 billion hours of leisure a year for those age 65+ and about 3.9 trillion hours over the next 20 years (Figure 5.2). If you consider this phenomenon across the developed and developing world, that's around 50 trillion hours of time affluence – and looking for fun, stimulating, nourishing, purposeful, even transformative, things to do.

That's a lot of leisure time, and Boomer retirees want to fill it differently than previous generations who were inclined to be less active in retirement, had fewer options, and were far more frugal. Boomers want to stay active and explore their options, and they're willing to spend. As one Boomer retiree told us, "I want to keep growing and trying new things. I don't want to be as old as my parents were when they were this age."

Several years ago, we conducted a first-ever series of global studies on "The Future of Retirement" in partnership with London and Hong Kong headquartered HSBC Bank. We surveyed thousands of people in 20 countries, representing two thirds of the world's population. We asked people all over the world if they saw retirement as "a time to wind down," "a time for rest and relaxation," "a whole new chapter in life," or "the beginning of the end." We were fascinated to see that "a whole new chapter in life" rose to the top of Boomers' preferences in the United States, Canada, Sweden, France, Germany, Japan, and China. They view retirement as a

Figure 5.2   U.S. Total Hours of Leisure 2021–2040

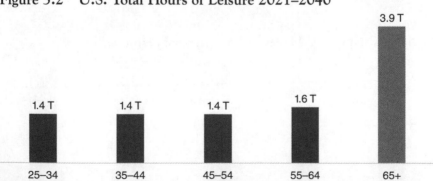

Source: U.S. Bureau of Labor Statistics, 2018; U.S. Census Bureau, 2018; Age Wave calculations

new starting point, not a finish line. They want to rev up with new activities and adventures and are eager to have peak experiences in their newfound leisure time. But for this to happen, there's an addiction to be overcome.

The No-Vacation Nation

For most of history, leisure was primarily the province of the wealthy elite. To the ancient Greeks, leisure was an opportunity for higher-order activities like scholarship, contemplation, and self-development. To the Romans, it was more associated with recreational pursuits. In the Judeo-Christian tradition, leisure centers on the Sabbath as a day of rest and religious activities. In the industrial era and per the Protestant work ethic, leisure came to mean rest from work so you could then work harder. Working harder is still the name of the game for many people, especially during their prime working and childrearing years. But older Americans – even those continuing to work part time in retirement – have much more leisure time, including the huge increase upon retirement.

That transition to time affluence can be abrupt and challenging, because for many Americans, workaholism – a round-the-clock addiction to work – has become a way of life, a big part of personal identity. We often define ourselves by our professions or titles or even how hard we work. And many Americans are out of practice or even unskilled at knowing how to take time off and what to do with themselves when they're not working. Compared to other industrialized countries, where the norm is 25 to 30 vacation days each year, Americans are, at 14 days, vacation deprived (Figure 5.3). And unlike the governments of most other countries, the U.S. government doesn't mandate *any* paid vacation or holidays to employees. The Center for Economic and Policy Research has dubbed the United States the "no-vacation nation."

To make matters worse, over half of employed Americans who receive paid time off don't take all their vacation days. A record 768 million U.S. vacation days went unused in 2018, and 236 million of them were forfeited completely, equating to $65.5 billion in lost benefits.[1] And when Americans do take vacations, most still

Figure 5.3   Average Number of Annual Vacation Days Offered by Employers

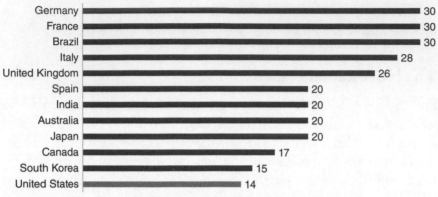

Source: Expedia, Vacation Deprivation Survey, 2018

work. Seventy-percent say they check their work emails regularly and do other work activities while on vacation.[2] If they can't escape the job, they can't fully enjoy the rest-and-recreation benefits of leisure. It's no wonder that those who stop working "cold turkey" or take a career intermission can find the early days of retirement disorienting.

Most retirees are so unaccustomed to unhinging from work that they don't know what to do with all their free time. Sadly, in America last year, the average American age 65+ spent close to 50 hours a week – more than a traditional work week – watching television.[3] So there's plenty of opportunity for community organizations, recreation services providers, and family and friends to encourage more people to get off their couches and get involved in the myriad everyday leisure activities that are popping up in their communities and online.

Perhaps in the years ahead, there will be detox centers or 12-step programs for people trying to break their workaholic addiction and learn how to "be here now" in their retirement years. At the very least, perhaps Tony Robbins and Deepak Chopra will take note of this challenge and attempt to help people relearn how to let go and have some fun.

Retirement Transforms Leisure – and Leisure Transforms Retirement

As we described in Chapter 3, time affluent retirees are entering into a "freedom zone" where many will have more fun and greater emotional well-being than at any earlier stage of their lives. In this zone, they have *freedom from* old constraints as well as *freedom to* explore and enjoy themselves in new ways. Nine in ten retirees, regardless of wealth level, say they now have the freedom to do what they want on their own terms. Those who enjoy retirement most are more likely to be socializing with family and friends, traveling, attending cultural and sporting events, and volunteering. As retirees multiply in the decades to come, every sector from technology to match-finding to fitness clubs to ecotourism to hobby crafts will see demand multiply.

Leisure in retirement is far different from leisure before retirement in a variety of ways (Table 5.1). Most of the changes are very positive: more choice, more purpose, more social connection, and, of course, more time. The exception is that health becomes more of a constraint on leisure for most of us as we age. While pre-retirees view free time as precious and scarce, eight in ten retirees tell us that they now have the amount of free time they desire – and they like it.

For the newly retired, organizing one's time can be a real challenge. Most retirees want to stay busy but not too busy. They want a balance of structure to avoid boredom and non-structure to enjoy the freedom and spontaneity that retirement makes possible. One retiree shared the feeling: "It is a little scary because you are so used to structure – for 35 years I got up every day to go to work. And then suddenly you have to put your days together and figure out where you are going to go and what you are going to do. It's a little scary until you find your niche, and you find things that you like doing."

We found that retirees' freedom and enjoyment are not dependent on wealth. Eighty-six percent of all retirees say they find it relatively easy to find inexpensive leisure activities they enjoy.[4] They take advantage of free or low-cost programs at schools, community centers, churches, libraries, and social clubs. Mary Furlong, EdD,

Table 5.1   Leisure Is Different in Retirement

Leisure *before* retirement	Leisure *in* retirement
Leisure is restricted, mostly to evenings, weekends, and vacations.	Leisure time is abundant.
Leisure is often about relaxation and de-stressing.	Leisure is often about engagement, connection, and activity.
Health is less likely to be a constraint on leisure.	Health is more likely to be a constraint on leisure.
Technology interferes with leisure; people want to (but can't) unplug.	Technology enhances leisure through social connection; people want to be plugged in.
Travel is often short.	Travel can be longer and more immersive.
Work and family responsibilities constrain leisure timing, activities, and involvement.	People have more freedom and flexibility to do what they want to do when they want to do it.
Planning horizon is usually the next vacation.	Planning horizon can include a portfolio of trips and activities.
Leisure is an adjunct among life priorities.	Leisure can be central to people's identity.

Source: Age Wave / Merrill Lynch, *Leisure in Retirement: Beyond the Bucket List*

author of *Turning Silver into Gold* and a leading authority on the longevity marketplace, describes the everyday freedom: "It's like living as a college student again because our schedules are more flexible and in many cases are far more under our own control than ever before. You might go shopping mid-morning or go to dinner a little bit earlier. My friends shop the happy hour for the best appetizers and the best deals."

Boomer retirees are driving massive growth in the experience economy – products and services that enable them to enjoy themselves in new ways in retirement. Nearly every aspect of the leisure travel industry is positioned to prosper. More customers with more time, more flexibility, and more money to spend equals a growth industry. Retired Boomers spend more per capita on leisure travel than any other generational cohort,[5] and Americans age 65+ already spend $200B a year on leisure travel. As their ranks continue to grow dramatically, so will that annual spend (Figure 5.4), reaching a cumulative total of $5.2T between 2020 and 2040. And that's just Americans. Many experts multiply that number by 10+ to get a sense of what's about to unfold worldwide.

Leisure travel may just be the tip of the iceberg. Retirees find plenty of ways to spend leisure close to home. There are countless opportunities to serve them in entertainment and media (both traditional and social), gaming (both online and casino-based), health and fitness, technology and education, recreational equipment and vehicles, and even financial services to help retirees plan and manage their new leisure hopes, dreams, and spending.

Futurist and award-winning travel writer Don Mankin, PhD, aka, "The Adventure Geezer," who before he became a renowned expert on travel was a psychology professor and college dean, says, "The Boomer generation was extremely adventurous in their youth from attending Woodstock, to backpacking through Europe, and experimenting with mind-altering drugs. In retirement with newfound freedom, they're looking to rekindle that adventurous spirit." Whether it's a day trip or an immersion experience in a foreign culture, an extensive cruise or a visit to the grandchildren, Boomer retirees are increasingly on the move.

Figure 5.4   Annual Leisure Travel Spending by Americans Age 65+

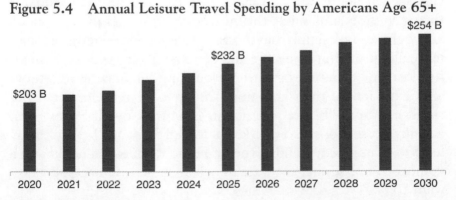

Source: Age Wave / Merrill Lynch, *Leisure in Retirement: Beyond the Bucket List*

And compared to previous generations, wherever possible they're after *authentic* experiences. Larry Pimental, Chief Strategy Office for Royal Caribbean, is an industry veteran and a legendary travel visionary. He has noted that yesterday's retiree traveler wanted to follow the rules and be met with few or no surprises. Boomers, on the other hand, want to get off the usual routes in order to really see, feel, and experience the world. They want some surprises (as long as they're safe). For example, in their travels, over half say they would like to eat meals in locals' homes and almost a quarter say they would like to stay with them.[6] Richard Weiss, Former CEO of Mountain Sobek Travel, shares his experience: "My wife and I went on a river cruise down the Nile where we got to see and do all kinds of amazing things from a visit to King Tut's Tomb to a hot air balloon ride – but the most memorable part of our trip was the homecooked meal we shared with a local Egyptian family." This is good news for Airbnb and others who allow travelers to become immersed in local neighborhoods and customs.

For some Boomers, the sky isn't necessarily the limit. Twenty-seven percent of Boomers said they'd be interested in traveling into outer space.[7] Former Astronaut-Senator John Glenn, who flew to space for the second time at the age of 77, has company.

Ultimately, retirement leisure can be transformative on many levels. Personally, retirees have time for learning and pursuing new interests, for challenging and reinventing themselves. Physically, they can enjoy both exercise and relaxation. Socially, they can deepen family ties and make new friends. And emotionally, they can stop and smell the proverbial roses, enjoying beauty and culture and simply having fun. Life in retirement becomes more about having enjoyable and beneficial experiences. Ninety-five percent of retirees say they would rather have more enjoyable experiences than buy more things. One retiree shared her transformation: "Before retirement, I defined myself by my work and my possessions. Now, I define myself by what I do with my leisure – I'm now a grandmother, a French student, a cook, and a volunteer. I seek out new ways to define myself, to become who I want to be."

The Leisure in Retirement Journey

As people move into and through retirement, the role of leisure in their lives continues to evolve. We can use the five stages of retirement that we introduced in Chapter 1 to trace how retirees' leisure experiences and priorities change along the journey. Leisure services providers who recognize these stages can catch customers at the right times, be it with new leisure experiences or useful leisure planning tools.

> *Stage 1: Imagination.* Decades before retirement begins, most people are totally time constrained, raising then launching their children, advancing their careers, and sometimes caregiving their parents. Vacations and leisure during this period of life are usually short and must be organized around work breaks and children's school schedules. However, bucket lists begin forming during these years, and people begin to imagine all of the things they might do when empty nesting and retirement liberate their lives a few years down the road.

> *Stage 2: Anticipation.* In the five years or so prior to retirement, many pre-retirees begin to actively look forward to more time off and the activities they'll fill it with. Leisure travel in this stage is often for purposes of escape from work and recharging one's batteries. However, there's a dip in people's leisure travel and spending in the two years before retirement. Many are gearing up mentally and saving up financially for the retirement celebration trip or cruise.

> *Stage 3: Liberation.* Newly minted retirees, in the first two years or so of retirement, are enjoying their newfound time affluence. The sense of liberation and thrill of self-discovery can be enormous, and more than three-fourths of new retirees feel they finally have enough free time. However, during this transitional period, significant numbers feel unsettled, anxious, or bored. More than a third say it's harder to structure their time than it was before they retired, and nearly half say they feel guilty about not using their leisure "productively."

Stage 4: Reorientation. The sense of freedom enlarges. Spanning the period from years 3 to 15 of retirement, the enjoyment of leisure continues to grow and deepen. The large majority (72%) want to try new leisure activities, not just do things they've already done, and there's an uptick in activities involving personal growth, learning, adventure, and the outdoors. They establish everyday leisure routines: exercising, shopping, reading, volunteering, taking classes, socializing with friends. As they seek immersive experiences, they travel more, from weekend trips to visit their grandkids to international excursions.

Stage 5: Reconciliation. Fifteen years into retirement, and later for many, the focus of leisure gradually shifts more to maintaining health and enjoying familiar activities. More of retirees' leisure is spent relaxing and connecting with family and friends. While they are often happy, relaxed, and content, health conditions and caregiving responsibilities can limit leisure activities and keep them close to home. Travel is more often with family and multigenerational, sometimes on "heritage trips."

We've heard many retirees reflect upon their journeys. One described the adjustment in Stage 3: "When you retire, after taking some time to simply crash, the initial 'woo-hoo' wears off, then you have to create your own meaning and purpose somehow. For me, that involved getting out of the house, taking classes, and making sure that I was keeping my head going and working toward some kind of goal." Another recounted the pleasures of Stage 4: "Right now, I'm really enjoying retirement. I'm feeling good, happy, respected, and I'm thrilled to be reaping the fruits of my labor." As Stage 5 begins, they begin to anticipate what lies ahead: "My husband and I are currently very active and footloose because we can be, and a little later on, I still want to be open to new experiences. We might be slowing down physically toward the end, but hopefully we'll still be doing things we enjoy and that are mentally stimulating." One retiree shared a pithy perspective: "When you can't any longer climb the pyramid, you can stand at the base and enjoy looking at it."

Everyday Leisure and Staying Healthy

The wide spectrum of leisure activities fall in two base camps. *Everyday leisure*, as the name suggests, is how people spend most of their leisure time – relaxing or exercising, socializing or enjoying hobbies, reading or watching TV. *Special occasion leisure*, in contrast, is more of what we now think of as a "vacation," and involves going places or doing things out of the ordinary, often after some serious planning and anticipation.

Geoffrey Godbey, PhD, Professor Emeritus of Leisure Studies at Penn State University, described Boomer retirees' aspirations in leisure: "Technological literacy and willingness to learn are much higher among Boomers than older generations. They are more willing to pick up new hobbies in retirement and to go for the unconventional. And Boomers want both up- and downtime in leisure. They want to go for hikes or rafting, but they also want time to recuperate and relax later that day."

When we asked retirees what they most seek in their everyday leisure, staying healthy and relaxing top the list, followed by the three F's – family, friends, and fun (Figure 5.5).

Retirees' options for everyday leisure are many, and public and cultural institutions increasingly have programs and services – often with discounts – for older adults. Libraries commonly offer book clubs, classes, and technology access, education, and assistance. The New York Public Library's programs include art and website design

Figure 5.5   Everyday Leisure Priorities of Retirees

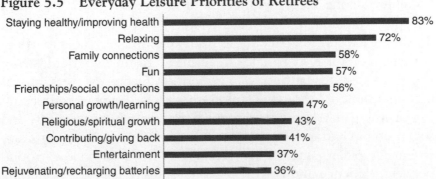

Staying healthy/improving health	83%
Relaxing	72%
Family connections	58%
Fun	57%
Friendships/social connections	56%
Personal growth/learning	47%
Religious/spiritual growth	43%
Contributing/giving back	41%
Entertainment	37%
Rejuvenating/recharging batteries	36%

Source: Age Wave / Merrill Lynch, *Leisure in Retirement: Beyond the Bucket List*

workshops, film discussions, and chess night. Many museums offer classes in drawing and art criticism. For example, the Met offers a program for visitors with dementia and their care partners to participate in hands-on art activities. Recreation and "senior" centers often provide opportunities to learn, exercise, stay fit, and volunteer. Churches sponsor social gatherings, outings, volunteering, and support groups, sometimes in collaboration with local businesses. Colleges are increasingly offering non-credit, low-cost courses to older learners. Osher Lifetime Learning Institutes is a network of more than 120 college campuses that have designated programs for those over 50. The University of California Berkeley offers dozens each semester, including "The Joy of Singing" and "Exploring Your Identity Through Writing." Most parks and nature preserves are free to everyone or offer senior discounts. There's little excuse to stay on the couch.

The most enjoyable leisure activities can be those people invent and organize themselves. Meetup.com is a network for creating groups, hosting events, and finding others with similar interests. A Tucson, Arizona, group called "50plus Moderate to Easy Nature Hikes and Social Events" organizes hiking trips and social gatherings.

Online Leisure and Recreation

Four in ten Americans over age 50 play games online, but they're not the games teenagers and young adults are playing. An AARP-sponsored survey found the most popular games to be solitaire and scrabble (among men), mahjong and monopoly (among women, who play a bit more).[8] They mainly play for simple diversion and fun. There are exceptions, of course. GrndPaGaming, age 66, is a celebrity gamer on the e-sports live-streaming platform Twitch. Master of the Apex Legends battle royale game from Electronic Arts, he has a couple hundred thousand followers. Online games are (depending on the game) good for mental sharpness, physical agility, and social collaboration. We envision that there's ample opportunity to engage older gamers with offerings in the vast middle ground between Patience and Fortnite, likely games that involve building more than destroying.

Libraries and community organizations commonly offer technology classes, sometimes geared toward older adults. One of the most experienced educators is Senior Planet, part of Older Adults Technology Services (OATS), which has held more than 35,000 classes over the last 15 years. Their mission is to provide courses and programs to help older people learn how to use computers – and in the process be both more independent and more connected with others. Dr. Thomas Kamber, OATS Founder, says, "We view technology as an entry point for older adults to engage in new ideas, make friends, and take on challenges." There are courses on how to start online businesses. A recent partnership with T-Mobile seeks to address senior isolation with new programming in largely rural northern New York.

Virtual reality technology holds vast recreational and therapeutic potential for older people. You can visit Paris or a favorite vacation spot, see a Broadway musical or a holiday parade, participate in family celebrations – all without leaving home. But the headsets and interfaces have been designed for young gamers, and many older users can find them disorienting. Two companies with virtual reality technology designed specifically for older adults are Rendever and MyndVR. Chris Brickler, CEO of the latter, says, "We set out to reimagine a very senior-friendly interface and content streaming platform so we can offer them this world of immersive content."[9] Both companies are focusing on senior and assisted living communities, where the technology is proving to reduce social isolation and increase happiness, and Rendever is expanding into the home care market. As it incorporates more of the principles of universal design, we see the technology in general use as a media and entertainment channel for older people.

By the way (and moving offline), the other "gaming," casino gambling, is also popular among older Americans. The American Gaming Association reports that 20% of current (within the last year) gamblers are retirees, and older women are a fast-growing customer demographic. We hear widespread concern about elder gambling addiction and financial loss, as well as the marketing-to-seniors practices of casinos. But the large majority of older gamblers seem to be casual, not competitive. They largely stick to the slots, and, while it's nice to win sometimes, they also enjoy the entertainment, change of scene, and socialization.

Healthy Leisure

With health such an important objective in retirees' everyday leisure, public and private fitness services are expanding. The broadest-based fitness program for retirees is Silver Sneakers, a program designed for people age 65+ that is included in many Medicare Advantage and Supplement plans. Available in more than 16,000 locations, including YMCAs, the program includes branded fitness classes emphasizing balanced, low-impact workouts that enhance both strength and flexibility, including "gentle yoga" and dance. Participating centers often supplement the offerings with, for example, Tai Chi. And participants have access to the other facilities of participating fitness centers for more of their exercises of choice.

Silver Sneakers isn't limited to the gym. "FLEX" fitness classes are held in parks, community centers, churches, and other public places. Participants can also exercise at home with the guidance of online classes and video workouts. But the program tries to get people out and exercising together, creating a supportive community.

The program is a win all around. Participants want to maintain fitness. Insurers know that fitness reduces claims costs. Gyms fill their facilities during off-peak daytime hours when other members are at their jobs. And the need is certainly there. Nearly one-third of older adults do not spend any leisure time on physical exercise. Having pioneered fitness movements doesn't guarantee that Boomers are fit. With higher rates of chronic conditions, many are less fit than their parents were at the same age. At the same time, a growing number of people are becoming personal trainers and fitness instructors in their 60s, often specializing in working with older adults. A retirement job that pays off in many ways!

Independent fitness centers are also focusing much more on serving older clientele. For example, at Welcyon Gyms, the tagline is "Fitness After 50" and the background music, from the '50s and the '60s, plays at lower-than-your-typical-gym volume. There are no free weights, but rather carefully calibrated equipment. Exercisers adjust their workouts and track activity with smartcards. Group classes include yoga and Zumba, seated volleyball, and even "cane-fu" self-defense.[10]

In many Chinese public parks, more than half the users are older adults (in most U.S. municipal parks, it's under 15%). Early in the morning, Chinese elders gather for exercise routines, including Qiqong and Tai Chi, and to use colorful exercise equipment designed for light cardio and gentle strength training workouts. Morning exercise is a popular component of traditional Chinese medicine, and collective group exercise was being promoted by the government when today's elders were young. Also in China, in recent years, a new phenomenon has emerged. Thousands of older women and men gather in local parks and other public spaces to ballroom dance. When Ken and his wife Maddy were recently in China to visit their son Zak, who was living in Beijing, they were surprised to see crowds of stylish older men and women, dressed to the nines, dancing their way through the afternoons to big band and swing music. Groups of these "damas" have also assembled to dance in Moscow and Paris.[11]

In recent years, London, Berlin, Toronto, and other cities have built what some are calling "senior playgrounds" (we object to the term). For example, the Lion Wellness Park outside Vancouver opened in 2007 and has increased exercise rates among older residents. Its most popular exercise machines help with age-related issues like balance and dexterity. In British Columbia alone, the Lion model has been replicated in 18 locations. Jay Maddock, professor of public health at Texas A&M University, cites the benefits of such facilities and their use: "More and more studies show that elderly people need exercise, social connection, and nature. Senior parks are a really low-cost investment that hits each of these."[12] In the United States, AARP and the nonprofit FitLot are working together to bring to public parks in every state fitness equipment that is adaptable for people of all ages and abilities. In addition to specially designed exercise equipment, the installation in Bilboa, Spain, also has a series of stations with cognitive games to exercise memory, attention span, and mental math. Going to the park is a physical, mental, and social experience. We applaud this activity and hope these environments and programs proliferate.

Bicycling has been gaining popularity among people ages 60–79, sometimes with a mechanical assist.[13] A recent *Fast Company* article examined how new, lightweight models of e-bikes, motorized to enable people to peddle farther with less effort, "are helping keep seniors young and, in some instances, even alleviating the symptoms of Alzheimer's and Parkinson's."

Healthy activity needn't be strenuous. Many studies have found both psychological and physiological benefits for older adults who have creative outlets, such as painting, singing, and dancing.[14]

Health problems can, of course, constrain everyday leisure activities, more so as we age. Three-fourths of retirees say that health limitations do not substantially limit their leisure activities now, but they're prepared to adjust the activities to accommodate their physical conditions. If we're looking for role models, on the back of the Ruth Bader Ginsberg calendar it shows the exercises that she does every day.

In Search of Peak Experiences

Special occasion leisure is breaking out of the ordinary with experiences that are memorable. The first thing that comes to mind may be travel. That's high on the agenda for many retirees, but so are family gatherings or simply attempting something new and challenging. What retirees say they most want is adventure, fun, and plenty of "peak experiences" (Figure 5.6). They want to create moments that matter and realize that they might need some help in optimizing the likelihood of success with these pursuits.

Abraham Maslow described peak experiences as "moments that stand out from everyday events. Think of the most wonderful experience of your life: The happiest moments, ecstatic moments,

Figure 5.6   Special Occasion Leisure Priorities of Retirees

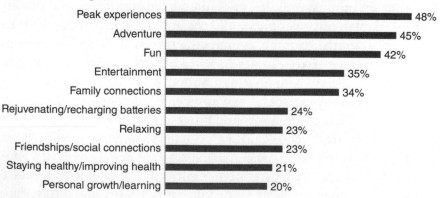

Peak experiences	48%
Adventure	45%
Fun	42%
Entertainment	35%
Family connections	34%
Rejuvenating/recharging batteries	24%
Relaxing	23%
Friendships/social connections	23%
Staying healthy/improving health	21%
Personal growth/learning	20%

Source: Age Wave / Merrill Lynch, *Leisure in Retirement: Beyond the Bucket List*

moments of rapture, perhaps from being in love, or from listening to music or suddenly 'being hit' by a book or painting, or from some creative moment."[15] Peak experiences can happen any time, but they are often purposefully sought out through special occasion leisure. For some, having a peak experience means traveling around the world and spending lots of money. For others, it's watching a sunset with a grandchild in the local park. Regardless of which type of peak experience people are pursuing, having time affluence raises the importance of creating new, powerful memories, often shared with loved ones.

An Experience for Every Mood and Taste

In the "freedom zone," retirees enjoy far more flexibility to travel where they choose, when they choose, and for however long they choose. Though extensive travel is easier when people have greater resources, leisure travel doesn't have to be long, far away, or expensive. Retirees explore their travel options. They are often able to take advantage of off-season rates and make last-minute decisions to travel. Boomers are more likely than younger generations to take part in loyalty programs offered by airlines, hotels, cruise lines, and other travel providers. Globally, almost one million Airbnb users are over 60. About a quarter of retirees find RV trips appealing, and RV sales are expected to continue to grow as Boomers retire.[16]

A variety of companies cater to older travelers, such as Eldertreks, Walking the World, 50Plus Expeditions, and Smithsonian Journeys. Some specialize in trips and tours for the growing numbers of women who travel alone or with their friends, including Women Traveling Together and Adventurous Wench. And travel services cater to retirees' special interests: educational, culinary, sporting, musical, volunteering, even medical services.

For example, Road Scholar knows how to engage and support retirees in lifelong learning. Founded as "Elderhostel" in 1975, this nonprofit provides educational travel experiences geared toward older adults at affordable prices. Elderhostel was an ingenious creation. Realizing how much many people had enjoyed their college experience, and also taking note of the fact that during summer months, most campuses were quiet, with empty dorms, they simply put two and two together. Today Road Scholar offers roughly 5,500 educational tours across all 50 states and 150 countries, and each year more than 100,000 people participate in a Road Scholar learning journey. Trips are organized not only by location and learning opportunity, but also by activities and groups, including women-only tours and even some programs for grandparents and grandchildren. All trips come with their "assurance plan" that includes everything from assistance with lost baggage to emergency medical services. They also offer scholarships and grants to caregivers.

Most participants range in age from 50 to 100. In a relaxed atmosphere of intellectual stimulation, elder students not only discover new ideas, but also new friends. Debates begun in the classroom carry over into the dining hall and the dorm rooms. Skills and insights accumulated over long careers are brought to bear on new facts and new ideas. Professors accustomed to classes of cell-phone-distracted 20-year-olds are presented with people who debate important points, ask thoughtful questions, and bring in new perspectives from their own life experiences.

For those whose peak experiences tend toward adventure, there's Mountain Travel Sobek, a travel company that designs packaged adventure excursions. Half of their customers are over 50.[17] They offer hiking, safari, rafting/kayaking, cruising, cultural, and wellness expeditions. Plus they offer trips designed for families and for solo women. Each trip is rated on a scale from 1–5 based on the activity and fitness level involved, and includes the full package of experienced guides, accommodations, meals, and local transportation – even some sightseeing as a respite from more strenuous adventure.

Peak experiences may also be found close to home. The Over the Hill Gang ski club at Copper Mountain in Colorado was founded in 1976 with the vision of encouraging skiing as a lifelong sport for people over the age of 50. Membership includes daily group skis tailored to skiers' ability, instruction, special lift privileges, and perhaps most importantly, a supportive community of peers. Many skiers are in their 80s and some beyond. One participant says of the Gang, "It is the only and real reason my wife and I come to ski. We have different skiing abilities. It was tough for us to ski together, so this way I go with my group, she goes with hers, and then we meet up at lunch time and just have a blast."

Foodies have many options. Tour Radar offers over 350 food and culinary vacation packages around the globe. Their Taste of Sicily tour, for example, features eight stops in as many days, a cooking class, and tastings of wine, olive oil, cheese, and produce. Viking River Cruises knows how to cater to their target clientele of "culturally curious" people age 55 and older. They offer relatively small vessels, lots of comfort and amenities, and many occasions "to get close to local life."

Retirees also indulge their fantasies and their nostalgia. At the Chicago Cubs Fantasy Camp, participants spend two days at Wrigley Field warming up and playing with former Cubs stars. Campers sign a one-day contract with the Cubs and receive a full personalized uniform. Similarly, at Rock 'n' Roll Fantasy Camp, campers get to jam with and learn from gold record musicians like Joe Walsh and Slash, with careful consideration of their skill level and musical preferences. Other camps include a Space Academy, a Broadway Fantasy Camp, and a Sonoma Grape Camp.

Finally, "voluntourism" that enables people to contribute in the places they are visiting is especially popular with Americans over age 60. For example, Projects-Abroad.org helps travelers to find volunteering opportunities as well as arrange accommodations and travel. And medical tourism is also on the rise. Patients Without Borders estimates that 1.4 million Americans travel to another country annually for everything from dental work to knee or heart surgery. Medical conditions permitting, they can make a vacation of the trip. They're seeking lower cost treatment services not available in the United States. Rio de Janeiro is now known as the "World Capital of Plastic Surgery."

Don Mankin offers good advice to the travel industry: "Many travel companies think about marketing to older travelers in terms of the limitations that come with age. Understanding these are important, but that's a narrow way of thinking. They also need to recognize that Boomer retirees are experienced and educated consumers who want a *multidimensional* travel experience: a lecture on the history of a place, a meal with locals, a manageable hike or bicycle tour." Geoffrey Godbey recommends dealing with travelers' limitations realistically: "Companies should fully disclose the intensity of an activity because people want to be surrounded by those of similar ability levels. So get real feedback from older consumers. Do a test run with 60-, 70-, and 80-year-olds."

Family, Friends, and Especially Grandkids

Geoffrey Godbey also told us, "Leisure activity often runs secondary to socialization. It's not so much the activity itself, but with whom you do the activity." The clear majority of retirees (61%) tell us that *whom* they spend time with is more important than *what* activities they do. Retirees have much more time available to spend with family and friends. Leisure activities provide occasions to have fun, deepen ties, share experience, and make new memories.

Matthew Upchurch of Virtuoso reflects on the opportunities that surface when you take note of the celebratory side of leisure: "Meeting the needs of Boomers is a critical part of the burgeoning travel industry worldwide. With their newfound time affluence, they're entering a unique stage in their lives where they have the greatest concentration of milestones." Jim Bendt agrees: "They're celebrating not only their individual moments such as retirement, anniversaries, and birthdays, but also milestones for their friends and two or three generations of the family – graduations, weddings, births, and so on. It's also an important time in their lives where they have a deeper appreciation for growing relationships and special memories."

More travel today is multigenerational. Virtuoso's survey of 1,000 travel advisors named multigenerational travel the number-one travel trend of 2019, with Italy, Mexico, Hawaii, and Orlando, Florida, the top family travel destinations.[18] While the multigenerational excursion may be the "greatest trip ever," there are common challenges in determining destinations, dates, logistics, and especially activities that appeal to everyone. "Grandtraveling" is also becoming more popular, with 32% of grandparents having taken solo trips with a grandchild and 15% planning a trip in the next year. Sierra Club, Road Scholar, Disney, and Smithsonian have trips designed for grandparents and grandchildren to take together. We were amused when in one of our surveys most retirees said that spending time with their grandchildren was more fulfilling than spending time with their children.

A massive retiree solo travel market is also emerging. Twenty million retirees are single, including those who are divorced, separated, never married, or widowed. More than two-thirds of them are women. Single retirees report that they enjoy their leisure experiences with friends or by themselves. About 10% of all leisure travelers go alone. Many travel companies – Mountain Travel Sobek, Road Scholar, and G Adventures, to name just a few – now offer specially designed trips for solo travelers and allow the traveler to choose private accommodations or to be paired up with a roommate. Forty percent of travelers with the age 50+ adventure travel company Overseas Adventure Travel go solo.[19]

Help Needed: How and Where Can Fun Be Found?

Retirees need Wanderlist-type assistance. Roughly half tell us they have done some planning for leisure in the next year, but only 10% say they've done a lot. One-fourth have done some planning farther out, but only 4% an extensive amount (Figure 5.7). Most revealing is that two-thirds of retirees with a spouse/partner have not discussed and agreed on how much leisure time to spend together or

Figure 5.7   Retirees' Time Spent Planning Leisure Activities

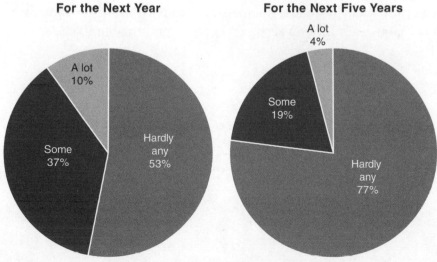

Source: Age Wave / Merrill Lynch, *Leisure in Retirement: Beyond the Bucket List*

how much money to spend on it. While most retirees have dream vacations or peak experiences in mind, only 15% report having the proverbial "bucket list." Many don't even like the phrase because it says "before I die" rather than "enjoying my life."

As the ranks of active and adventurous retirees swell, we anticipate that leisure planning will become a more regular part of retirement preparation and life-in-retirement discussions. There are opportunities for financial and other advisors and services to help retirees shape and fund their ongoing leisure programs, not just their individual excursions. And there's another reason to plan for retirement leisure – those who plan report having more fun. Much of it comes with the anticipation, as one retiree told us: "Travel planning is two-thirds of the fun. It takes longer than the trip itself and it just builds the experience. You are looking forward to it and then you are reliving it afterwards."

We have academic tutors for kids, mentors and career counselors for workers, clergy for spiritual guidance, doctors for medical care, and psychologists for mental health guidance. We have no doubt that there will be a growing opportunity for leisure planning "coaches." We anticipate that Boomer retirees will be looking for Wanderlist-type help making the most of all their leisure time, not just their travel adventures – everything from how and where to volunteer, to how and where to meet new friends, to where to live to enjoy their lifestyles. Boomers are ready to use their time affluence, like their other assets, purposefully and in abundance.

Actions and Opportunities for Organizations and Entrepreneurs in the Leisure Sector

1. In the spirit of Don Mankin, make travel – and leisure generally – hands-on and multidimensional, incorporating culture, health, learning, and creativity.
2. Offer multigenerational experiences where people can do things together or apart as the spirit moves them. And market across generations – you can't be sure who is picking up the tab.
3. Accommodate older people's needs and limitations – physical, nutritional, medical – discreetly and respectfully. Self-consciousness can inhibit their participation in and enjoyment of leisure.
4. Offer activities graded by degree of ability, interest, and available time.
5. Don't over-program or over-schedule activities. Boomer retirees value freedom, independence, authenticity, and socializing – all of which need some spontaneity.
6. Make it easy for people to participate in groups or singly with the opportunity to connect and group up.
7. Develop activities for those who most need a break and change of scene – such as widows and caregivers – and market to them with empathy.
8. Help retirees discover and try out new activities and destinations, plan their leisure activities, anticipate beforehand, and document and celebrate afterwards.
9. Everyday leisure providers can steal a page from the travel loyalty programs. Encourage participation by "keeping score" and conferring rewards in a friendly way.
10. Recognize where people are in their retirement journeys and find the "sweet spot" at each stage. Just don't assume that age determines interests.

6

Searching for the Fountain of Health

Can We Match Healthspan to Lifespan?

MEDICAL SCIENCE IS making astounding progress with the diseases and conditions of aging. Robots are conducting eye surgeries. Robotic underwear can assist the hips and lower back to support mobility and posture. Smart pills can monitor gastrointestinal functioning, and genetic editing will be able to improve digestive health by altering the microbes in people's guts. Deep brain stimulation, including with the help of virtual reality, is helping patients regain motor function after being paralyzed by strokes. Genetically reengineered T cells are returned to a patient's body as part of an immunotherapy approach to cancer treatment. 3-D bioprinters can produce living tissue, bone, blood vessels, and soon entire organ systems.

Artificial intelligence is getting into the game. Canadian health-monitoring platform BlueDot alerted its customers to the Wuhan coronavirus outbreak a full *nine days* before the World Health Organization notified the public. BlueDot's AI algorithm combed through foreign-language news, information on disease networks, and official proclamations to pinpoint the outbreak. In addition, with its access to global airline data, BlueDot accurately predicted when and where the disease would spread.[1]

Just as notable is who's entering the business of health these days. As *The Verge* has reported,[2] Amazon acquired PillPack and with it a medical records software platform. Apple, which has long partnered with medical and government institutions, continues to expand its Apple Health medical records app, and the Apple Watch can take one's EKG. Alphabet's Verily Life Sciences company pursues medical research collaborations, for example, with ResMed to tackle sleep apnea. And Google is consolidating its health industry initiatives, including AI assistance to physicians and health-monitoring technology for nursing homes.

Health providers can now book rides for patients or caregivers through Uber Health, and Lyft has partnerships with BlueCross BlueShield. Some early setbacks notwithstanding, IBM continues to make Watson artificial intelligence and natural language processing technology a centerpiece of its health division. Microsoft Azure is partnering with Epic Systems to provide cloud-based artificial intelligence and predictive analytics to health care organizations. And Stanley Healthcare, part of the Stanley Black & Decker tools empire, offers patient safety and security solutions to health care providers.

Why is everyone flocking to the health care space? Mary Furlong, EdD, author of *Turning Silver into Gold: How to Profit in the New Boomer Marketplace* and a leading pioneer on the longevity marketplace, puts it concisely: "Every dissonance of aging – from joint pain to diabesity – is a market opportunity."

At $3.65 trillion annually, health care is one of the largest industries in the United States. It is also inefficient and fragmented, with many potential niches to fill. It's no wonder that major corporations in other industries, especially technology, are getting into the health care business. But for all these investments and advances in technology and techniques, staying healthy as we age remains a problematic proposition.

In the United States we spend over $10,000 annually per capita on health care, more than any other country and 25% more than Switzerland in second place. Over one-third of that spending is on people age 65 and older (who represent about 17% of the population). But, as we mentioned in Chapter 1, that spending does not necessarily buy results in terms of longevity, where the United States ranks 33rd (almost six years behind Japan), or overall health of the population, where it ranks 35th (Spain is first).[3] Promising treatments are always on the horizon, but we await breakthroughs against the leading causes of death, starting with heart disease and cancer (Figure 6.1), and what has become the most debilitating and feared condition of age, Alzheimer's.

Retirement's Biggest Wild Card

Health is the biggest wild card in a happy and fulfilling retirement. It can make the difference between a retirement of activity, happiness, independence, and financial security – or of worry, unhappiness, constraint, and financial insecurity. Boomers are a very health-conscious cohort and, compared to past generations, they can look forward to longer and healthier retirements, perhaps extended by breakthroughs in disease prevention and medical care. But at the same time, more of them may spend more years later in retirement fighting the chronic and often debilitating diseases of aging.

Which will it be? Are we approaching Shangri-la, the fictional valley where people don't age, with longer and healthier lives and accessible and affordable care? Or are we headed to Geriassic Park,

Figure 6.1 Leading Causes of Death in the United States

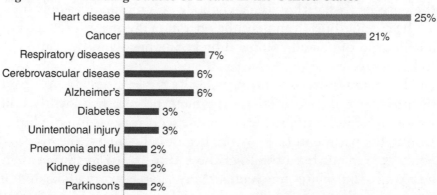

Source: National Center for Health Statistics, Health United States, 2017

with tens of millions constantly beset by chronic and degenerative diseases, taking a toll on themselves, their families, and their finances? The fields of health science and health care may be moving fast, but the jury is still out.

In the meantime, what do Boomer retirees say they want? To take charge of their health because they don't trust the system to take care of them. To prevent or manage their chronic conditions so they can live the active lifestyles they want. To avoid cognitive decline. And to stay healthy and look and feel their best without breaking the bank. Do they want to live to be 100 or more? It's an intriguing prospect, but only 22% of Americans say yes. Among those already 65 and older, twice as many say no (35%) as yes (17%). The most common response, of course, is "it depends on quality of life."[4]

The real issue is not lifespan but *healthspan* – how long people live in "full health" without disabling illnesses or injuries. In ancient Greek mythology, Eos, the beautiful goddess of the dawn, falls deeply in love with the warrior Tithonus. Distraught over his mortality, she goes to Zeus to request a special favor: she wants to love Tithonus until the end of time and begs Zeus to grant her lover immortality. "Are you certain that is what you want for him?" Zeus challenges. "Yes," Eos responds. But as she leaves Zeus's chamber, she realizes in shock that she forgot to ask that Tithonus also remain eternally young and healthy. With each passing year, she looks on with horror as he grows older and sicker. His skin withers and becomes cancerous. His organs rot, and his brain grows feeble. As the decades pass, Tithonus's aging body becomes increasingly frail, yet he cannot die. Ultimately, the once-proud warrior is reduced to a collection of pained, foul, and broken bones – but he continues to live forever.

Tithonus's story is a fitting allegory for what is occurring in health care today. Until recently, most people died swiftly and relatively young of infectious diseases, accidents, or in childbirth. During the past century, however, health care breakthroughs have eliminated many, but not all, of those threats. Today, rather than worrying about dying too young, many people worry about living too long without sufficient quality of life. In the United States and most of the industrialized world, the difference between life expectancy, or lifespan, and healthy life expectancy, or healthspan, is almost 10 years.[5] Whether we're headed toward Shangri-la or Geriassic Park is a matter not just of extending life, but of better matching healthspan to lifespan. That requires progress against both the infectious and the often debilitating chronic conditions associated with aging, and progress toward the behaviors that protect our health and well-being.

The Health-Wealth Convergence

Retirees say the key ingredients for a happy retirement start with good health and financial security, with good health in the lead by a significant margin (Figure 6.2). But the two are closely related. Those with wealth can invest more in their health. And it's harder to enjoy wealth – and all the activities it enables – if you're in poor health. At the same time, unpredictable health care costs can quickly unravel financial preparations for retirement and deplete one's wealth. As more people spend more years in retirement, they'll need more care, and as health care costs continue their rise, health and wealth become more intricately intertwined.

Even with many people postponing retirement in order to build their nest eggs or simply because they enjoy their work, nearly four in ten (39%) retirees globally and nearly three-fifths (58%) in the United States retired sooner than planned, and the number-one

Figure 6.2 Most Important Ingredients to a Happy Retirement

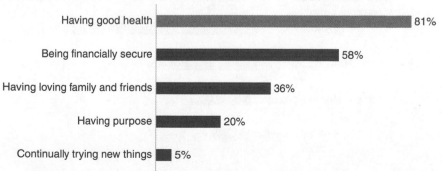

Having good health	81%
Being financially secure	58%
Having loving family and friends	36%
Having purpose	20%
Continually trying new things	5%

Source: Age Wave / Merrill Lynch, *Health in Retirement: Planning for the Great Unknown*

reason is due to their own ill health (Figure 6.3). Early retirement is for some a sign of financial success, but today it's more often driven by health issues. That's a double whammy: a shorter career means less in earnings and retirement savings to start retirement with, especially for people who haven't saved enough and had hoped to plump up their nest egg by working longer. Then those savings must be tapped earlier than planned and health expenses may deplete them faster.

What catches many people off guard are the out-of-pocket health-related costs they'll face throughout their retirement. The longer they or their partner live, the higher the accumulated cost. So it's no wonder that health care costs, unpredictable and potentially high, are retirees' greatest financial worry.[6] And those financial concerns are a family affair. Spouses and partners naturally worry about each other's health, and women, who are likely to live longer, often after having spent savings on the spouse's care, are more worried than men about the long-term financial impact of health care expenses. One retiree expressed the concerns shared by many: "My husband and I have always tried to do the right things – save money, maximize our 401(k)s, even delay retirement a bit. But who knows how long we'll live and what might happen to our health? Will that make us outlive our savings? It's a scary thought."

Figure 6.3   Reasons for Early Retirement Globally

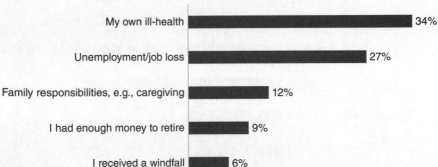

Source: Aegon Center for Longevity and Retirement, *The New Social Contract: Empowering Individuals in a Transitioning World*, 2019

Ken Cella, who leads the Client Strategies Group for Edward Jones, describes the growing role of health in retirement preparation:

> Longevity planning is so much more than simply an investment discussion. So many of our clients talk about health as a key focus in their retirement, so we are having more and more conversations about how our clients want to age with dignity, using long-term care solutions that allow them to receive in-home care. We also train our financial advisors to recognize the 10 warning signs of Alzheimer's, for example. And we have a responsibility to have trusted contacts named for our clients, so we can reach out to those contacts if we are concerned about issues such as elder abuse or fraud. We have to go beyond helping our clients create wealth to helping them navigate the often complex journey to and through retirement – so they can experience meaning and purpose during this third phase of life.

Taking Charge of Health: The Self-Care Revolution

Their approach to health is one of the pronounced differences between Boomers and their parents. Boomers were behind the fitness movement that saw the proportion of adults who exercise regularly more than double between the 1960s (25%) and the 1980s (60%).[7] They have helped drive the growth of health club memberships from 53 million to 71 million over the last decade.[8] And they are driving the current growth of alternative, complementary, and holistic medicine. But as singer Al Jolson famously said, "You ain't heard nothing yet."

Americans over 50 account for 64% of all expenditures on vitamins.[9] Boomers are more open than older generations to alternative treatments to beat cancer. Nearly 80% of Boomers say they support medical marijuana use.[10] The global complementary and alternative medicine market, which includes botanicals, acupuncture, and mind/body/yoga therapies, is expected to grow from $60 billion in 2018 to $211 billion in 2026.[11]

Precision Medicine

Boomers want more precise and holistic care of body and mind, not just treatment of their symptoms. So integrative and precision medicine are gaining traction fast. An early pioneer is Dr. Andrew Weil, author of *Healthy Aging* and founder and director of Center for Integrative Medicine at the University of Arizona. Integrative medicine is a healing-oriented approach that takes account of the whole person (body, mind, and spirit), including all aspects of lifestyle. Dr. Weil created an anti-inflammatory diet to ward off diseases like heart disease, Alzheimer's, and some cancers. Its principles include maximizing intake of fresh fruits and vegetables and minimizing processed and fast foods. True Food Kitchen, a restaurant chain based on the anti-inflammatory diet, plans to have close to 40 locations by 2022.

One of the most courageous pioneers in the field of preventive medicine for healthy aging is Ken's longtime friend Dr. Dean Ornish. President and founder of the nonprofit Preventive Medicine Research Institute in Sausalito, California, and a Clinical Professor of Medicine at the University of California, San Francisco, Ornish disrupted the nutrition and medical fields in 1995 with the publication of his bestselling book *Dr. Dean Ornish's Program for Reversing Heart Disease: The Only System Scientifically Proven to Reverse Heart Disease Without Drugs or Surgery*. Over the decades, he has been an unrelenting advocate for using diet and lifestyle changes to treat and prevent heart disease. Ornish's approach, which he now recommends for a wide range of chronic conditions from heart health to prostate cancer to dementia to aging itself, incorporates a primarily plant-based diet, smoking cessation, moderate exercise, stress management techniques, including yoga and meditation, and holistic psychosocial support.

Another influential figure in the Boomers' quest for the fountain of health is Dr. Mark Hyman, author of *Food: What the Heck Should I Eat* and many other popular books. He is the Medical Director of the Cleveland Clinic's Center for Functional Medicine, which seeks to identify and address the root causes of disease, and views the body as one integrated system, not a collection of independent organs divided up by medical specialties. Functional medicine treats the whole system, not just the symptoms. Programs include functional-based approaches to weight loss and blood sugar control that incorporate lifestyle changes, dietary guidelines, and a specific supplement regimen.

The SHA Wellness center may provide a glimpse into the spa of the future. Located in Alicante, Spain, SHA positions itself as a pioneering clinic, focused on improving people's health and well-being "through the fusion of natural therapies, mainly originated from millenarian Eastern wisdom with Western techniques." In addition to what a typical spa would offer – massage, facials, manicures, and body wraps – SHA offers cutting-edge treatments including cryotherapy, pressotheraphy, oxygen bars, and electro-lymphatic drainage. Offerings now include a seven-day program on healthy aging. Participants begin the week with a multitude of tests to create a biological health profile based on 88 determinants. Throughout the week, they have consultations with various specialists including in anti-aging medicine; they receive acupuncture, hydrotherapy, massage, or other treatments; and they follow personalized macrobiotic nutrition plans and supplement regimens aimed at optimizing cell function and strengthening the immune system.

They won't spread like McDonald's restaurants starting when the Boomers were teenagers, but can we imagine a worldwide chain of health and rejuvenation clinics? Definitely.

Within a few short years, through advancements in artificial intelligence, we believe there will be a transformation from today's somewhat chaotic state of health diagnosis and treatment to an era of "precision medicine." We're going to see scientific breakthroughs that will enable us to arrive at a far deeper and richer understanding of the interactions among our genes, nutrients, and molecular activity – indeed, our brain-body interactions – so that we'll be able to holistically track thousands of biomarkers. And if the AI is informed by a wide range of potential solution paths – allopathic, naturopathic, homeopathic, ayurvedic, and others (always evolving based on outcomes research) – it could be far more effective at precisely diagnosing what's not working right – even novel coronavirus – and then proposing the ideal constellation of solutions for each individual. This will create an entirely new science and practice of medicine, geared to optimizing physical and mental health, enhancing well-being and happiness, and maybe even fore-stalling aging.

These breakthroughs may also present us with a serious market-driven ethical issue. If precise and optimal health is available to everyone, that would be grand, but if it's only available to Silicon Valley billionaires, that doesn't seem fair. Access to quality care and the best that medicine has to offer has been and remains tied to wealth and social factors. However, in the years ahead, the dispari-ties could multiply. If we think "income inequality" is a big deal (and we do), just imagine how folks will feel about "longevity inequality."

Personalized Care and Customer Service

Boomers have also taken charge of how they consume health care services. They expect, and often demand, plenty of information and explanation from their doctors, not just a diagnosis and instruc-tions. They expect doctors to go beyond the physical and ask them about their feelings and concerns, something most doctors are still shy of doing. And those who can afford it are driving the growth of concierge medicine.

With concierge or direct-pay medicine, individuals pay a retainer for more direct and personalized access to physicians and services. Most of the medical costs may still be covered by insur-ers or Medicare, but patients pay extra for a different kind of rela-tionship with their physicians. Founded in 2000, MDVIP is one of the oldest and largest medical concierge companies in the United States, a network of more than 900 physicians in more than 40 states. A typical MDVIP practice has 600 patients, compared to 2,300 for an average group practice. Patients pay an annual fee from $1,650 to $1,800. Membership benefits usually include no-wait, same-day, or next-day appointments, on-time visitations, and after-hours direct access to one's doctor. Even what can turn out to be minor medical issues may seem big at first, and concierge medicine ensures that treatment happens in the patient's time frame, not the medical establishment's.

Concierge medicine can add value to any traditional medical services model. Concierge Choice Physicians is expanding from the

United States into the U.K., which already has universal health coverage. Patients will pay roughly 100 pounds per month to have better access to their physicians.

Individual Responsibility

Boomers' approach to health and health care are rooted in the fact that, rightly or wrongly, they now place more faith in themselves than in the health care system. In our study *Health and Retirement: Planning for the Great Unknown*, we were surprised to see that Boomers believe their lifestyles – starting with diet, exercise, and activity in general – have far more influence on their health in retirement than having a great doctor (Figure 6.4). They also believe that retirement is enhanced if they can take excellent care of their health, and they're correct. Surveyed retirees who reported being in good health are more likely to be exercising, eating nutritiously, watching their weight, and staying connected socially.[12]

When asked to compare themselves to their parents, Boomers say they are more than twice as likely to be proactive about their health, to question their doctors' orders, and to view their doctors as partners in managing their health. And, thanks in large part to the internet, they are four times more likely to do their own research on

Figure 6.4 Boomers' View on How to Maintain Health in Retirement

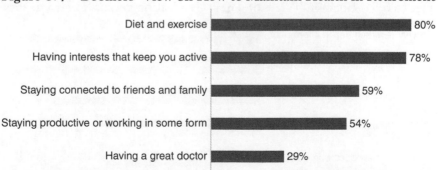

Source: Age Wave / Merrill Lynch, *Health in Retirement: Planning for the Great Unknown*

health matters (Figure 6.5). As one retiree summarized for us: "My parents believed that the doctor's word was gospel. You didn't question it. Now you need to be your own health expert and advocate."

It turns out that health is a matter of personal attitude as well as individual responsibility. One of the keys to better health is a positive attitude toward oneself and the process of aging. As Dr. Charlotte Yeh, Chief Medical Officer at AARP Services, Inc., told us, "Studies have shown that if you have a positive view of aging, you live seven-and-a-half years longer, and you're 44% more likely to fully recover from a disability. These are correlations, not causal. But those who view aging positively have 55% lower risk of hospitalization and fewer plaques and tangles at autopsy indicative of dementia. One study calculated that the stress of negativity around aging costs the United States $63 billion a year in health care costs."

Four Boomer Health Styles

Knowing what it takes to promote good health does not, of course, always translate into good practice. While some Boomers are very health conscious, many are not. For example, Boomers have higher rates of obesity than older generations.[13] Our survey found four basic health styles among Boomers, based on their condition and approaches to health itself, getting health care, and preparing for

Figure 6.5   Boomers' View of Their Generation versus Their Parents'

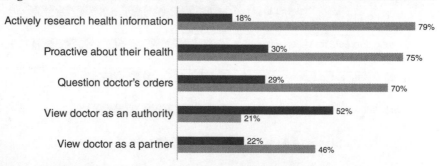

Actively research health information — 18% / 79%
Proactive about their health — 30% / 75%
Question doctor's orders — 29% / 70%
View doctor as an authority — 52% / 21%
View doctor as a partner — 22% / 46%

■ Boomer view of their parents' generation ■ Boomer view of their own generation

Source: Age Wave / Merrill Lynch, *Health in Retirement: Planning for the Great Unknown*

health expenses in retirement.[14] Providers of health products and services may benefit from engaging these segments differently.

Healthy on Purpose Boomers consistently do what's good for their health, both physically and financially. They engage in healthy behaviors, including exercise and eating well, and don't let things interfere with their discipline. They take pride in their health. Half say they are nonetheless concerned about the financial impact of an illness, and they learn what they can about costs and insurance.

Course Correctors are motivated to take better care of their health, often by the onset of a condition that is not yet a serious impairment. The wake-up call has them paying more attention and learning more. More than half are diligent about their health behaviors, but the majority also say they still let things get in the way of attending to their health. They are very concerned about potential health costs and very interested in technology that can help them manage their health.

Health Challenged Boomers have conditions, often chronic, that keep them from doing many things they enjoy. They are the most concerned about their health and how to pay for it, yet only two in five are actively attending to their health. A majority say that other responsibilities and worries interfere with taking care of their health. They express greatest concern about health care costs, and the majority say that they are confused by costs and insurance options.

Lax but Lucky do not take great care of themselves but manage to remain somewhat healthy. They likely have their genes to thank, not their behaviors. Only about a third try to engage in healthy behaviors or to seek out information on improving their health. Like everyone else, they are concerned about the financial impact of health problems, but they are doing little to prepare financially.

Roughly 30% of Boomers fall into each of the first three categories, leaving 10% Lax but Lucky. Women are in the majority in the first three categories, men among the Lax but Lucky.

Helping Boomers Look and Feel Their Best

Today's retirees want to stay healthy, with all the parts in working order. They also want to look good and feel comfortable in their own skin. Unlike their parents who were relatively stoic, most Boomers want their comforts to continue indefinitely. They want to age agelessly, reasonably free of aches and pains and robust enough to live the lifestyles they want. And they'll spend money to try to bring this about. Health-related products and services that have framed a positive attitude toward aging and deliver aspirational messages will reap the marketplace rewards.

The number-one ad campaign of this century is Dove's Campaign for Real Beauty. As *Advertising Age* introduces it, "Many ad campaigns over the years have sold soap. Fewer have tried to change societal notions about beauty."[15] The worldwide campaign, launched by Unilever working with Ogilvy & Mather in 2004, included advertisements, videos, workshops, events, a book, and a play. The first forays of the campaign were billboards at busy intersections in London and Canada with photos of women of all shapes, colors, and ages and the invitation for motorists to vote on whether they were "fat or fit" or "wrinkled or wonderful." That turned heads and started conversations. The campaign really took off with the 2006 "Evolution of Beauty" video showing at accelerated speed the complete makeover, photography, and photoshopping of a young woman to turn her into a billboard image. The concluding message: "No wonder our perception of beauty is distorted." The video went rapidly and globally viral, also generating extensive coverage by the traditional media. The ongoing campaign has continued to thrive on social media.

The campaign had a strong foundation. Dove had always used a variety of "real" women in its ads, and the brand identity included honesty and transparency. The welcome message on dove.com says, "For over a decade, we've been working to make beauty a source of confidence, not anxiety. . . . Beauty is not defined by shape, size or color – it's feeling like the best version of yourself."

The campaign's impact has been both commercial and cultural. Sales increased from \$2.5 billion to well over \$4 billion, and not just in soap and shampoo. Nancy Vonk of Ogilvy explains, "We found out that the women and men exposed to [the campaign] became much more interested in buying anything the brand was selling. That was about, 'I really appreciate what the brand is doing in the world.'"[16]

The Dove campaign succeeds in large part because it fits the modern ambitions, purchasing patterns, and attitudes of Boomer women. They are most interested in achieving a healthy, authentic look. And they are experienced and realistic as consumers of personal care and beauty products. They know what they're looking for, and they don't believe most product claims. Today's women over 50 say they feel more beautiful in midlife than they felt when they were in their twenties. They object to use of younger models or phony celebrities in advertising targeting them. And, interestingly, they define beauty in terms of confidence.[17]

Finances expert Kerry Hannon, author of *Never Too Old to Get Rich*, reflects, "The Dove campaign gave a message to the rest of us that, you know what, you're attractive just the way you are." Colin Milner, founder of the International Council on Active Aging, said, "They were looking at the inner spirit of these older women as opposed to the outer look." And Karyne Jones, CEO of the National Caucus and Center on Black Aging, told us, "Too many marketers are saying to avoid your age. Improving my look is appealing, but trying to make myself look younger isn't. They should all be appealing to people's individuality to make them feel good about who they are."

Unfortunately, plenty of brands have stuck with the formula of serving up guilt and shame with an ageist spin. Contrast Dove's stance with a Dior campaign, widely and rightly criticized, that used an unblemished 25-year-old model in ads for an anti-aging cream called "Capture Youth." Much of the criticism flew on Instagram with the hashtag #ThatsNotMe. Like many gerontophobic ads in that product category, it created anxiety by stressing what's wrong with the consumer. And it set an impossible ideal standard of beauty rather than encouraging consumers to be their own version of beautiful. Then there are the ubiquitous – and ageist and sexist – ads for Peloton exercise equipment. Featured exercisers are young and already in perfect condition. As *USA Today* reported, "Every person portrayed in Peloton ads is in great shape, lives in a lavish home, and chooses to make the Peloton workout bike the centerpiece of said home. Sure, it's a commercial, but it might as well be parody."[18] Older exercisers need not apply.

A wide range of health products and services can engage older consumers by helping them look and feel their best – beauty and personal care, fashion and everyday attire, pharmaceuticals and medical services, food and nutrition, fitness and wellness. Some campaigns use generational anchors sharing their need for care, just like the rest of us. The Novartis "See Me" campaign places Cyndi Lauper amid a variety of everyday people showing how their skin has improved as they manage the chronic condition of psoriasis. Bon Jovi's "Advil Story," declares that there's no room for pain in his busy schedule as singer, songwriter, philanthropist, and father because "life's a juggling act."

Coming Breakthroughs in Longevity?

Will we see practical and affordable medical protocols to slow, or even partially reverse, the aging process? Many scientists believe it's a question of when, not if. A big breakthrough may come too late for most Boomers, but some experts predict that a majority of the children born today will live past 100, thanks to advances in chronic disease prevention, precision medicine, and new biotechnologies.

CRISPR (pronounced "crisper") stands for Clustered Regularly Interspaced Short Palindromic Repeats, which are the hallmark of a bacterial defense system. It forms the basis for a revolution in genome editing that could change every aspect of our lives in the decades ahead. Some experts believe that we're heading toward an era when revolutionary gene-editing methods may be able to correct almost 90% of disease-causing genetic variations, and the global CRISPR market is projected to reach over $7.6 billion by 2026.[19] The cost of sequencing an individual's DNA will soon be down to around $100. That will open floodgates of diagnosis, preventive treatment, and customization of wellness plans: the diets, supplements, exercises, and behaviors that work best for individuals.

The field of anti-aging medicine is coalescing and expanding rapidly. The American Academy of Anti-Aging Medicine

(A4M), co-founded by physician and sports medicine author Bob Goldman, and physician/researcher/inventor Ronald Klatz, is dedicated to the advancement of tools, technology, and transformations in health care that can detect, treat, and prevent diseases associated with aging. The organization has more than 26,000 members, primarily MDs, and hosts educational events all over the world.

Some promising protocols aim for rapid recovery. For example, platelet-rich plasma therapy (PRP) uses injections of a concentration of a patient's own platelets to accelerate the healing of injured tendons, ligaments, muscles, and joints. A blood sample from the patient is centrifuged to section out the platelet-rich plasma, which is then delivered to the targeted area of the body. Other protocols try to influence the aging process itself. Senolytics is an emerging class of drugs that targets senescent cells, those which in the natural aging process have ceased to divide. Unity Biotechnology, backed by Amazon founder and billionaire Jeff Bezos, is developing therapies intended to selectively eliminate senescent cells to slow age-associated disease and restore tissue to healthier states. Diseases being addressed include osteoarthritis, macular degeneration, COPD, and glaucoma.

Living Longer in Blue Zones

At the opposite end of the technological spectrum are decidedly low-tech ways to increase lifespan. A 2005 *National Geographic* story by Dan Buettner profiled five "Blue Zones," geographic regions with three times higher than average rates of living centenarians. The zones were in Greece, Sardinia, Japan, Costa Rica, and California. Researchers talked with centenarians and identified the common key practices which make for a longer and healthier life.

In Blue Zones, people's daily activities keep them moving naturally; they don't make special trips to the gym. They eat in moderation, heavy on various types of beans and greens and light on meat, and they drink alcohol moderately. They are closely connected to family, faith, and friends who reinforce each other's healthy behaviors. And they have a strong sense of purpose, worth up to seven years of life expectancy. In Okinawa, the key word is "Ikigai," which translates generally as "purpose" and specifically as "why I get up in the morning."

The value of this approach is being put to the test today. The organization Blue Zones has partnered with 48 cities to improve health metrics and life expectancy for residents. Their ten years of work in Albert Lea, Minnesota, is projected to have collectively increased individual life expectancy by 2.9 years and saved employers $8.6 million in health care cost, in large part by reducing the number of smokers.

The Blue Zones highlight healthy behaviors that we're all familiar with. Regular exercise helps fend off chronic disease, depression, and physical and cognitive impairment. Healthy diet and weight improve heart and bone health, and reduce the risks of stroke, type 2 diabetes, and cancer. Quitting smoking at 65 adds an average of two to four years to life.[20] Failure to take medications consistently and correctly correlates with increased hospital and nursing care admissions.[21] Lack of social interaction is as bad for health as lack of exercise.[22] Even small improvements in health behaviors in later life can contribute to a more active and fulfilling retirement.

Battling and Coping with Chronic Conditions

Many health problems are acute – brief illnesses like the flu or injuries like broken bones that can heal fairly quickly. However, the conditions that tend to arise with age are chronic – arthritis, hypertension, COPD, heart disease, diabetes, cancer, and Alzheimer's. As the term "chronic" implies, there's no complete cure, but rather an ongoing process of trying to manage the underlying causes and mitigate the symptoms. Conditions like Alzheimer's, Parkinson's, and ALS cause steady and often prolonged decline.

Fernando Torres-Gil, PhD, is director of the Center for Policy Research on Aging at the Luskin School of Public Affairs at the University of California, Los Angeles. In 1993, he was appointed by President Clinton as the first Assistant Secretary for Aging in the Department of Health and Human Services. In 2010, President Obama appointed him vice chair on the National Council on Disability. He is a board member of AARP. He is also a Latino Boomer who contracted polio as a child. His personal and professional experience gives him a unique perspective on what Boomers face as their health declines:

> I'm really happy to talk about my personal story because I'm thrilled I made it this long. I have a huge advantage over all our Baby Boomer friends who are now discovering a variety of chronic conditions and disabilities, whether it's a stroke, or high blood pressure, or a knee replacement. I've had a lifetime to go through the psychological and emotional transitions to accepting and adapting to my limitations. Now at 71 I'm very happy, even though my polio is going to lead me to be in a motorized scooter or a wheelchair. I've been practicing for this all my life, as I've been aging with a disability.
>
> Our generation is going to go through a major collective crisis as they move into their 70s, 80s, and 90s and are suddenly confronted with the vicissitudes of aging. They're not all going to grow to be 85 and hiking and doing marathons and essentially acting like they're 25. The Baby Boomer cohort is going to have the largest number of individuals who will grow older on their own, either divorced, never married, or estranged from others. We're going to have a real social crisis with a large portion of our generation at risk of isolation and depression, with all the consequences for mental and physical health.

Organizations would be wise to pause and reflect on Torres-Gil's thoughtful concerns and try to imagine products or services that can help assuage either the physical or psychological challenges of what's ahead for so many.

Chronic conditions among older adults are very common (Figure 6.6). Atop the list is hypertension, commonly known as high blood pressure. Nearly six in ten Americans age 65+, over 33 million in total, have hypertension, and it is one of the most common health conditions among older adults globally.[23] Hypertension is called a "silent killer" because it usually goes unnoticed unless blood pressure is measured. Two in five Americans with hypertension are not aware they have it,[24] even though it can lead to heart failure, stroke, and kidney failure, three common causes

Figure 6.6   Most Common Health Problems Among 65+

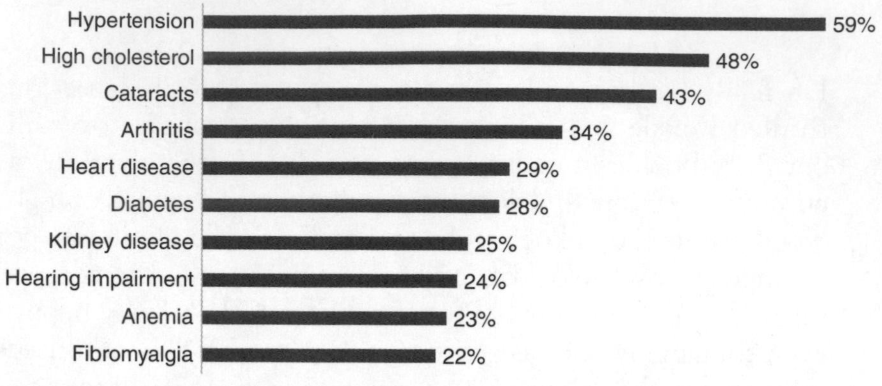

Health Problem	Percentage
Hypertension	59%
High cholesterol	48%
Cataracts	43%
Arthritis	34%
Heart disease	29%
Diabetes	28%
Kidney disease	25%
Hearing impairment	24%
Anemia	23%
Fibromyalgia	22%

Source: National Center for Health Statistics, Health United States, 2017

of death. The risks can be reduced by diet and exercise, specifically more fruit and vegetables, less salt, fats, and alcohol, and avoiding tobacco.

Those with hypertension should monitor their blood pressure regularly, and sales in the United States of smart devices for doing so are projected to grow from $85 million in 2018 to $122 million in 2022.[25] Omron Health released the first monitor built into a wristwatch. HeartGuide uses an inflatable cuff in the watchband to take an actual blood pressure reading (where other wearables provide only an estimate). HeartGuide's smartwatch functionality tracks activity levels (steps, aerobic steps, distance covered, and calories burned), monitors sleep (bed time, sleep time, and deep versus light sleep), and communicates (email and call and text notifications). The companion app tracks health data and provides customized coaching. Users have a more continuous and comprehensive picture of their heart health.

You can look at Figure 6.6 and do the math. If 59% of those 65+ have hypertension, and more than one in three has high cholesterol, cataracts, or arthritis, then a lot of older Americans must have multiple chronic conditions. In fact, 81% have two or more (Figure 6.7). That's unpleasant news if you are a sufferer, but for the nutraceutical, vitamin, pharmaceutical, diagnostics, and biotech sectors, it presents a world of opportunity.

Figure 6.7   People with Multiple Chronic Conditions by Age

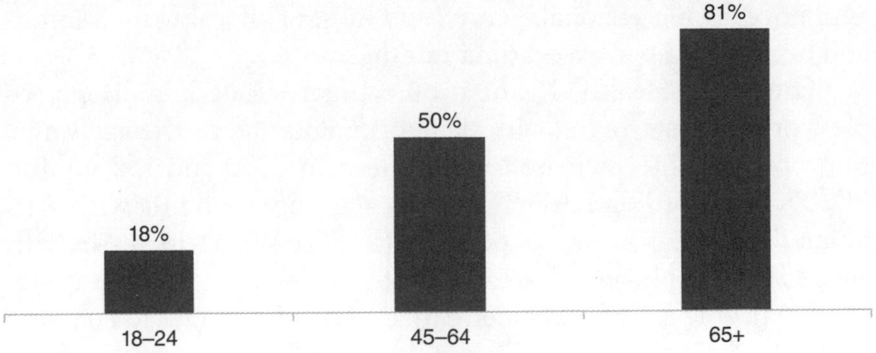

81%

50%

18%

| 18–24 | 45–64 | 65+ |

Source: Rand Corporation, Multiple Chronic Conditions in the United States, 2017

Maintaining Brain Health for Life

Retirees' greatest fear regarding living a long life is losing physical and cognitive abilities.[26] Presented with a forced choice, 75% say that functioning well mentally in retirement is more important than functioning well physically.[27] And Alzheimer's has become the most feared condition of old age. Cancer, stroke, and heart disease are frightening for sure, but more Boomers now fear Alzheimer's than all the other major diseases combined (Figure 6.8). What they

Figure 6.8   The Scariest Disabling Condition of Later Life

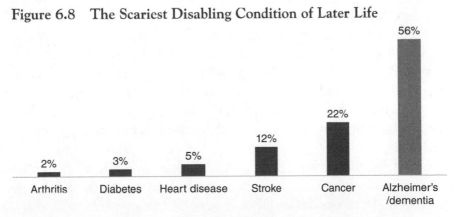

56%

22%

12%

2%   3%   5%

| Arthritis | Diabetes | Heart disease | Stroke | Cancer | Alzheimer's /dementia |

Source: Age Wave / Merrill Lynch, *Finances in Retirement: New Challenges, New Solutions*

really fear are the specific repercussions of the disease – losing independence, losing personal dignity, and most of all losing their minds and becoming a burden on their families.

The World Health Organization estimates that 50 million people worldwide are living with dementia, and due to the age wave, that's projected to increase to 82 million in 2030 and 152 million in 2050. Over 10% of Americans over age 65 are living with Alzheimer's. The percentage of people with Alzheimer's increases with age: 3% of people age 65–74, 17% of people age 75–84, and one-third of people age 85 and older. Since so many people will be living well into their 80s, Alzheimer's will become a challenge that most families – and nations – will face. Women are far more likely to develop Alzheimer's at some point – a one-in-five chance (21%) for a 65-year-old woman, but closer to a one-in-ten (12%) chance for a 65-year-old man – partly due to their longer lives. The projected number of people with Alzheimer's in the United States is expected to grow from 5.8 million in 2020 to 15 million in 2050.[28] Unless there's a true breakthrough, and we are surely hoping there will be, it could become the mental, physical, social, and economic sinkhole of the twenty-first century.

Dale Bredesen, MD, author of *The End of Alzheimer's*, is an optimistic voice in the fight against Alzheimer's while acknowledging the complexity of the challenge. He explained to us that a person with Alzheimer's and other related dementias may have 10 to 25 different factors contributing to their condition, and those all need to be understood at the individual level to come up with an effective treatment: "It's not going to be a one-pill, silver bullet solution that ends Alzheimer's. It's got to be a much more comprehensive approach." He is hopeful and believes that with continued scientific and clinical progress worldwide, rates of Alzheimer's and other dementias will start to decline within the lifetime of the Boomer generation.

Bredesen currently serves as Chief Science Officer at AHNP Precision Health. The firm trains practitioners in the ReCODE protocol. After a series of lab and genetic tests on the individual, practitioners customize a program including dietary guidelines, sleep goals, stress reduction techniques, cognitive training, hormone therapy, and other actions that work together to fend off cognitive decline. To date, more than 100 patients have seen documented improvements in cognitive functioning based on Bredesen's ReCODE Protocol.

Others are also taking multidimensional approaches. Based on the work of psychiatrist and self-help guru Dr. Daniel Amen, Amen Clinics opened their doors in 1991, and are now popping up all over the country. They look at the biological, psychological, social, and spiritual aspects of their patients' lives in order to come up with a comprehensive approach to lifelong mental wellness. One of their signature tests is a SPECT (single-photon emission computed tomography) to analyze blood flow inside one's brain. They work with a multitude of mental conditions including Alzheimer's, ADD, bipolar disorder, depression, and PTSD. Their website claims that 85% of their patients report improvements from their treatments and prescribed supplements.

Lisa Genova, PhD, a Harvard-trained neuroscientist, speaker, author, and yogi, broke away from her scientific background and wrote the bestselling novel *Still Alice*, which has now been published in 37 languages. It also won Julianne Moore an Academy Award for her portrayal of Alice in the popular movie. Genova told us, "I think people have become very comfortable with the idea that they can influence their health and their future health from the neck down. So people wear Fitbits, they know their blood pressure, they know their cholesterol level, and they are managing those numbers by what they eat and how they conduct their lifestyle. But most have the sense that there's nothing they can do about their health from the neck up. And in truth, there's a lot we can do."

When we asked for some examples, she shared, "We know that exercise does so many important, healthy things for everyday brain function and memory and has been shown to reduce the risk of dementia by as much as fifty percent. In addition, getting enough sleep, reducing stress, and supporting a healthy heart are all going to help fight off the accumulation of amyloid that could lead to Alzheimer's. All of these also help keep the brain running really well. But it's more than that," she added. "Having a sense of belonging, staying cognitively active, and learning new things also help your brain develop new neural pathways. It's a way of taking advantage of neuroplasticity. Every time you learn something new, you're actually building a bigger, more elaborately connected, Alzheimer's-resistant, healthier brain."

One of the other common mental difficulties among older Americans is depression, which is often linked to social isolation and loneliness. Social isolation also raises the risks of hypertension, heart disease, obesity, weakened immune system, and cognitive decline. Conversely, people who engage in activities with others tend to feel better, have greater sense of purpose, and live longer. Steve Cole, director of the Social Genomics Core Laboratory at the University of California, Los Angeles, said, "Loneliness acts as a fertilizer for other diseases. The biology of loneliness can accelerate the buildup of plaque in arteries, help cancer cells grow and spread, and promote inflammation in the brain leading to Alzheimer's disease. Loneliness promotes several different types of wear and tear on the body."[29]

Living with Everyday Health Problems

Some of the most common health problems of older people cause everyday discomfort or impairment. While remedies exist today, we expect that market forces will bring many more on the way, some effective and others snake oil. We're concerned that for most consumers, since so much of what's coming will emerge on the outskirts of traditional medicine and nutrition, it will be hard to know the difference.

Pain

One in three Americans over 55 has a diagnosed pain condition, commonly associated with arthritis. The majority of Americans rely only on over-the-counter medications to treat it, about 20% on prescription drugs.[30] The fast-emerging trend in self-managed pain treatment is CBD (cannabidiol), which is said to have anti-inflammatory and pain-relieving effects. CBD was legalized across the United States in 2018. The global CBD market, roughly half of which represents medical uses, was estimated at $4.6 billion in 2018 and is expected to grow to $23.6 billion in 2025.[31]

We're finally aware that far too many people have been pre-scribed opioids for their pain, and many have become tragically addicted or died. Increased awareness of the opioid epidemic is driv-ing a decline in prescription pain medication use. Among Ameri-cans with reported pain, 21% used a prescription in 2017 compared to 35% in 2013.

Sleep

Regular and adequate deep, restful sleep is vital to physical and men-tal health, and lack of sleep is associated with a variety of chronic medical conditions including hypertension and diabetes.[32] In *Sleep Revolution*, Arianna Huffington writes: "Scientists are resoundingly confirming what our ancestors knew instinctively: that our sleep is not empty time. Sleep is a time of intense neurological activ-ity. . . . Getting the right amount of sleep enhances the quality of every minute we spend with our eyes open." However, nearly half of Americans 65–80 report that they regularly have trouble falling asleep. And an estimated 22 million Americans suffer from sleep apnea. Its prevalence increases with age, and an estimated 80% of cases are undiagnosed.[33]

More older Americans means more sleepless Americans. The market for OTC sleep remedies nearly doubled between 2011 ($217 million) and 2015 ($420 million).[34] Global sales of sleep aids and technology, including smart beds and pillows, are expected to grow from $60 billion in 2018 to $95 billion in 2025.[35]

Hearing Impairment

Nearly 25% of those aged 65 to 74, and 50% of those 75 and older, have disabling hearing loss. Although many could benefit from hearing aids, fewer than one in three (30%) has ever used them, as they feel they'll be stigmatized as old.[36] However, hearing aids have come a long way from the big clunkers that debuted in 1956. Thanks to advances in miniaturization, some of today's options are virtually undetectable because they're positioned largely or completely in the ear canal or hidden away right behind the ear. And they'll soon do more than assist hearing. Valencell, with a wearable biometric sensor technology, and Sonion, with a new micro-acoustics and micro-mechanics technology, are partnering on a biometric sensor hearing aid. In addition to improving hearing, it will measure heart rate, electrocardiogram RR interval, activity levels, and energy expenditure – and provide a platform for future innovations in health monitoring. All that sounds promising, but Medicare doesn't cover hearing aids, and Supplement plans are unlikely to cover the most advanced and expensive kind.

Falls

Slipping and falling is not, of course, a medical condition. But it's a major cause of serious injury among older people, as well as a cause of general decline when the aftereffect is decreased mobility. Three million older Americans are treated in emergency departments for fall injuries each year,[37] and falls are contributing to the steady rise in hip and knee replacement surgeries around the world.[38]

A 2018 Centers for Disease Control study estimated the medical cost of falls at $50 billion annually, including $38 billion paid by Medicare and Medicaid. Yet basic interventions – home modifications like handrails in the shower, better medications management, or doing Tai Chi exercises – could prevent falls and avert medical costs.[39] The U.S. market for "ambient assisted living technology," primarily fall detection and emergency alert systems, is expected to grow from about $450 million in 2017 to nearly $2 billion by 2022.[40]

Age-Related Tech Is Ramping Up

The migration of health care processes into the home, and onto or even into the body, has unleashed a torrent of technological innovation. We're just at the beginning of this revolution, but here is a sampler of relatively new tech solutions. 23andme can test DNA for health predispositions, ancestry, carrier status, and other DNA traits for $199. Habit, a California start-up, is creating custom nutrition plans based on an individual's genetic makeup. Pillo is a home health robot for medication management. It can use facial recognition technology to interact with and dispense the correct pills for different individuals at the appropriate times, as well as order refills and connect with health care professionals. Mixfit is an app and a drink dispenser, producing a drink that is personalized to a user's nutritional and vitamin needs. Triple W has a wearable to help people with incontinence by using ultrasound to notify them when the bladder is getting full.

The Apple 4 Watch can detect irregular heartbeats and falls. ReSound controls hearing aid settings via an iPhone or Apple Watch. Xandar Kardian offers a contact-free (via radar technology) monitoring device that can keep track of a user's vital signs, detect a fall, and measure for sleep apnea. WiseWear jewelry does much the same, plus GPS location, with a fashionable bracelet connected to a smartphone. Care Predict Home is a wearable that uses kinematics to quantify daily activities, including eating, walking, drinking, toileting, and bathing, as well as predicting health issues. Healium tracks a user's brain patterns and heart rate, and then transfers the patterns into a visual mindfulness and stress-reduction app that is compatible with Oculus Go, Gear VR, and Google Daydream headsets.

Finally, general-purpose voice assistants, starting with Amazon Echo and Google Home, can perform or assist with tasks and issue reminders. Reminder Rosie gives reminders in the recorded voice of a family member, friend, or caregiver.

In one of our studies, we asked people of all ages how interested they were in new health technologies. Their responses (Figure 6.9) reveal high interest in everything from anti-aging therapies to replacement organs to home care robots. We expect that these will all be lively markets in the near future.

Figure 6.9   Interest in New Health Technology

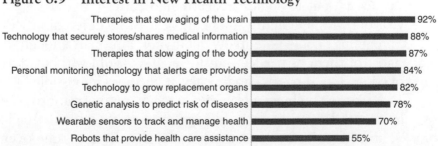

Source: Age Wave / Merrill Lynch, *Health in Retirement: Planning for the Great Unknown*

Waze to Help People Out of the Maze?

The U.S. health care system is a maze. Worse, it's a 3D maze. A maze that is costly in terms of expense, time, efficiency, patient outcomes, and public health. It is in no way user-friendly.

One dimension is the provisioning and receiving of care. Physicians and facilities are specialized and clinic and remote care options are multiplying. This fragmentation of services is hardest on older patients because they need more care, they have more combinations of conditions, and they are more likely to be receiving care from multiple organizations.

The second dimension is paying for services. Given the cost of health care, maximizing insurance coverage and minimizing out-of-pocket expenses are necessities. Yet insurance options and processes are complicated, to put it mildly. Retirees may be dealing with three parts of Medicare, widely variable supplemental plans, and a lucky few with employer-sponsored retiree health plans. Only a small fraction of today's retirees (19%) say they feel knowledgeable about Medicare and its options. That's unconscionable.

Even the small stuff can cause confusion. Ken recently received a note from Medicare about his coverage. In the upper left of the document, in large letters, it proclaimed, "This Is Your Medicare Premium Bill." However, in the upper right, also in large letters, it proclaimed, "This Is Not a Bill." Hello? Is anybody there?

A third dimension is the often-overlooked challenge of accessing – and making sense of – supportive and social services at the local, state, and national levels. Agencies are separate organizations with often overlapping missions and little by way of coordination. Housing doesn't talk to home care. Fernando Torres-Gil told us, "As a 71-year-old with a disability, there are at least 20 different offices for 20 programs I could potentially qualify for. I'm smart enough to work most of them as needed, but for a 71-year-old without that kind of education, support, or advocacy, it becomes impossible."

The Waze app helps people navigate to where they want to go – by car, on a bike, or on foot. It negotiates traffic, avoids roadblocks, and helps us reach destinations in the shortest time over a minimally complicated route. Perhaps it's time for a retiree "Health Waze." On the care dimension, it could assess one's condition quickly, determine and recommend the right provider or service, identify the best nutrition and exercise protocols for every individual, and thereby help people stay healthier and get better sooner. Such a technology could help avoid roadblocks like competing diagnoses or prescriptions as well as confusion regarding all of the lifestyle modification possibilities. On the insurance and payment dimension, it could submit complete and correct claims quickly, thereby causing faster payment processing while minimizing out-of-pocket expense.

Although we're still a far cry from Health Waze, we do see and applaud steps toward easier navigation. Major hospitals and health systems have website portals to patients' health information, appointments and physician communications, billing, and other resources. Insurance companies have increasingly clever mobile apps. Aetna helps customers find services and manage benefits, and it integrates with the health and activity monitoring functions of an Apple Watch. UnitedHealthcare's app offers video chat with a doctor 24/7. These services are local to the institution, and they tend to be task-based, not objective-based. The user still puts the pieces together and does most of the navigating.

AI will probably need to advance for a few more years before there's a smart and user-friendly app to rule them all. But there are opportunities everywhere for providers, insurers, and agencies to deliver more of what retirees want – and sometimes desperately need – by way of navigating the system. And there may be opportunities for organizations to band together on technological capabilities without running afoul of patient data privacy regulations.

Once again, Fernando Torres-Gil helps us look at the big picture:

America has evolved a health system based on a categorical approach as opposed to a universal approach, a system with many categories of providers, insurers, and patients. Most other nations have created or are creating public policy approaches to their aging populations based first on a set of universal principles. These may be simply saying that everyone has the right to health care, everyone has the right to long-term care, everyone has the right to grow old without having to be on the street. From those principles, they move forward and create systems of services and benefits that are more universal – and can have one access point.

We agree 100%, and we're hoping that folks in the government sector will bring in a few skilled marketers and communicators to help them make Medicare and other services far more understandable and user-friendly. The long-term solution may be to simplify and better integrate the system, but for now retirees need a lot of help just navigating it.

A Looming Geriatric Medical Crisis

Two-thirds of Americans age 50+ believe that today's health care system isn't ready for an aging population.[41] They're correct.

Even as the demand for geriatric medicine is growing rapidly with an aging population, geriatrics remains a relatively obscure medical specialty. By way of contrast, trained pediatricians outnumber trained geriatricians by more than ten to one. There is one active pediatrician providing patient care for every 1,393 children age 18 and under, but just one geriatrician for every 10,732 adults age 65 and over.[42] The American Geriatrics Society projects that we will need more than 30,000 geriatricians by 2030. As of 2018, there were only 7,300 board-certified geriatricians. It's highly doubtful that supply will catch up to demand, since only 66 of the 5,349 medical school graduates in 2018 went into a geriatrics program.[43] The reason is largely economic. In an era of highly specialized medicine, the disciplines that attend to people's health across the lifespan – pediatrics, family medicine, and geriatrics – are the least compensated (Figure 6.10). Plastic surgeons and orthopedic specialists earn about 2.5 times what geriatricians do. The incentives have got to change – this is an institutional failure. Many people today are speaking out about how our economy is "rigged." We believe that our health care system is "rigged" to favor the rich, the young, and the connected.

Compounding the problems of health care delivery at large is the retirement wave of Boomer physicians. As of 2016, 52% of the one million professionally active physicians in the United States were over the age of 50, and 29% were in their 60s or older. More than one-third of currently active physicians will be 65 or older within the next decade, and 17% plan to retire within the next

Figure 6.10   **Annual Physician Compensation by Specialty**

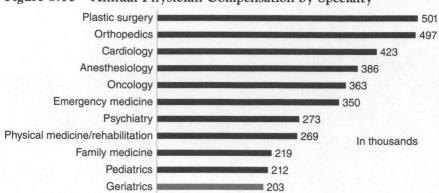

Source: Medscape, Physician Compensation Report, 2018; Medpage Today, 2018 Geriatrics Salary Survey

three years. That would remove approximately 136,000 physicians from the workforce during a period when about 85,000 physicians will complete residency and enter it. Overall, the supply of U.S. physicians is expected to grow by about 8% over the next 15 years, while the 65+ population is projected to grow by 53%.[44]

What will compensate for a severe shortage of physicians, especially geriatricians? Some medical schools are piloting tuition-free programs, funded by donations and grants, to attract students into lower-paying specialties. Kaiser Permanente opens its own medical school this year and is waiving tuition for the first five classes of students (but has no apparent focus on geriatrics). Those are laudable efforts but small steps. Against the backdrop of the demographic increase in older Americans, overall demand is not going to shrink, even if we see breakthroughs in the treatment of chronic conditions or in anti-aging medicine. Instead, the gap will need to be filled by more and better information, technology, and self-care.

Taking charge of one's health may not be just a generational trait of Boomers, but everyone's imperative. We believe we're in the first inning of a revolution in science, health, medicine, and self-care that could possibly transform the future of retirement more than any other factor.

Actions and Opportunities for Organizations and Entrepreneurs in the Health Sector

1. Build Waze-like navigation into your offerings. Retirees need help navigating their care needs, their relationships with providers, and their handling of payments.
2. Build motivation (e.g., through progress tracking), discipline (e.g., around meds management), and confidence (e.g., by feeling informed) into your offerings.
3. Make your offerings more holistic and integrative by showing how they fit with other treatments or into healthy behavior regimes.
4. Build social support into your offerings by connecting customers with family, friends, and people with similar health needs and interests.
5. Personalize your offerings to fit the precise needs and preferences of older customers, or to include concierge-style individual attention.
6. If your offerings are portable or wearable, make them unobtrusive, uncomplicated, age-friendly, even fun to wear and operate.
7. Have monitoring devices automate emergency response (e.g., after falls) by contacting care providers or designated family members, but without a "big brother is watching" aura.
8. Integrate offerings with technologies already in use, such as smartwatches and in-home voice-control devices.
9. Help retirees anticipate and plan for the cost of care, including being realistic about the options and costs of long-term care.
10. Adjust to retirees' very different approaches to consuming health services. They're in agreement about the importance of staying healthy, but not about how or how much they want to invest in it.

7

Retirement Isn't a Solo Project

The Entangled Endearments of Family Relationships

THE GILLETTE TREO™ is the world's first razor designed for shaving someone else. Developed with the help of caregivers, the award-winning design features an ergonomic handle suited to the person doing the shaving, a special non-foaming shaving gel conveniently stored in the handle, and even a safety comb to protect the skin. Gillette points out that there have been 4,000 variations on safety-razor design, but this is the first specifically for caregivers and care recipients.

At the center of the TREO's launch was a multiple-award-winning three-minute ad called "Handle with Care." It shows a middle-aged New Jersey man, Kristian Rex, together with his son Luke, caring for his widowed father, who had suffered a stroke and was unable to do many things for himself. Rex awakens his father and helps him to the bathroom for a shower, shampoo, and shave. Rex narrates the story, from how as a kid he admired the physique and "Popeye arms" of his tugboat-captain dad to the current role reversal: "Now he needs me to help him out. . . . It's actually an honor to do that for your father because he did it for me when I was a kid."

Shaving him carefully and conventionally had taken a while, "but I gotta be careful with that face." The story ends with the father looking good, the three men sharing some wine, and an affirmation of how the generations take care of each other. The camera draws in on Rex as he heartfully reflects, "After I've poured love on my dad all day, he says to me 'I don't know what I did to deserve you.' I tell him, 'I've got you dad. I've got you.'"

Gillette's slogan, "The Best a Man Can Get," winds up summarizing both the product and the relationship. The ad campaign and even elements of the product itself were created by marketing wizard Leo Savage. Gillette's TREO was named one of the greatest technological breakthroughs of 2018. Seeing the simplicity of this innovation and its appeal – it even won an award at the Cannes Film Festival – it's hard not to be frustrated that so few companies have entered into the caregiver marketplace. This is even more upsetting when you realize that, while 4 million babies were born in America last year, 20 million people became elder caregivers.

The TREO ad introduces many of the key family-related themes we explore in this chapter, including the growing strength of intergenerational connections within families and communities, the special relationships in grandparenting, the many challenges of widowhood and family caregiving, and the countless opportunities for companies and organizations to better engage and serve retirees through transgenerational appeal.

The Changing Family Lifescape

Increasing longevity and changing social norms are redefining "family." Today, about one American in three is part of a four-generation family – including parents, children, grandchildren, and great-grandchildren. There's even a growing number of five and six-generation families. In 2001 *The New York Times* showed the world a glimpse into the future. It wasn't an article about a Jetsons' future with flying cars and super-smart robots. What they featured was even more mind-boggling. It was a story about 118-year-old Sara Knauss. To get your attention, it featured a wonderful picture of Knauss surrounded by her 95-year-old daughter Kitty, her

73-year-old grandson Bob, her 49-year-old great-granddaughter Kathy, her 27-year-old great-great-granddaughter Kristina, along with her adorable 3-year-old great-great-great-grandson Bradley. Welcome to the future!

Partly because of our increasingly mobile and modular lifestyles, blended families have become more common, with two-thirds of remarriages involving children from previous marriages and 40% of Americans having at least one step-relative. One-parent households and LGBTQ-parent households are also on the rise. So are single-person households – including among older Americans who are divorced, widowed, or always single. At the same time, one in five Americans, some 64 million and rising, live in households containing multiple generations of adults (Figure 7.1).[1] And 4.6 million children live in the same household as their grandparents, almost half of them with no parents on hand.[2]

In a recent article in *The Atlantic*, David Brooks concludes that we're seeing the most rapid changes in family structure in history. He describes how the still-idealized "nuclear family" of married couples and 2.5 young children was a twentieth-century phenomenon – and a step in the fragmentation of family structures. Brooks writes:

> If you want to summarize the changes in family structure over the past century, the truest thing to say is this: We've made life freer for individuals and more unstable for families. We've made life better for adults but worse for children. We've moved from

Figure 7.1   Americans Living in Multigenerational Households

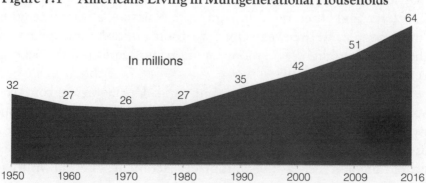

Source: Pew Research Center, 2018

big, interconnected, and extended families, which helped protect the most vulnerable people in society from the shocks of
life, to smaller, detached nuclear families . . . which give the
most privileged people in society room to maximize their talents
and expand their options.[3]

Today nuclear families are in the minority, and we need new
ways to recreate the interconnection, society, support, and resilience that extended families provide. Mutigenerational households
and cooperative living arrangements are steps in a positive direc-
tion, and the support they offer can be especially important to older
people at risk of isolation and loneliness.

Family structures are widely varied and in flux, and organizations seeking to serve retirees should not make assumptions based
on yesterday's family structure and relationships. Chances are high
that the assumptions will be wrong.

Deepening Relationships and the Reemergence of Interdependence

In our studies, when we asked what facet of life – health, home,
work, leisure, giving, finances, family – has been most satisfying,
the number-one answer was always "family."[4] In fact, more retirees
said family than all those other facets of life combined. Retirees
have more time for family and friends, and they relish it. In retirement, while some couples separate – we've all heard the line, "I
married you for life but not for lunch" – most couples report growing closer, and other friendships grow more active, especially among
single people. Retirees get closer to their children and especially
their grandchildren. The most common motivation for relocating
is to be closer to family.

As Patricia Thomas, Hui Liu, and Debra Umberson, the
authors of "Family Relationships and Well-Being" explain, "Family relationships may become even more important to well-being
as individuals age, needs for caregiving increase, and social ties in
other domains such as the workplace become less central in their
lives." At the same time, "Family relationships often become more
complex, with sometimes complicated marital histories, varying

relationships with children, competing time pressures, and obligations for care."[5]

We're seeing a rise not just in multigenerational living, but in transgenerational interdependence. It goes up, down, and sideways. Boomer retirees may be supporting or caregiving their elderly parents, who may move in rather than go into assisted care. They may also be supporting adult children who are still trying to gain their financial independence and may "boomerang" back home for a while. The parents are usually happy to receive them, because parenthood doesn't retire. Or retirees may be helping siblings or close friends in need of support. In all these relationships, the feelings of commitment are mutual, with younger generations saying they are ready to support older ones when the time comes.

Intergenerational connection can be core to retirees' happiness and sense of purpose. As Encore.org founder and CEO Marc Freedman told us, "The research about socioemotional connectivity shows we get better at relationships as we age, with more empathy and emotional regulation, and the impulse to express feelings of connectedness. All that adds up to happiness. In this phase of life, people form deep connections that nurture the next generation, and that process not only alleviates social isolation and loneliness, but also provides a deep sense of living a worthwhile life."

The Generosity of Grandparents

Grandparenting is growing ever more important to family life. By age 65+ over 90% of Americans have grandchildren. That's over 70 million grandparents total, and six in ten are members of the Boomer generation.[6] Christine Crosby, founder of *GRAND Magazine*, told us that grandparenting today is like never before: "We are the first generation of grandparents to hit the planet that has lived this long, and we'll be in the lives of our grandchildren for an average of 30-plus years. There are no roadmaps for us to follow. This is a new path." Lori Bitter, author of *The Grandparent Economy*, adds, "Grandparenthood is a time when the future comes into sharper focus. There is a realization of mortality, and of family life continuing after they are gone. Relationships take on greater meaning and a sense of selflessness takes over."

Eighty percent of grandparents call their grandchildren a top priority in their lives.[7] Nearby grandparents regularly provide child-care, and they are the primary childcare arrangement for one in four children of preschool age.[8] A recent AARP study found that 45% of grandparents keep in touch with older grandchildren by text, 38% by video chat, and more than 25% each by email and Facebook.[9] When grandparents help raise grandchildren, it makes a big differ-ence, as Crosby points out: "There has been tremendous research showing the value that grandparents who play an active role have on the upbringing of their grandchildren – from lower truancy and drug usage to greater confidence in life."

Grandparents have become a market force unto themselves – and one that's almost always overlooked. For example, when we think of a target consumer population for children's toys, clothes, or technology, the automatic reaction may be to think of their parents. Think again. In America alone, grandparents spend an estimated $18 billion annually on apparel for their grandchildren, $15 billion on toys, and almost $10 billion on vacations.[10] In fact, they purchase 25% of all toys, 40% of all children's books, and 20% of all video games. Today's Boomer grandparents aren't just purchasing clothing, sports, and entertainment products for grandchildren when young, but also for them as teenagers and early adults. They may travel regularly to visit the grandchildren. And they invest in grandchildren's futures by contributing to college savings plans. Almost 20% of surveyed grand-parents had contributed to a grandchild's college savings or expenses in the past year, an average of $2,337.[11] We estimate grandparents' total annual contribution toward college savings at $34.2 billion.

Disney has honed the techniques of marketing to grandparents – and there's a lot that can be learned from them. One in five grand-parents has taken a Disney vacation with their grandchildren.[12] Walt Disney World's "Grand Adventure" web page provides tools for grandparents planning visits, right down to choosing activities, skipping long lines, making the most of resort and park services, getting tips from insiders, and otherwise "childproofing" the vaca-tion plan. Part of the appeal to grandparents is reliving the fun of earlier Disney adventures as parents with their young children, or even as children themselves.

Several years ago, Ken and his wife Maddy, co-founder of Age Wave, were noticing that many grandparents spent a lot of time reading children's books to their grandchildren. Because they had also read many books to their own kids when they were little, they had noticed that in children's books, there were no elders, or if there were, they were weird old geezers, or nasty crones who were trying to fatten up kids to put them in the oven to eat. They felt that a story was needed for grandparents to read, and even discuss with their grandkids, that would feature the idea that more and more people are choosing to reinvent themselves in maturity. You know, the mom who goes to law school at 45, the person who comes back from a health crisis to run a marathon at 60, the couple who falls in love at 80, the retiree who starts a whole new career.

Ken and Maddy got to work creating a children's book that would tell the simple yet wonderful story of new beginnings. They were fortunate to be joined by an extraordinary illustrator and artist, Dave Zaboski, who had been a senior animator at Disney and had worked on projects like *The Lion King*, *Aladdin*, and *Beauty and the Beast*. What emerged was *Gideon's Dream: A Tale of New Beginnings*, a modern fable, in the spirit of Aesop, about a caterpillar grub who, after falling off a leaf one day, always dreamed of flying. Then when he got older instead of becoming a worn out old caterpillar, he transformed himself into a butterfly. Since the book was published over a decade ago, they have received countless letters from grandparents thanking them for the magical book and describing how it allowed them to share stories with their grandkids about their own reinventions.

Lori Bitter offers several pieces of advice for marketers trying to engage grandparents. First, like older consumers generally, grandparents are experienced and perceptive. They know when depictions of family interactions ring true and when they do not. Second, the experiences don't have to be expensive, just together with the grandkids – like learning to cook or going fishing. And third, other children are often recipients of grandparents' generosity as they volunteer, donate, and support causes that serve the needs of children generally.

Why Not Turn the Tables?

Thoughtful marketers have noticed that grandparents love to give to their grandchildren, but here's an example of a massive opportunity that's hiding in plain sight. Why not activate the marketplace for grandparents as the *recipients* of generosity? With those 70 million grandparents in the United States and over a billion worldwide, and with the average grandparent having 4+ grandchildren, why is "Grandparents Day" such a snooze? You may not even know when it is. Hardly anyone does. Since it was established in the United States in 1978, some two dozen countries around the world celebrate Grandparents Day in some form. But the emphasis is on honoring grandparents' contributions, not generosity toward them, and the day isn't a big deal anywhere.

There's four billion grandparent cards waiting to be bought. But let's imagine more than that. What kinds of running shoes might Grandma like? Which new books would Grandpa like to read? And if you can afford it, does he need new golf clubs? Would Grandma like a ticket to Las Vegas? Just as brilliant Chinese entrepreneur Jack Ma hit the bullseye when his Alibaba retail platform promoted "Singles Day," which swiftly became the biggest and most lucrative annual selling event in the world, there must be a massive grandparent market waiting to be envisioned and unleashed around the world.

Who's the Buyer?

Recognizing grandparenting as a lifestage and tremendous market opportunity raises a key question: who's the buyer? Are elders always the buyers for their children and grandchildren or, as with Grandparents Day, does it also go the other way around?

Lifeline was the first and is still the leading medical alert system, designed to let people summon help at the press of a button on a necklace or wristband. Today such systems are standard fare in medical facilities, senior communities, and the homes of older people living alone. But the product got off to a slow start.

It was developed in the early 1970s by gerontologist Dr. Andrew Dibner. Initial sales to individuals, the target market, were slow, though hospitals showed interest in using it within their facilities.

How could such a good idea achieve even more success? The answer lay in the sales data. Checks coming in for the monthly subscription fee weren't always from the persons using the device. They often were from the daughters or sons, the ones who wanted to be sure that Mom or Dad was okay. Lifeline's product was conceived as an alert system for older adults, but they were fascinated to realize that they were also selling peace of mind for the families. The buyers spanned generations and were often happy to pay for such a service to meet both their parents' and their own needs. The product's positioning was adjusted, and the rest is history. Lifeline Systems went public in 1983 and was acquired by Philips in 2006. The latest product generation includes fall detection, advanced location technology, and voice communication. Nearly every technology company has taken note. Even Apple Watch now has an alert system for those – more likely older wearers – in need.

Retirees in their 60s are buying things for their parents, their children, their grandchildren, and of course, themselves. That's four generations. Who is paying for the oldest generation's health and caregiving services? Often the adult children. For the multigenerational family trip? Could be the elders, the adult children, or even the grandchildren. And who's paying for the grandchildren's education? Increasingly the grandparents. For their favorite toys? Same. Who is buying the TREO razor supply? Most likely the son. Businesses would be wise to realize that the retiree market is not just silver-haired consumers buying things only for themselves; it's a far more lively and transgenerational marketplace, unlike anything we've ever seen.

Transgenerational Appeal: No Need for Age-Ghetto Marketing

In Chapter 1, we discussed generational "anchoring," the use of emblematic people, music, or events to connect with the shared attitudes and experiences of a generation, specifically Boomers. In Chapter 3, we discussed how "universal design" doesn't stigmatize older men and women. Rather it's design that is smart and inclusive of everyone. Appeals to intergenerational relationships can be just as engaging, and numerous financial services firms are getting very adept at this.

For example, in Principal Financial's "We can help you plan for that" marketing campaign, retirement dreams turn out to be about family generosity. A 2017 ad had retirees moving from their lifetime home to the big city to help their daughter and son-in-law raise the grandchildren, with the tagline, "Be where you're needed most." A 2019 ad had a young woman moving in with her grandparents to finish her senior year of high school. The grandfather shelves buying the yellow sportscar of his dreams in favor of buying a car for his granddaughter, explaining, "This is my dream now." Another tells the story of a man taking his father to look at assisted living facilities, then instead building a small house for his dad in the backyard, harkening back to the treehouse his father had built for him. In all cases, empathetic financial advisors make cameo appearances to help make it happen.

In 2017 MassMutual rebranded around the theme of "interdependence," reaffirming its deep roots as a mutual, or customer-owned, company. The rebranding campaign portrayed interdependence in family, community, and society. For example, the "Two Ways" ad portrays contrasting images of the isolated – a solitary hiker, a tiny International Space Station traversing the moon – and the interdependent – a father helping his son fix a bike, a well-lit Earth at night seen from space. The narration is poetic: "We come into this world needing others. Then we are told it's braver to go it alone, that independence is the way to accomplish. But there is another way to live. A way that sees the only path to fulfillment – is through others." MassMutual is also incorporating the theme of interdependence into an expanded employee benefits package with more for caregivers, widows and others bereaved, new mothers and fathers, and those wishing to volunteer.[13]

The Prudential campaign featuring Professor Dan Gilbert is thoroughly multigenerational, without focusing on specific families. The question posed in the commercials is, "Will you be financially ready for a long retirement? One answer is provided by a crowd of people of all ages putting stickers on a large wall indicating the age of the oldest person each has known. It turns into a graph of how long people live past 65. In another ad, people unroll on an athletic field ribbons whose length corresponds to how many years their planned retirement savings will cover. Lori Bitter explains why the campaign is so effective: "It brought people of every age into the conversation about getting older and what that means in term of your finances. You saw children in that ad. You saw older people. You saw Millennials. You saw somebody from every generation taking part in kind of a street event."

Other products and services, like the Gillette TREO, tap into family connections and transgenerational appeal. A very effective Volkswagen ad portrays family bonds and the power of personal legacy. *Adweek* recounts the storyline: "A family loses its grandfather. But the tribe bonds during a cross-country trip that their late patriarch never made, driving the brand-new seven-seat 2018 Atlas SUV from one coast to another – through a series of stunning landscapes – to throw his ashes into the great Pacific Ocean."[14] The soundtrack (note the generational anchor) has Simon and Garfunkel tenderly singing "America."

In 2018 Ralph Lauren celebrated its 50th anniversary with a multigenerational fashion show in Central Park that included babies, adolescents, several gray-haired models, and entire families walking the runway.[15] We applaud these kinds of efforts. In 2019, Ralph Lauren's global advertising campaign took the theme one step farther, "Family is who you love," portrayed eight different families, including a grandmother and her two granddaughters, a father with his three adult children, a father with his adult daughter, a lesbian couple, and families with young children. In one ad, they share definitions of "family," including "home," "everything," and the "center of my world." But the consensus definition is "who you love."

Chief Marketing Officer Jonathan Bottomley describes the campaign as "a celebration of the fact that family means different things to each of us – we live in a world where the meaning of family is bigger, broader, and more personal than it has ever been before." He continues, "While family, love and inclusion have always been the core values that underpin the brand, they're particularly resonant with our consumer today."[16]

Challenges Aging Families Face

Connections and commitments may run deep, but family can be a major source of worry as well as satisfaction for retirees. Marriage and family therapy, including intergenerational counseling and mediation, is a fast-growing field. Family issues often involve money, but overcommitment can be personal as well as financial. Retirees can feel stretched too thin, or "sandwiched," by their commitments to their parents, children, and others. Let's look at two common challenges, one to family finances, the other to family structure.

The Family Bank: Open 24/7

One of the biggest financial – and often emotional – complications in retirement comes from serving as what we've termed the "family bank" and lending, or more often simply giving, money to family members. The web of family interdependencies can keep the bank open 24/7. The family bank may help meet a one-time need such as an extraordinary medical expense, or it could provide ongoing everyday assistance over the course of many years. The most common recipients are adult children, but others include parents or in-laws, grandchildren, and other relatives. Six in ten Americans over age 50 we surveyed have provided financial support to family members in the last five years. Among those who have given or loaned money in the last year, the average amount is $6,500.[17] Globally, HSBC reports that 50% of parents provide regular financial support to their children over 18, and 54% provide support to their parents.[18]

Why do people nearing or even in retirement take on the role of family bank? Generational generosity, whether they can afford it or not. Eight in ten told us, "It's the right thing to do." And half say they felt an obligation.[19] Unlike regular banks, in the family bank the money is typically provided without expectation of repayment. About a third of the time, the banker provides funds without even knowing how they will be used.

Who serves as the family bank? Sometimes the role is predetermined, as when parents support their adult children. But beyond that, family members turn to the person who seems to have the most money, who seems most financially responsible, or who seems most approachable. More than half of those surveyed said they can name the family member who serves as the bank. Being the fiscally responsible and approachable one can backfire.

A surprising number of retirees provide financial support to their adult children. Those who delayed having children or had children in second marriages are increasingly likely to have early adults on the family bank books. And those early adults are taking longer to establish their own financial footing. Seven in ten early adults received financial support from their parents – who are usually in their 50s or 60s – in the last year, and half of them continue to receive support into their early thirties. While most of the financial support is for everyday expenses such as cellphone plans, groceries, rent, health insurance, and automobiles, some parents provide help with big-ticket items like down payments on houses. The total is enormous. The aggregate annual amount spent by all parents on early adult children is over $500 billion – or twice what they put into their retirement accounts. And while we hear a lot about the strain on young people to pay down their college debt, for many it's their parents or grandparents who are footing the bill. Educational expenses for adult children account for one-fourth of that $500 billion.

Some retirement age family bankers feel cornered. One told us, "I thought I would be supplementing my grandchildren's college funds. It turns out I *was* the college fund." Another said, "I paid down my mortgage and didn't run up my credit cards. Now everyone in my family is turning to me for money." Overall, however, generosity prevails: "I'm not looking to get back the money I loaned my daughter. I'm just happy I could help her when she needed it." But generosity can backfire in a big way when people sacrifice their own retirement savings and financial security to support family members. And it can backfire down the road when today's generosity means being strapped tomorrow, perhaps to the point of needing help in return and becoming a burden on family members, something that people from all walks of life tell us they dread.

Few retirees or pre-retirees anticipate and plan for providing financial support to family members. Nine in ten have never budgeted for such support, including the easily anticipated need to assist aging parents. So support is given without careful consideration of what they can really afford and how much they may be compromising their own retirement finances. An underlying problem is lack of discussion, hence clarity of terms, between giver and recipient. In retrospect, the family bankers often wish they'd established clearer expectations and limits, especially with adult children. And that there were ways to educate family members on how to be more financially independent.

Gray Divorce

People today feel greater permission to move on if relationships aren't working out. Consequently, increasing numbers of retirement-aged couples and their families are disrupted by divorce. In fact, between 1990 and 2015, the rate of "gray divorce" (among those 50 and older) doubled, and among those 65 and older it has tripled.[20] Over 30% of Boomers have been divorced at least once, and among the oldest Boomers, born before 1952, it's 37%.[21] "The Baby Boom generation was responsible for the extraordinary rise in marital instability after 1970," say Sheela Kennedy and Stephen Ruggles in their study, "Breaking up is hard to count." What's behind the instability? "The loosening of legal constraints and declining social stigma has reduced barriers to divorce, and the opening of new economic opportunities for women allowed many to escape bad marriages."

Gray divorce complicates retirement, both personally and financially. After a divorce, networks of friends shrink, especially for men. And financial assets shrink, especially for women. The average gray divorced woman experiences a 40% decline in household assets.[22] And there's less time to catch up, as Susan Brown of Bowling Green State University explains: "You're on the downslope of your career, so your ability to recoup any financial losses are lower compared to if you get divorced at age 35, when you've still got a good 30 more years potentially in the labor force."[23]

While divorce is among the most stressful life events, it comes as a relief for some. And while most people try to keep matters private and quiet in a divorce, others benefit from making the event a bigger deal. And there's a market in that. Christine Gallagher, author of The Divorce Party Handbook, has organized more than 200 such parties. The playful celebrations can include cathartic rituals – tossing the wedding ring into the ocean or burning the bridal veil – or fun and games mocking the ex. The divorce party supplies site named "Unknotted" offers "I Don't" cake toppers.

***

In the remainder of this chapter we explore in depth two more family challenges, two common situations where lives are stressed and families rally in support: when retirees serve as family caregivers and when they are widowed. Both can be anticipated but not completely prepared for. And both offer occasions for attentive and empathetic organizations to grow their business while serving and deepening relationships with retiree customers.

The Responsibilities and Rewards of Caregiving

The ultimate display of family interdependence, generosity, and sacrifice comes when a family member needs care. Providing it can be physically, emotionally, and financially draining on the caregivers, but we found in our studies that the overwhelming majority find the experience ultimately rewarding. Most family caregivers say that it brought them closer to their loved one, and they gained satisfaction from knowing that the recipient was being cared for well.[24] More than three-fourths say that they would gladly care for another loved one if needed.

Consider three things: increasing longevity, the aging of the enormous Boomer generation, and the significant gap between healthspan and lifespan. Add them up and we see the growing need for caregiving. As former First Lady and Carter Center co-founder Rosalynn Carter put it, "There are only four kinds of people in this world: those who have been caregivers, those who currently are caregivers, those who will be caregivers, and those who will need caregivers." Many younger retirees are caregivers, many older ones care recipients.

Almost seven in ten Americans turning 65 today will need long-term care services at some point in their lives, and nearly one-quarter of those will need support and services for longer than five years.[25] Because the cost of professional care is high (prohibitively so for many), family members step in as informal and generally unpaid caregivers. These informal caregivers provide 1.3 billion hours of help per month to people aged 65+ who are not in nursing homes, and about 40% of that effort serves older adults with dementia.[26] Nearly two-thirds of caregivers are women.

One in four retirees say they have dedicated a significant amount of time in retirement to serving as caregiver.[27] Their care recipients are most often spouses or parents, although care for other relatives and friends is also common.[28] Caregiving expert A. Michael Bloom points out, "With life expectancy rising and medical improvements, people live longer with illness. That means the caregiving journey is longer as well. One out of five caregivers passes away before their care recipient."

The Variety of Caregiving Responsibilities

Caregiving can begin suddenly when the recipient suffers a setback like a fall. Or it can increase gradually from occasional help to daily assistance to continual care. The duration can be brief – the recipient who fell had a hip replacement and recovered nicely. Or indefinite if the recipient has a gradual debilitating condition like Alzheimer's. Care most often takes place in the recipient's home, and 14% of the time the caregiver lives there as well, but one-third of the time the recipient moves into the caregiver's home.[29]

The caregiving process depends on the recipient's mental and physical condition and trajectory. As the recipient's needs increase or communication capability declines, caregiving can become more physically difficult and emotionally stressful. Yet most family caregivers let the load increase without getting additional support, and social isolation can become a problem for caregivers. Another big variable is the relationship between caregiver and recipient. Caring for a parent usually involves more of a role reversal than caring for a spouse.

Caregiving can include a variety of services (Figure 7.2). We may think first of physical care – help with eating, bathing, dressing, toileting, getting around. But the heart of caregiving can be emotional and social support, including companionship, conversation, everyday leisure activities, and transporting the care recipient to see friends. A recipient who does not need much personal care

Figure 7.2   Services Provided by Caregivers

Service	Percentage
Emotional/social support	98%
Financial caregiving	92%
Household support	92%
Medical care	84%
Care coordination	79%
Physical care	64%

Source: Age Wave / Merrill Lynch, *The Journey of Caregiving: Honor, Responsibility and Financial Complexity*

may still need household support, like cooking, cleaning, shopping, or medical support, such as managing medications and appointments and performing some basic nursing procedures.

Another important role is care coordination, organizing and monitoring the activities of the caregiving team. With that much potential work to do, many families make caregiving a group endeavor, where one person serves as primary caregiver and usually coordinator, and other family members fill in on a regularly scheduled or as-needed basis. As we'll discuss in more detail in Chapter 8, paid professional caregivers are part of the team in about one-quarter of caregiving situations, most often to help older recipients with physical care.[30]

Family caregiving is the most common situation. But what happens if no family is around? The emerging and expanding "share the care" model organizes local volunteers to collectively provide care and serve as the recipient's extended "family." When we talked with Michael Adams, a Stanford-trained lawyer and CEO of SAGE, the advocacy and services organization for LGBTQ older adults, he explained, "Because many LGBTQ people don't have adult children, they can't expect built-in care from family or family caregivers as they get older. Many are recognizing that at some point, they may well need community support and care. Some people I know are thinking about and exploring ways of creating their own kind of Share the Care communities." SAGE research finds that 30% of older LGBTQ people are very or extremely concerned about not having someone to take care of them, and 32% are just as concerned about being lonely and growing old alone. Among older heterosexual, cisgender people, less than 20% share those fears.[31] This creates both challenges and opportunities to serve the LGBTQ community.

Financial Caregiving

Caregiving is an intensely personal commitment. It can also be a major financial one. Our studies have revealed that over 90% of caregivers are also financial caregivers, contributing money directly or performing financial coordination tasks on behalf of the care recipient (Figure 7.3). Nearly two-thirds of caregivers do both.

Those making direct financial contributions average $7,000 a year.[32] The money usually pays for a mix of personal, medical, and general living expenses, with the biggest categories household (41% of the total) and medical expenses (25%). But out-of-pocket expenses can be a lot higher, especially when caring for someone with dementia. Three in ten family caregivers who contribute financially say it causes them financial difficulty.[33] But the majority aren't tracking and don't even know how much they are spending, especially for background expenses like their own transportation.

Financial caregivers also pay bills and manage bank and credit card accounts, and they commonly handle insurance policies,

Figure 7.3   Financial Coordination Tasks of Caregivers

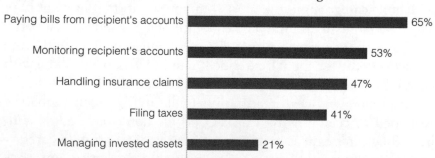

Paying bills from recipient's accounts — 65%
Monitoring recipient's accounts — 53%
Handling insurance claims — 47%
Filing taxes — 41%
Managing invested assets — 21%

Source: Age Wave / Merrill Lynch, *The Journey of Caregiving: Honor, Responsibility and Financial Complexity*

prepare taxes, and manage investments. They should also be a major line of defense against elder financial abuse, starting with monitoring accounts of all kinds. As a recipient's condition declines, these responsibilities expand. The financial caregiver may play an ongoing role getting and keeping the recipient's financial and legacy affairs in order.

Nearly 12 million care recipients need full assistance managing their finances. But nearly half of their financial caregivers do not have the legal authorization, such as a durable power of attorney, to perform all the roles they play.[34] And three-fourths of family caregivers haven't even discussed their financial roles with the care recipient. That reticence may be due to the recipient's mental condition, but more often it's a matter of family taboos about discussing finances, plus the fact that the caregiver just gradually assumed financial roles. In short, financial caregiving merits more acknowledgment and discipline than it generally receives. And we must note that, although it's unconscionable, financial abuse of elders is on the rise, with some of it perpetrated by family members who take money or possessions or try to force changes in their favor in the care recipient's will.

Serving Caregivers

Caregivers' personal finances can be stressed by contributing directly to the recipients' care and by the opportunity cost of the time spent in caregiving. The latter can be very high if the caregiver must cut back on work, reducing both income and retirement savings. Seventeen percent of Boomer caregivers have retired early or quit their jobs, and 21% have reduced hours or job responsibilities as a result of becoming caregivers.[35] Caregiving can also take a toll on the caregiver's health, and thus health expenses. Two-thirds of caregivers said they could benefit from financial advice.

A variety of services and guides are appearing to ease the work and challenges of caregivers. Target's "Caregiver Essentials" web page curates useful products, such as pill planners, blood pressure monitors, and over-the-counter drugs. For caregivers, they offer smart home products, stress-relief products, organization and planning tools, and helpful books on caregiving. They also provide caregivers with flexible shopping options including subscription service, same-day delivery, and curbside pickup. We expect to see many more services customized to caregivers' needs in the future, and whatever the products or services may be, 40 million family caregivers, and 20 million people becoming caregivers each year, is a very large market.

Caregiving may be a high-touch activity, but a wide range of rapidly evolving high tech can help make caregivers' work and lives easier. For example, in-home patient monitoring and treatment can revolutionize the medical side of caregiving. Caregivers can monitor recipients remotely, check in with them electronically, and be alerted by medical response services when called. Through telemedicine, physicians and nurses can "visit" patients in their homes. And caregivers can use apps for tasks including monitoring the recipient's medications, refilling prescriptions, and making medical appointments. For everyday health services, CVS in-store Minute Clinics provide basics. Most CVS stores have a Higi Station, a wheelchair-accessible booth where caregivers and recipients can get health readings such as blood pressure, pulse, weight, and BMI. Caregivers can also now get online training and real-time assistance when performing nursing tasks. Recently, after caregiving her mom who had early stage Alzheimer's, Carrie Shaw created the Embodies Labs company, which uses cutting-edge virtual reality technology to teach caregivers – both family and professional – how to empathically understand the world from the point of view of their loved one, and thereby provide more respectful and sensitive care.

Services are also cropping up to assist the financial caregiver. The Care.com HomePay service helps family members who hire home care workers with payroll, tax, and other mandated tasks. It also provides access to financial professionals and assistance in hiring home care workers. The True Link service provides prepaid cards for care recipients with settings to prevent certain purchases, such as from telemarketers, and alerts to family members about large purchases. The cards can also be issued to caregivers to make specific purchases.

At the end of caregiving, caregivers may need to reset their own personal and family finances, especially if the recipient has passed away, because caregivers are often heirs. A widowed spouse-caregiver is often the primary or sole heir, and it's common for children-caregivers to receive special consideration in the recipient's will. The experienced retiree-caregiver is better prepared should another loved one need care and has had an advance look at what life would be like as a care recipient. For many retirees, caregiving ends with the death of a spouse, and they enter our next personal and financial crossroads, widowhood.

The Journey of Widowhood

When couples grow old together, the marriage ends with the death of a spouse. The death may be anticipated, but the transition to widowhood is almost always highly upsetting and traumatic. On the Holmes and Rahe life change scale, the most stressful life event is the death of a spouse.[36] Fortunately, family and friends can provide immediate and ongoing emotional and pragmatic support, and those relationships often deepen.

Fifteen million Americans are currently widowed, and five million more have been widowed and then remarried.[37] Each year, 1.4 million Americans are newly widowed (Figure 7.4). In half the cases, the new widow had been serving as caregiver to the deceased spouse. And over three-fourths of the currently widowed are women.[38] That's because women have superior longevity and tend to be, on average,

Figure 7.4   Prevalence of Widowhood: Americans Widowed in 2019

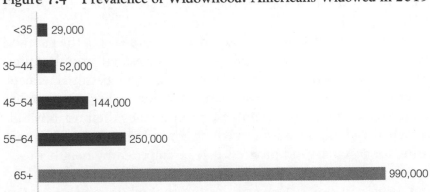

Source: U.S. Census Bureau, 2018 American Community Survey, and Marital Events of Americans, 2009

2.5 years younger than their husbands. It's also because widowed men tend to remarry more than widowed women do. Among all Americans over age 65, 32% of women and 11% of men are widowed.[39]

The new widow is suddenly the primary – or lone – decision maker, and there are so many decisions and actions to take. Two-thirds of widows say that in the beginning of their grief they had too many things to do and didn't know where to start.[40] Funeral arrangements to make, death certificates to obtain, financial accounts to reassign, and eventually an estate to settle. Paperwork and logistics intrude upon the chance to grieve. One widow articulated the common plight: "The world is not sympathetic to what you're going through. They don't give you any time to grieve properly. . . . Your life is suddenly in probate. You can't take even a few days to process what's just happened to you because the business demands taking care of, and the business is not simple."[41]

Emotional Adjustments

Widows make emotional and practical adjustments at different paces. Although some widows never recover from the loss of their spouse, our research showed that after approximately three years of grieving and adjusting, the physical and emotional health of widows typically returns to normal levels, or we should probably say to "new normal" levels. Many widows discover resilience they weren't sure they had, and more than three-quarters of widows said that after losing their spouse, they discovered courage they never knew they had.

Many widows deal with tension between preserving the past and creating a future. Their progress may be measured in milestones: When to deal with the spouse's clothing and personal effects. Whether to take the trip they'd planned. When to begin to socialize as a single person. Progress can be complicated by their responsibilities when widows have jobs, have children living at home, or are caring for parents. And progress can be impeded by health issues. Especially early in widowhood, the chances of serious illness and depression can rise.[42] It's worth noting that while modern society has a wide range of products and services to help people plan for and adjust to both marriage and parenthood, the other side of the lifeline is far less attended to and creatively supported. This ties in to Dr. Robert Butler's notions about gerontophobia. Because we're uncomfortable with death, many needs go avoided or even unnoticed by youth-focused service providers.

Financial Challenges and Surprises

The financial transitions and challenges of widowhood are several and significant (Figure 7.5). While widows commonly experience a drop in income, they also often see a substantial rise in assets as bank and investment accounts, real estate, and other assets transfer mainly into their control. Many also become the recipients of life insurance payouts. So there are many widows at each end of the economic spectrum, including with high home equity or net worth. Ironically, at present, the highest concentration of poverty is among single older women, while at the same time, the highest concentration of wealth is also among single older women. However, even the affluent widow can face the immediate challenge of lack of cash because assets in the late spouse's name may not be accessible until the estate is settled, and assets like real estate aren't liquid.[43]

At the start of widowhood, many feel stressed about immediate expenses, with funeral costs coming on top of regular housing and health and other costs. Widows may need to remix their everyday

Figure 7.5   Financial Challenges of Widowhood

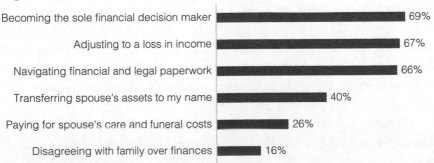

Source: Age Wave / Merrill Lynch, *Widowhood and Money: Resiliency, Responsibility and Empowerment*

finances and eventually make bigger adjustments to maintain their lifestyles and protect their assets.

The key word is "eventually." Many widows report feeling pressured to make financial decisions quickly, including from well-intentioned family and friends offering unsolicited advice. The experts say it's important to distinguish decisions that need immediate attention from those that don't. Big decisions should wait: "Don't put your house on the market. Don't give away money to your children or charity. Don't sell stocks or bonds. Eventually, any of these steps may make perfect sense. But take a breather in the overwhelming weeks and months after a spouse dies."[44] Experienced widows advise new ones to avoid making major financial decisions.

Over time, widows prove resilient financially, just as they do emotionally. Only 14% of widows say that they were making financial decisions on their own before the spouse died. As widows, 86% do so.[45] They adjust their everyday finances and then they look ahead. Widows are much more likely than married couples of the same age to have wills, advanced health care directives, and designated powers of attorney. Experience brings confidence. Over 70% of widows consider themselves more financially savvy than other people their age.

Serving the Newly Widowed

Organizations that recognize widowhood as a distinct and important lifestage are developing innovatively pragmatic services. For example, Peacefully is a service that takes care of the "loose ends" of life, so that surviving loved ones can focus on what matters. It helps people deal with tasks including notifying Social Security, canceling utilities, dealing with social media, and transferring bank accounts. The start-up was inspired by a Millennial entrepreneur's experience watching her family struggle with all the immediate burdens after they lost her grandmother.

Created in 2001, Everest describes itself as "a funeral concierge service rolled up into a life insurance plan. When help is needed, we are one call away. We are there to guide families through a very emotional, complicated, and confusing time in their lives. . . . Everest has combined on-demand, personalized service, technology and

consumer advocacy to revolutionize traditional funeral planning."
When help is needed, Everest advisors are ready to personalize the
funeral plan, compare and negotiate prices on funeral homes and
products, and work with life insurance companies to get monies
to the beneficiary quickly. Families can make informed decisions
without having to research their options. Everest can be purchased
directly, obtained as an add-on to a life insurance policy, or sometimes accessed as an employee benefit. More than 25 million people
in the United States and Canada are covered by Everest.

Other services to ease the immediate challenges of making
funeral arrangements include Parting.com, launched in 2015, and
Funerals360, launched in 2017. Both help people find the right
funeral home, comparing the services and costs of funerals and cremations by local area.

Undertaking LA brings the funeral director to the home of the
deceased and walks family members through the death rituals, such
as washing and dressing the body and holding an in-home wake.
The entrepreneurial pioneer of this enterprise is Caitlin Doughty.
In addition to her years as a mortician, she has taken on our modern
discomfort with death and travels the world speaking on the history of death, including its culture, rituals, and the funeral industry.
In 2011, Caitlin founded the Order of the Good Death, a death
acceptance collective that has been featured everywhere from NPR
to the BBC to the *LA Times*. She produces a web series, "Ask a
Mortician," and wrote a book, *Smoke Gets in Your Eyes: And Other
Lessons from the Crematory*, which was a *New York Times* bestseller.

Financial services firms try to ease the complexity of widowhood with services specifically designed for when a loved one passes
away. For example, specialists on the Survivor Relations Team at
USAA create a "dashboard" overview of the steps necessary to manage and settle accounts, including how to submit required documents electronically. A variety of other resources provide guidance,
and USAA offers survivorship consultation with specially trained
financial advisors.

When a spouse passes away, money and other assets go in
motion to the widow and also to children or other family members in many cases. That makes it a delicate time for financial services firms because many widows change banks and almost half of

widowed women change their advisors.[46] Sometimes they switch under the influence of family or friends. Kathleen Rehl, financial planner, author, and widow, points to another cause: "In that early stage of widowhood, it is critical to have someone that you can think things through with – not tell you what to do. That's why many widows leave the advisors because the advisors try to tell you what to do." Rehl is a faculty member of the Financial Transitionist Institute, where they teach advisors to establish "decision free zones®" by helping clients understand what decisions can be placed on hold while they're grieving and where an immediate decision is really needed.

The widows we surveyed offer good advice to the financial professionals trying to serve them (Figure 7.6), starting with turning down the pressure to make decisions.

Of course, the best way to protect the customer relationship is to have been serving the couple all along, including helping them prepare for the eventuality of one of them dying. That includes the seemingly mundane details of making sure that accounts are in both names, key documents are accessible, and cash can be available. Couples need that basic help: more than half of widows say that they and their spouses did not have a plan for what happens when one of them passes away, and three-quarters of married retirees say they would not be financially prepared if their spouse died.

Figure 7.6   Advice from Widows to Financial Professionals

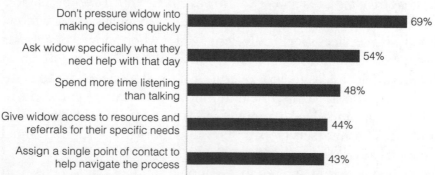

Don't pressure widow into making decisions quickly	69%
Ask widow specifically what they need help with that day	54%
Spend more time listening than talking	48%
Give widow access to resources and referrals for their specific needs	44%
Assign a single point of contact to help navigate the process	43%

Source: Age Wave / Merrill Lynch, *Widowhood and Money: Resiliency, Responsibility and Empowerment*

Actions and Opportunities for Organizations and Entrepreneurs in the Family Services Sector

1. Pay attention to intergenerational purchasing patterns, including by grandparents for grandchildren and by retirees who may be supporting both their parents and their children.
2. If your enterprise is in consumer services, find opportunities to package and customize offerings to make the process of caregiving and the lives of caregivers easier.
3. If you are in health care technology, deliver products and services that benefit caregivers and recipients alike, and that increase the competence and confidence of caregivers in their medical-related tasks.

If your enterprise or organization is in financial services:

4. Offer information, tools, and services to help caregivers in managing their own money and compensating for the direct and opportunity costs of providing care.
5. Package services for financial caregivers to monitor and manage the recipient's accounts, including preventing fraud and abuse.
6. Also make it easy to expand those services, sometimes to incorporate estate management, as the financial caregiver takes on more responsibility.
7. Offer packages of services that ease the burden of the new widow, starting with access to accounts and cash, and that minimize the burden of paperwork and bureaucracy.
8. Then stand ready with services to help widows adjust to their new mixes of income and assets, and to help reestablish their financial bearings.
9. Offer financial-reset services for newly divorced retirees, whose financial pictures often change dramatically. But don't confuse the circumstances of widowhood and divorce.

8

Home and Community

Stay, Go, Remodel, or Find Roommates?

TODAY'S BOOMER RETIREES have far more choices regarding their preferred home and community than did past generations. They are renovating or relocating, downsizing or upsizing, creating homes that support their evolving family and social lives, and choosing communities that support their interests and avocations.

In today's long arc of retirement, it can begin with new freedom regarding where to live and what kind of home to occupy. It can often end with health issues that dictate living where needed care is available. We've learned that many retirees relocate twice, first to a place desirable for lifestyle, climate, or proximity to family. Later in life, they're far more likely to move to someplace offering needed support and care, often assisted living facilities, close to family care, or moving in with family. Those who choose to stay in their pre-retirement homes just make the latter move, if any.

Home renovations follow a parallel pattern. Early in retirement, the objective is to make more of a dream home, with an entertainment or exercise room, a home office, a gourmet kitchen, more rooms for the grandkids. Later on, renovations accommodate declining mobility or other health conditions and make the home a safer and more functional place to age. Health and home are closely intertwined late in life, and some retirees opt for continuing care communities where they live independently until assistance is needed, and where everyday and long-term care are bundled into the living arrangement.

Supporting retirees in all of these endeavors is already a big business, and it will grow bigger as the number of age 65+ households in America grows by over 10 million in the next decade. How and where Boomer retirees choose to live will reshape how homes are designed and renovated, how extended health care is provided, and how communities support our aging population.

Crossing the Threshold into the Freedom Zone

We've described the new retirement as the "freedom zone." With respect to where they live, retirees cross a specific threshold into this zone when their housing requirements and determinants shift (Figure 8.1). Throughout our working lives, where we live and when we relocate are determined predominantly by work and family responsibilities. When we're getting started in adult life, home needs to be affordable, in reasonable commuting distance, often for two partners. A growing family may need a larger home and

Figure 8.1   Freedom in Where to Live

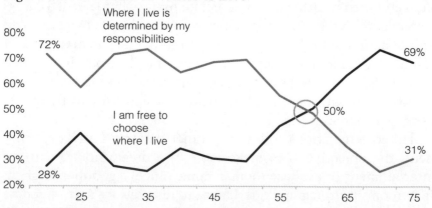

Source: Age Wave / Merrill Lynch, *Home in Retirement: More Freedom, New Choices*

proximity to good schools. When we become empty nesters, school district loses importance. Then in retirement, most people cross the threshold into a world of choice over where and how to live to match their hopes and dreams for this new stage of life.

Should We Stay or Go?

Not surprisingly, people are very emotionally attached to their homes, especially when the home has been occupied for decades and has been the nest for raising a family, gathering with friends, and generating innumerable memories. The majority of Americans age 60+ have lived in their homes for more than 20 years.[1] Younger homeowners tend to see a home's financial value as more important than its emotional value. But for older homeowners, it's no contest – emotional value far outweighs financial.[2] As one retiree told us: "Our home is everything we put into our house materially and emotionally over the years. It's us, and we love it."

Many retirees, especially older ones, intend to stay put (Figure 8.2), what's called "aging in place." When we asked why, most simply said because they love their homes. They also feel that moving and relocating might be a big hassle. Other common motivations include proximity to family, love of community, and the desire to remain independent.

These attachments to the family home notwithstanding, many retirees are in motion. In 2017, 2.8 million people over age 60

Figure 8.2   Future Living Preferences

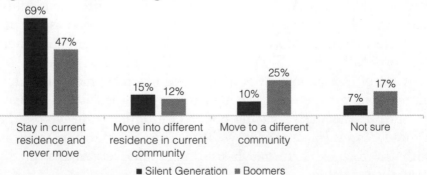

Source: AARP, 2018 Home and Community Preferences Survey

moved. Personal circumstances can lead retirees to move, including health challenges and changes in marital status through divorce or widowhood. Many relocate to save money through lower living costs and local taxes. But the most common motivator is getting closer to family.

Determining whether, when, and where to move is a big decision with long-term personal and financial implications. But part of retirees' freedom of choice is *not* having to decide right away. They can experiment by exploring potentially attractive locations and communities with extended visits or brief rentals.

Where Retirees Want to Live

Retirees can follow their own compass to different parts of the country and the world. Common perception has retirees flocking to warmer climes, and those destinations are indeed preferred. The greatest net migration gains from 2012–2017 were in Phoenix, Tampa, Riverside (CA), Las Vegas, and Jacksonville. The areas with the highest numbers of people 55+ moving away were New York, Los Angeles, Chicago, Washington D.C., and San Francisco.[3] Interestingly, Los Angeles and Riverside are not far apart. Four in five retiree moves are within the same state.

More retirees may move away from the major cities, especially in the north, but there is traffic in both directions. Clare Trapasso of Realtor.com writes, "Instead of migrating south en masse to retirement communities in the Sunshine State or the wilds of Arizona, more and more baby boomers – a particularly urban-savvy group of Americans – are moving back to the metro areas they abandoned when they began raising families. And in leaving their suburban homesteads, these empty nesters are redefining the urban centers they now call home."[4] We're convinced that's a trend to watch.

Cost of living, not just of housing, can be a big factor in determining where to live and whether to move, especially on a fixed income. The effective buying power of a dollar varies across the United States (Figure 8.3). We'll explore this further, together with the role of an owned house in funding retirement, in the next chapter.

Figure 8.3   The Value of $1.00 in Each State

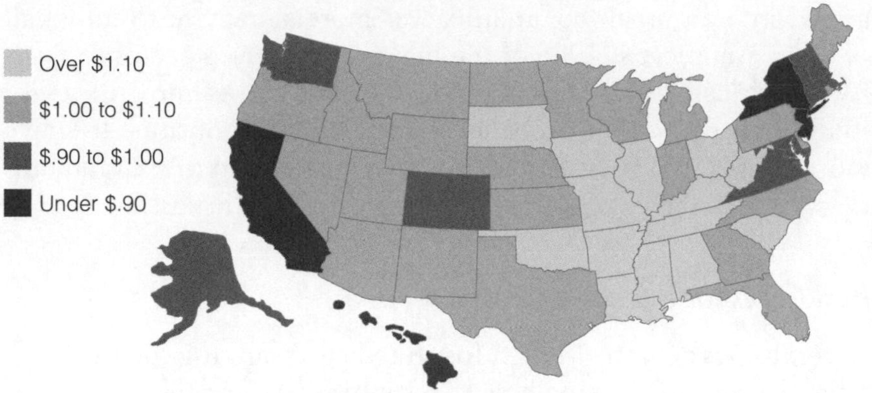

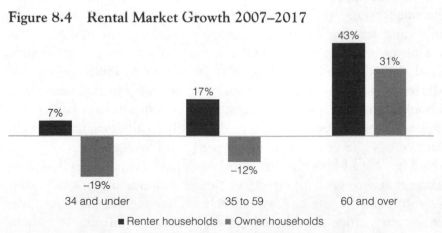

Over $1.10

$1.00 to $1.10

$.90 to $1.00

Under $.90

Source: 24/7 Wall Street, "The Value of a Dollar in Every State," January 12, 2020.

In addition, as Figure 8.4 shows, the renter market is growing faster than the owner market among all age cohorts. More and more Boomer retirees are planning to sell their homes and rent, which provides immediate cash without some of the responsibilities of homeownership. If this happens at large scale, it could deflate the housing market and add an additional and relatively unanticipated thrust to the rental market throughout the United States and abroad.

Figure 8.4   Rental Market Growth 2007–2017

43%

31%

17%

7%

−12%

−19%

34 and under   35 to 59   60 and over

■ Renter households   ■ Owner households

Source: U.S. Census Bureau, ACS 1-Year Estimates 2007-2017

A 2019 survey by Perkins Eastman found that housing integrated into an urban community was more attractive to fully half of older Americans.[5] One of the major attractors is access to quality health care.[6] Bill Petit, President of the real estate and senior living firm R. D. Merrill, believes "Seniors will continue to crave more connection to walkable, intergenerational living. Communities that are islands of old age will be a thing of the past."[7]

Best Cities for Successful Aging

Several years ago, the Milken Institute began ranking the best U.S. cities for successful aging based on sophisticated analysis of factors ranging across nine categories, including general livability (cost of living, safety, and weather), access to and quality of health care services, wellness of the population, financial strength, educational opportunities, safety and security, public transportation, employment possibilities, housing, and community engagement (cultural, recreational, civic, and religious). While some of these attributes might be similar to the ones sought by young adults, there's much more focus on access to quality health care, safety, and security, and far less on childhood education and night life. Atop the latest rankings are Provo-Orem, UT, and Madison, WI, among large metro areas, and Iowa City, IA, and Manhattan, KS, among smaller cities.[8]

Paul Irving, chairman of the Milken Institute Center for the Future of Aging, puts the research in context: "We don't necessarily advocate moving to these places. We encourage municipal leaders and organizations to look at some characteristics that enable healthy and productive aging, and figure how to replicate some of those characteristics in their cities and counties. The real messages – about strong family relationships, sense of community, healthy eating, walkable streets, and so on – can apply to all of us, including in large cities like Los Angeles, New York, and Washington."

The World Health Organization's Global Age-Friendly Cities Project also works with cities to establish policies and practices that enable older people to "age actively." That means they can "live in security, enjoy good health, and continue to participate fully in society." The project focuses on cities because three-fourths of older people in the developed world live in them. Its guidelines to service providers, public officials, and businesspeople include recognizing the diversity among older persons, promoting their inclusion in community life, respecting their decisions and lifestyle choices, and anticipating their needs.[9]

International Destinations

Over half a million retired Americans lived abroad in 2019 and the numbers are steadily growing.[10] International Living's Annual Global Retirement Index highlights the best countries for retirees to relocate. The 2019 top choices, all very affordable compared to living stateside, are Panama for mountains, beaches, and friendliness; Costa Rica for a healthy, active lifestyle and access to health care; Ecuador for climate and geographic variety; and, farther away, Malaysia for beautiful landscape and abundance of amenities, including great restaurants. Ex-pat American retirement communities are also expanding into Canada, the U.K., China, and India.[11]

Futurist and travel writer Don Mankin, PhD, The Adventure Geezer, recommends international retirement destinations beyond those on the most-popular lists. His evaluation criteria include the usual ones – climate, safety, cost of living, and access to quality and affordable medical care. Based on his travels and interactions with local communities, to these he adds five more: "access to physical activity, cultural attractions, transportation with international connections, English is widely spoken, and the place is attractive to, but not overwhelmed by, tourists."[12] His recommendations include Victoria, British Columbia, Canada; Chiang Mai, Thailand; Split, Croatia; Adelaide, South Australia; and Puerto Varas, Chile.

For those who like to be in motion, The World is not your average cruise ship. On board are 165 luxury condos, plus stores, restaurants, movie theater, spa, and a variety of health and fitness facilities. Residents vote on where the 664-foot vessel sails, and some segments feature scientists, anthropologists, and field experts who educate the residents about the chosen route and ports. The World is the largest passenger ship to traverse the Northwest Passage. Some residents are onboard full time while others join for whatever segments they wish. Their average age is 64.

The World caters to multi-millionaires, but classic 3–4 month world cruises cost $200–500 per person per day. We can envision a market for extended-stay cruises that are shorter and less programmed, centered on everyday living and leisure rather than vacations and nonstop activity. Even non-millionaires are choosing to live year-around on cruise ships. With discounts and negotiated longer term rates, the nightly cost of some cruise ships is around $100 per night. That can compare favorably with the cost of senior living communities. People say that on the cruise ship, there's great service, nightly entertainment, and a chance to meet lots of interesting people.

Another option for a nomadic retirement is RVing as a second traveling home, or even a full-time residence. Steve and Mona Liza Lowe retired in 2012, sold their home, and moved into a 40-foot Winnebago RV they named Betsy. They chronicle their travels all over North America on lowestravels.com. In the beginning they had to get rid of nearly all their possessions. Mona Liza reflects, "Downsizing and simplifying sounds crazy and terrifying, but as it turns out, letting go was truly liberating. . . . This journey of ours is about living a dream, existing simply and enjoying every moment of life." Steve echoes the sentiment: "Daily life is simple now, and even though I must clean and maintain the motorhome and car, it's such a joy to have so little to worry about on a daily basis." The website also shares Steve's experiences modifying and repairing the RV.

How Retirees Want to Live

Relocation is a matter both of where and how – a comfortable home, desirable location, and the style of life it provides. Retirees now have many community and living options, some established and some emergent, that can meet their needs and aspirations for social engagement, learning, and personal fulfillment. For example, college towns are popular places to retire, and not just for the alums. They accounted for 11 of the top 25 locations in Forbes' Best Places to Retire in 2018. "People do like to move to college towns to retire," says Lauretta Fogg of Coldwell Banker in Gainesville, FL, home to the University of Florida. "And between sports, concerts and lectures, they get access to great medical care. Another plus is that there are a lot of young people that stimulate them and keep them vibrant."[13]

Neighborhood really matters. Many retirees want to be active in their neighborhoods and communities. They volunteer for local organizations, use libraries and other community facilities, take classes, and often simply get to know their neighbors better. As one retiree told us: "Since I retired, I rediscovered my neighborhood. I developed new friendships and started volunteering in my community." Among Boomer home buyers, the most important factor for home location is the quality of the neighborhood, ahead of even proximity to family and friends. And the importance of convenient access to shopping and health facilities increases with the buyer's age.[14]

Do retirees prefer to spend their time with people their own age? That's the case for some, and age-restricted living communities and leisure activities serve their preference. However, most want just the opposite. One retiree told us, "I may have funny vision because I don't see my age. The idea of a 55+ community doesn't appeal to me. I want to hear children and see them." Two-thirds of Boomers say they prefer neighborhoods with people of diverse ages and generations. It's actually younger people who more often say they prefer communities of a similar age.

Multigenerational Living

As we mentioned in Chapter 7, one-fifth of Americans live in households with multiple generations of adults. Due to both adult children returning home and older parents moving in, the percentage of multigen households nearly doubled between 1980 and 2016, from 12% to 20%.[15] Asian (29%), Latino (27%), and Black (26%) families are much more likely than White (16%) households to live in a multigen home. As the population becomes more ethnically diverse in the years ahead, we're likely to continue to see growth in multigen living.

This increase in multigenerational households is prompting new kinds of "duplex" housing. Kim Adams of the Brambleton Group says, "Builders are adapting their home designs to create additional living spaces that offer privacy and separation for either parents or college students – or both – moving back home, and ground floor suites for easy access for grandparents."[16]

Lennar's NextGen home is actually two houses in one, built for extended families who want to live in proximity but maintain some privacy. Its architect, Howard Perlman, received an innovation award from the HIVE (housing innovation, vision, and economics) conference. He says, "We decided with the design of this home to not only accommodate multigenerational living but also encourage it by creating a new type of house – one with a separate space for grandparents, or boomerang kids or 'failure to launch' kids, or nannies, caregivers or even a home office."[17] A NextGen building may not look like two homes, but each has its own driveway, entrance, kitchen, and living spaces. Lennar offers them in a dozen states, including California, Arizona, Texas, Florida, and the Carolinas.

Accessory Dwelling Units (ADU) are small-scale apartments, like pieds-a-terre, that can be built or purchased and installed in one's yard or a neighboring lot. They are designed to help those who require more frequent assistance to preserve as much independence as possible. Over 30% of American adults say they would consider building one on their property to have a place for a loved one who they'd like to live closer to or who needs care.[18]

Active Retirement Communities

There are more than 2,000 age-restricted active adult communities in the United States, most for those age 55 and up.[19] Danny Goodman of 55places.com explains their value proposition: "While personal needs and requirements will vary for each active adult, we've learned that at the core, affordability, attractive amenities, and social opportunities are the most important factors when searching for a new home in an age-restricted community."[20] Many are resort-style communities with facilities and programs for physically active lifestyles. The communities try to be both self-contained, with shopping and restaurants, and varied, with wide ranges of fitness, hobby, and community activities.

Some adult communities are very large. The Villages, a sprawling central-Florida retirement community, has more than 100,000 residents and was the fastest growing metro area in the United States in 2019. "The Villages has completely transformed that area," said Rich Doty, a research demographer at the University of Florida. "In 1970, the median age of that area was about 30. In 2020, it is about 67."[21]

Some have specific niches or themes. As a shining example of generation anchoring, Latitude Margaritaville in Daytona Beach is "inspired by the legendary music and lifestyle of singer, songwriter and best-selling author Jimmy Buffett." The emphasis is on food, fun, entertainment, and socializing. Facilities include a bandshell and a private beach club. The community bills itself as "a place where life rolls easy, neighbors are friends, and the party never ends."[22]

Because they are less likely to have children, LGBTQ retirees have more freedom in choosing where to live, but also more concern about who will care for them. Many have faced housing discrimination, and they want to avoid isolation, so they want to be around other LGBTQ people. A growing number of active adult communities are welcoming to or specifically designated for LGBTQ individuals and couples. Now 30 years old, the Palms at Marasota in Palmetto, FL, was the first community to actively welcome LGBTQ seniors. Down the coast in Fort Myers, the Resort on Carefree Boulevard was the first women-only community. Other well-known LGBTQ communities are in desirable locations including Pecos, NM; Santa Rosa, CA; Boone, NC; and Provincetown, MA. Other LGBTQ-friendly urban apartment communities are springing up in New York, Philadelphia, Chicago, Cleveland, Minneapolis, and other cities.

Colin Milner, founder of the International Council on Active Aging, shared some of the key industry trends with us: "There are always going to be people who just want to be around people like them, and then there are those who want the opposite. Del Webb is building ten comparatively small properties closer to city centers for retirees who want more urban and intergenerational living. But the biggest shift in the senior living sector is in perception. In the past, people worried that they might be moving into something like a hospital. However, six in ten communities that provide care services see themselves in the next five years as becoming primarily wellness-based rather than care-based."

Co-Housing, Villages, and NORCs

Fostering mutual support among neighbors makes a lot of sense for older retirees, especially those who live alone. Several innovative models are gaining traction.

Originating in Denmark in the 1960s, there are already more than 150 active and forming Cohousing Communities in the United States,[23] and we expect that there may be thousands in just a few years. The architectural firm McCamant & Durrett describes the approach as "recognizing the importance of having neighbors you know and break bread with. . . . Though the word 'cohousing' is relatively new, it really is the modern version of age-old community ideals where children were adored and elders were looked up to, and both were cared for by the community." Oak Creek in Stillwater, OK, has 24 individually owned homes and one common house. Community members range in age from 60 to 90. They have weekly meals together, share in decision making, and care for each other as they age. A resident describes the advantages: "I now feel very safe and have interaction with people, caring neighbors who are looking out for me (and I for them), opportunity to share my skills and benefit from the skills of others, a variety of activities from which to choose, and no more loneliness!"

The Village Movement started in Boston in 2002 with the formation of the Beacon Hill Village. Their goal is to "grow older better in the homes and neighborhoods we love." This member-led community offers services that enable healthy aging, including exercise and wellness programs, social events, resources and support services for independent living, and cultural and learning experiences. The Village database identifies for members trusted and vetted services, such as home health, legal and financial, maintenance and repair, and medical providers. The Village to Village Network strives to grow the movement internationally, and there are now over 350 Villages in the United States and around the world with their numbers growing every year.

Another option, with the strange sounding name NORCs (which stands for Naturally Occurring Retirement Communities), has residents of all ages but has evolved to have higher proportions of older individuals. New York has the highest documented number of NORCs with 35 in New York City alone.²⁴ Morningside Gardens is a private housing cooperative in Manhattan with 980 apartments. Residents organize group dinners and a variety of classes, activities, and excursions, including to nearby universities. Among the older residents are centenarians who have spent half their lives there. Facilities include a fitness center, gardens, and an arboretum, and services include both a preschool and a retirement and health center.

Roommates: A Cross Between Golden Girls and Friends

The Golden Girls was more than an acclaimed American sitcom of the late '80s and early '90s. The premise – four older women sharing a home, one of whom was the parent of another – was a harbinger of the future. A few years later, *Friends* not only introduced us to Jennifer Anniston, Courtney Cox, and Matt LeBlanc (among others), it also made it cool to share a residence with your buds. Living with roommates is hardly a new idea, but one gaining in popularity. As more older retirees live alone, many in houses they own, having roommates can make enormous sense socially, financially, and pragmatically.

People aged 50 and over are now the fastest growing demographic on SpareRoom, an apartment-sharing service that helps roommates find each other via online ads and in-person meet ups.²⁵ Other home-sharing matching services focus specifically on older adults. Silvernest has seen rapid growth since launching in 2015, expanding to all 50 states, growing its annual signup rate by 150 percent, and making nearly 40,000 qualified matches in its first three years.²⁶

Like some did decades ago with live-in nannies and au pairs to help with raising their kids, Boomers are now experimenting with providing low or no rent to younger individuals who are willing to help around the house or with caregiving responsibilities. For example, ALA's Shared Housing program matches two or more unrelated people to share a home in exchange for rent or services such as cleaning or cooking. The arrangements are especially popular in cities like Los Angeles, where there is a shortage of affordable housing. The average age of ALA housing providers is 75.

In Germany, the "Living for Help" association matches students on a budget with older people who have room to spare. The students provide some household help as part of the arrangement, and young and old enjoy the company. Similarly, the university town of Porto, Portugal, has a program that helps students find affordable housing while combating loneliness and isolation among older residents.[27] And at the Humanitas retirement home in Deventer, Netherlands, university students live rent-free in exchange for spending at least 30 hours a month acting as "good neighbors" to residents by doing simple activities together and providing company when older residents are ill.[28] These arrangements look like a win-win all around.

Louise Bardswich was in her 50s looking for a care facility for her mother when she decided that she personally wanted to take a different course: "I recognized that at some stage I was going to be living with other people, probably because at some point I would become infirm enough that my family said, we've got to move you in with somebody else." Bardswich didn't want to wait for that to happen: "If you recognize it's going to happen anyhow, you can take control, figure it out and live with people you want to live with." Together with three other retired women, she purchased and renovated a residential home. With the help of a local builder who specialized in designing homes for older adults, they built their own version of a retirement paradise. Their 6-bedroom, wheelchair-accessible, 5,000-square-foot farmhouse enables them to remain independent, enjoy the benefits of companionship, and have the security of knowing they can stay there forever, barring any unexpected changes to their lifestyle or health status.[29]

Golden girls, indeed. Back in the day, we'd call this a "commune." We are absolutely convinced that this style of living/housing will be commonplace for retiring Boomers.

The Upsize Surprise

People downsize their homes in retirement, right? Children have grown. The family home is too big for a couple or a single retiree. Maintenance has become a chore. And moving into a smaller home can save money in rent or taxes or free some of the equity in an owned home. Except that for some, the home may be *too small* for visits by children and grandchildren or extended family. Too small for gatherings of friends. Too small for the leisure and fitness facilities they've always wanted to add – gourmet kitchen, exercise room, entertainment room. Too small when an aging parent or in-law needs to move in.

Our studies revealed that half of those who move in retirement downsize. And they do so for the pragmatic reasons of cost and maintenance reduction, or as part of a program to simplify and declutter their lives. Not surprisingly, we're beginning to see web-based, community, and commercial (like Legacybox) services that offer to help people digitize their papers and photo albums as they clear out their garages and attics.

However, we also learned that a surprising 30% upsize into a larger home (Figure 8.5), and half of the higher-net-worth retirees surveyed intend to upsize. The rest change location but not home size.

Retirees most often say they upsize to have more room for family who visit. Some are anticipating that family members may move in, and one in four wants a more prestigious home, one that represents their success in retirement or that rewards them for a career's worth of effort (Figure 8.6). Downsize or upsize? Affordability aside, it comes down to the role of the home in retirees' family lives, social lives, and lifestyles.

Figure 8.5   Retirees' Most Recent Move was into a . . .

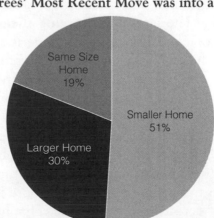

Source: Age Wave / Merrill Lynch, *Home in Retirement: More Freedom, New Choices*

Figure 8.6   Motivations for Upsizing in Retirement

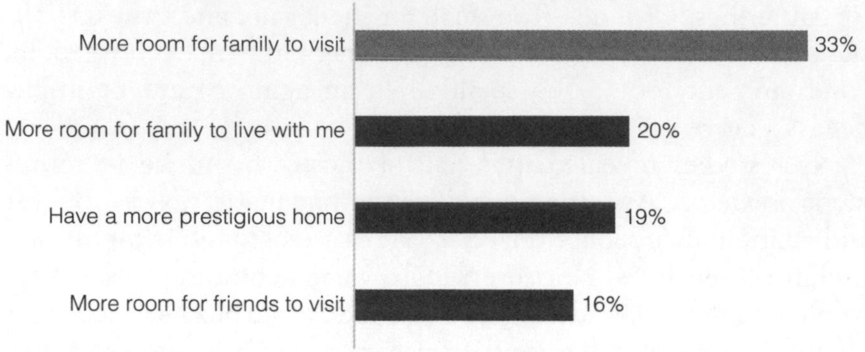

Motivation	Percentage
More room for family to visit	33%
More room for family to live with me	20%
Have a more prestigious home	19%
More room for friends to visit	16%

Source: Age Wave / Merrill Lynch, *Home in Retirement: More Freedom, New Choices*

Renovation and Home Services

When Americans think of home renovation, what often comes to mind are the endless array of fix-it-up shows on the HGTV network. The homeowners are young couples, straight or gay, and only the renovators show much age and experience. That's another example of ageism by omission, because a high percentage of retirees want to turn their houses into their dream homes for this new chapter in their lives. As one retiree told us, "We always had plans to make our home better, and to make it more of what we wanted. Now that we're retired, we have the time, flexibility, and savings to do just that."

Retirees may love their homes, but they also love to make their homes even better. The market for serving them is already massive and poised for continued growth. Americans 55 and older spend over $117 billion annually on home renovations. That's half the national total (Figure 8.7), and their spending is on the rise – although they remain largely ignored by modern media and marketing.

Most renovations make retirees' homes more functional, attractive, comfortable, and versatile. Upgrading kitchens and bathrooms are among the most common renovations by retirees intending to stay in their homes throughout retirement (Figure 8.8). But interestingly, atop the list is creating a home office. That makes sense given how many retirees choose to work or start businesses in retirement,

Figure 8.7 Home Renovation Expenditures by Age

< 35
9%
65+
25%
35–44
18%
45–54
23%
55–64
25%

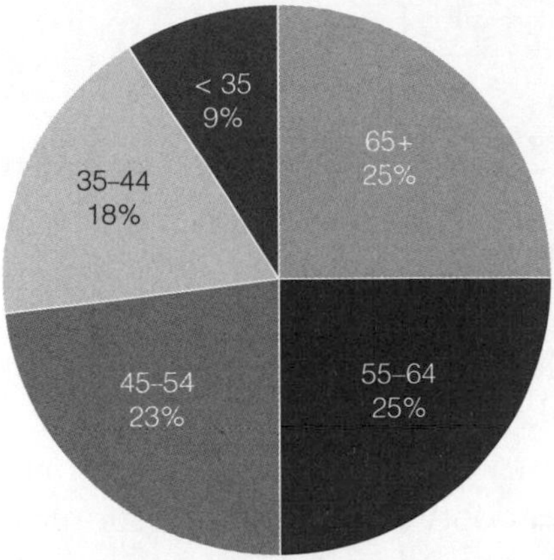

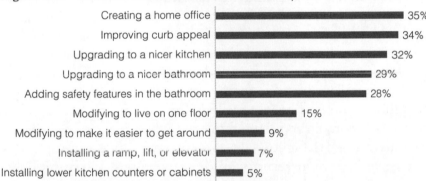

Source: Harvard Joint Center for Housing Studies, 2019

Figure 8.8 Retirees Renovate Their Homes by . . .

Creating a home office 35%
Improving curb appeal 34%
Upgrading to a nicer kitchen 32%
Upgrading to a nicer bathroom 29%
Adding safety features in the bathroom 28%
Modifying to live on one floor 15%
Modifying to make it easier to get around 9%
Installing a ramp, lift, or elevator 7%
Installing lower kitchen counters or cabinets 5%

Source: Age Wave / Merrill Lynch, *Home in Retirement: More Freedom, New Choices*

including those who work as independent consultants or contractors and those with jobs that can be performed from home.

Home Depot has recently begun responding to this longevity market phenomenon by increasing the staff and scale of its installation services, and in the process increasing product sales. They've learned that with the aging of the Boomers, many of yesterday's Do-It-Yourself customers are in retirement turning to Do-It-For-Me. An expanded set of installation programs includes flooring, windows, cabinets, and countertops. This is of particular appeal to retirees and especially older single women, who may have previously had a husband who handled these repairs.

Homes Fit for Life

Not yet as common, but increasingly important as retirees grow older, are renovations that accommodate declining mobility or otherwise make a home "safe and sound for life." Nearly 30% of retirees we surveyed have added safety features to bathrooms, such as handrails and walk-in showers. Far fewer have made adjustments that enable them to avoid climbing stairs (ramps or lifts) or use wheelchairs (wider doorways and lower countertops).

Such renovations tend to be postponed until needed, yet some adjustments – like installing lever door handles – are, as discussed earlier when we talked about universal design, conveniences to people of all ages. According to Harvard's Joint Center for Housing, among the most basic are zero-step entrances into the home, single-floor living, wide halls and doorways that can accommodate a wheelchair, electrical controls reachable from a wheelchair, and lever-style handles on faucets and doors."[30]

The complete list of potential renovations for improving age-friendliness and functionality is lengthy, from safety measures like installing bathroom grab bars (think about how dangerous a slippery bathtub can be), to functionality improvements like non-slip throw rugs, higher and more secure seats, lower counters, and better lighting. These potential needs are well documented, room by room, by AARP and by LifetimeHome.org. They're not just conveniences, they could be life savers. Another contribution from AARP is partnering with the National Association of Home Builders to create a Certified Aging-in-Place Specialist (CAPS) designation for remodelers and architects. For help with everyday remodeling and repairs, a variety of companies – Angie's List, TaskRabbit, Porch, Thumbtack – identify reliable contractors and service providers. Most also can find matches for smaller tasks like mounting and installing a TV, assembling furniture, and lifting furniture up the stairs.

Aging-friendly renovations are often prompted by witnessing the struggles of a parent, partner, or sibling. As one retiree reflected, "Watching my dad fall and break his pelvis and then get around in a motorized chair helped me to understand the challenges of aging, and to look for ways to improve my own home to prevent or meet those challenges and others before they occur."[31] Keep in mind that two-thirds of people over 65 fall each year, often in their own homes. Many of these falls are preventable with easy adjustments. With a growing population of aging retirees, these renovations will become much more commonplace. And there's a lot of catching up to do. According to Harvard's Joint Center for Housing, less than 2% of America's total housing stock is aging friendly.[32] That's ageism embodied!

Fernando Torres-Gil, director of the Center for Policy Research on Aging at UCLA, a leading spokesperson on aging and public policy, and a polio survivor, reminds us that extensive "renovations" are needed in public spaces and facilities as well: "So how do we adjust traffic lights to allow a person with a cane or a walker to cross? How do we create bus shelters and benches that are comfortable for frail older persons? How do we make sure that there's lighting so seniors feel reasonably safe on our city streets?" Ageism can be pervasive – and destructive – in our public accommodations as well as in our attitudes.

Smarter Homes

As technology makes homes smarter, it also makes life a lot easier for retirees. Automatic and remote-control thermostats keep the temperature comfortable, lighting can be controlled by voice, self-guided vacuum cleaners keep things tidy, neglected stovetops turn themselves off, cabinets automatically adjust their height, video doorbells and security systems make things safer, and a growing array of such technologies and services are controlled through listen-and-speak devices like Google Home and Amazon Alexa.

Security systems and technologies are especially important, and we see a lot of innovation. Video doorbells show a lot more than the traditional peephole. Biometrics like fingerprints and eye scans can open and close locks. Programmable locks can admit family and friends, or temporary Airbnb guests. Drones can operate as mobile security cameras. And all the activity can, of course, be transmitted to and controlled by smartphones.

Out of doors, robot lawnmowers and smart sprinkler systems save time and labor. In cold climates, heated driveways make walking and driving safer. By 2030, over 130 million Americans age 50+ will spend upwards of $84 billion a year on technology products.[33] While people might think that smart homes are the dream of Millennials, retirees are without a doubt the ideal target audience.

Just as important to retirees are the technologies of home health and personal safety. Personal Emergency Response Systems (PERS) have been around since the 1980s. Many remember the Life Call commercial with a woman calling, "Help, I've fallen, and I can't get up." It was a bit dramatic and many late-night hosts had some fun with it, but the situation it portrayed was real. Today there are many variations on PERS devices. The most basic have a button that transmits a signal to a base that can call an emergency responder, but recent innovations expand on that in many ways. In addition to emergency response functions, Alarm.com's Wellness tracker can detect if a person has left the home during odd hours, and it can monitor activity levels, bathroom use, eating habits, sleep patterns, and medication management. It can also enable caregivers to check on care recipients any time.

Transportation technologies, what we've nicknamed "transport-care," offer great convenience to retirees, including those who choose to forgo having a car, and they promise greater mobility to those with disabilities. Driverless cars are grabbing the headlines, but transportation providers are looking at the surrounding set of services that retirees need and appreciate. Let's think about this for a moment. Many older men and women live alone and value a human driver to say hi, open the car door for them, and maybe even make sure they get to where they're going safely. For example, Lyft enables older people without smartphones to arrange rides on a landline phone via GoGoGrandparent. Their CareRides partnership with Carelinx also enables family members and caregivers to arrange transport for the recipient, including with multiple stops and progress notifications. SilverRide's transportation services include full physical assistance for those needing help getting in and out of a vehicle. And many of these transport-care activities are now covered by Medicare.

Joseph Coughlin, Director of the Massachusetts Institute of Technology AgeLab, author of *The Longevity Economy*, and the world's guru when it comes to aging and technology, imagines "a convergence of sensor, communication and AI technologies that transform the home into a platform of services to keep us connected, provide convenience and deliver care as we age." We agree, and the eldertech marketplace has just begun to come alive. And then as the Global Coalition on Aging's Mike Hodin reminded us, there should be more older people on the innovation teams: "It's smart business."

Care at Home

The oldest retirees throughout the world need a lot of assistance and care services, and they'll need much more in the future. By the time they reach their mid-80s, many people have not only chronic conditions but also difficulty with one or several daily activities such as preparing meals, climbing stairs, or attending to their eating, dressing, toileting, or bathing.[34] Today, more than 25 million U.S. households have someone with a household-activity disability, a number projected to increase by more than 50% by 2040.[35]

When they need regular assistance and care, most retirees strongly prefer to receive it in their own homes (Figure 8.9) and almost no one ever wants to be moved into a nursing home. For the most part, it's becoming easier to do this, with the help of family, paid care, technology, or a combination. Retirees' second choice is an assisted living community, where they can remain semi-independent. Very few say they would want to move in to a friend or family member's home as they're very concerned about not being a burden on others.

The U.S. market for paid in-home care is expected to reach $187 billion in 2027, nearly doubling in the course of a decade.[36] There are more than 4.5 million home health services users, outnumbering nursing home residents three to one.[37] The industry is highly fragmented with the top-ten providers accounting for just 22% of the total market share, and no other provider with 1% share.[38]

Figure 8.9   Where Americans 65+ Prefer to Receive Extended Care

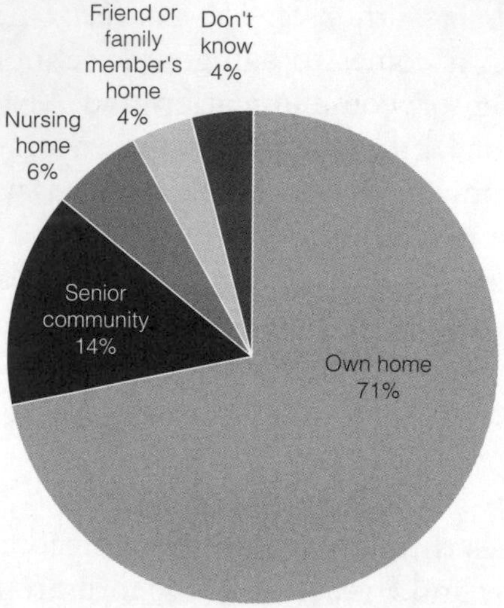

Friend or family member's home 4%

Don't know 4%

Nursing home 6%

Senior community 14%

Own home 71%

Source: The Associated Press-NORC Center for Public Affairs Research, *Long-Term Care in America: Expectations and Preferences for Care and Caregiving*, 2016

A highly respected franchise-based homecare provider is Home Instead Senior Care, which today provides more than 80 million hours of in-home care a year across 13 countries. We asked its entrepreneurial founder and now Chairman Paul Hogan why and how he created his company:

> The idea for Home Instead Senior Care came from my family's personal experience of caring for my grandmother Eleanor Manhart. Grandma Manhart was in her late 80s and her health was failing rapidly. At that time, my mother and her siblings held a family meeting and decided they would not place her into a nursing home. My mom volunteered to have grandma move in with her for what the doctors, and most of the family, thought would be the last year of her life. The family agreed. The move was made, and family members chipped in to help grandma with meals, medications, and personal care. Gradually, my grandma became stronger and more socially engaged. She began to garden again and even began to walk herself to church when the weather permitted. She literally regained her will to live.

And how did that lead to the company we now know as Home Instead?

Our family's experience led my wife Lori and me to ask the question, what do other families do to take care of older loved ones? We also learned that you didn't have to be a doctor or nurse to have a significant impact on the life of an older person. My grandma had 12 children, 50 grandchildren and 51 great-grandchildren – we had a lot of family to "share the care." So, in 1994, we started Home Instead Senior Care to help do for other families what my family was able to do for my grandmother.

How have Home Instead's services evolved?

From the start, we provided basic services including companionship, light housekeeping, meal preparation, incidental transportation, and medication reminders. Over our 25 years, our services have gotten much more sophisticated. We now provide personal care services such as bathing and toileting, medication management, and hospice support. And we now have specialized training for our CAREGivers to help them with all their responsibilities, including, for example, managing difficult behaviors associated with dementia. In the beginning our services took place exclusively in the client's home; now we also serve seniors who live in all types of care communities. While our CAREGivers do the tasks that need to be done to keep the senior safe and healthy, we train them to focus on "relationship over task." Relationships are at the core of our care.

Finally, we asked Hogan what he expects the impact of the aging of the Boomers to be on his sector. He reflected, "The oldest baby boomer turns 74 in 2020, and our average client is about 80, so we are clearly still at the beginning of this massive opportunity. Boomers, even more so than our clients today, will want to age on their own terms. They have always left a changed society in their wake, and their senior years will be no different. The one thing I do not

see changing, however, is their preference for their own homes –
especially with advances in technology."

The home care industry at large, however, faces a workforce crisis. Home care workers – not software engineers – are the fastest
growing occupation in the United States, generating a projected
7.8 million job openings by 2026.[39]

Other types of organizations are finding ways to help even those
with serious health issues remain at home longer. For example,
the Program for All-Inclusive Care for the Elderly (PACE) fosters
independence at home for as long as possible despite serious health
challenges. It incorporates interdisciplinary preventative, primary,
acute, and long-term managed care. The first program began in
the early 1970s in San Francisco, and today there are more than
240 PACE centers operating in 31 states. Legislation in 2015 to
encourage the development of more PACE centers permits them
to operate for-profit. InnovAge, the largest PACE provider, quickly
converted to for-profit and in 2016 received $196 million in private
equity funding.[40]

Perhaps no country will face more challenges with the demand
for eldercare than China, which saw 440 million births during their
baby boom, followed by their one-child policy. Add to that the fact
that one of the outcomes of their lightning-speed modernization is
that the average life expectancy has vaulted from 35 in 1950 to 75
today. At the same time, the availability of young family caregivers
has shrunk due to the one-child policy that was enacted in 1980 by
the Central Government of China and wasn't relaxed until 2016.
As a result of this 4–2–1 demography, China now has many elders,
but a shrinking pool of available family caregivers. Several Chinese cities have established "virtual nursing homes." At the push
of a button, older residents can summon help with shopping, room
cleaning, bathing, minor repairs, and various other services. An
online platform arranges these door-to-door services and serves as a
communications hub for senior citizens and medical services, with
updates to their children.[41] Faced with the massive demographic
challenges of a growing elderly population and smaller families to
support them, China needs to find such new ways to support older
citizens at scale.

Finally, an approach we hope will be widely imitated, postal workers in Japan and France have begun making regular visits to check on and interact with elderly citizens. Since so many elders live alone and their public workers are already in the neighborhoods every day, once properly trained, they're the perfect resource for regular check-ins. Japan Post is working with private-sector companies to provide the elderly with lifestyle support services from shopping to assistance alerts.

Communities with Care

Providing a combination of housing and health care is a $420 billion industry and growing.[42] In the United States, there are over 23,000 assisted living and nursing care communities with 25 or more units/ beds. More than 800,000 people reside in assisted living facilities, a majority of them women age 85 and older. The number of nursing homes has declined over the past two decades despite the increase in the older population, since more people prefer to receive care at home, where help is now more available, but revenues continue to grow.[43] The fastest growing segment is memory care – from approximately 1.5 million care facility residents in 2017 to a projected 11 million by 2027.[44] Years ago, these units were bluntly referred to as dementia lock-down wards. Renaming them "memory care" was both ingenious and appropriate.

As we've seen with other places to call home, retirees needing or anticipating the need for care have a growing array of sometimes innovative options. Continuing Care Retirement Communities (CCRC), also called Life Plan Communities, provide for independent retirement living, with home services and meal plans, plus stages of needed care – assisted living, nursing, and memory care. Many retirees choose to move into CCRCs in advance of needing regular care.

Colin Milner describes the upscale Moorings Park CCRC in Naples, Florida: "Of the roughly 1,000 residents, about 700 are independent, 200 in assisted living, and 100 long-term care. Their restaurant is like a fine dining establishment, their clubhouse like a private one you'd wish to belong to, their health club equal to any

I've seen. It's a top-notch community all around, and young or old, you'd probably want to live there. Even though their population is older, they're creating the environment that anyone would want to live in."

Colleges have begun taking advantage of their real estate and trusted brands and are building CCRCs for younger and more active retirees, offering lifelong learning opportunities and access to campus facilities and events. For example, Legacy Point is located on the campus of the University of Central Florida, where it fosters intergenerational connections in daily life. At Arizona State University, "Mirabella at ASU" is a 20-story, $250 million Life Plan Community for over 300 residents opening on the corner of campus in 2020. Every unit sold out in advance.

Belmont Village opened its first mixed-use property in Mexico City. In addition to 11 floors of senior housing with assisted living and memory care options, it also hosts a Hyatt Hotel and retail and restaurant spaces for people of all ages, and it is connected to a high-quality medical center. CEO Patricia Will describes the intent: "From our point of view, intergenerational senior living genuinely creates an environment where multiple generations are sharing in everyday life and activities, experiences, in a very rich and deliberate way."[45]

Stonewall Gardens in Palm Springs, CA, is the first successful assisted living facility catering to LGBTQ retirees, with an emphasis on community interaction plus personal and medical care services geared to the needs and preferences of individual residents. Fountaingrove Lodge in Santa Rosa, CA, was among the first to offer the full continuum of care.

Other types of communities also strive to integrate residents in memory care. De Hogeweyk in Weesp, Netherlands, is a gated model village of 152 elderly residents with dementia. Each of 23 houses has a half-dozen residents and a caregiver who cooks, takes people shopping or to social events, and watches over their safety. It looks like a normal village, complete with a market where residents buy groceries with in-house currency. The continuous practice of reminiscence therapy enables residents to be more active and need less medication. Each house has a style familiar to its residents, from city dwellers to craftspeople to homemakers.[46]

Dr. Bill Thomas is more than a leading and entertaining (as we described in Chapter 3) anti-ageism advocate. He is an influential innovator in housing and care for older adults. In the early 1990s, seeing the unfortunate quality of life in many nursing homes, he co-founded The Eden Alternative. Its purpose is to humanize nursing homes by eliminating what he viewed as the three plagues of loneliness, helplessness, and boredom. Then in the early 2000s, Thomas launched The Green House Project, an innovative new approach to long-term care "where nursing homes are torn down and replaced with small, home-like environments where people can live a full and interactive life."[47] With over 200 Green House homes across the United States, their evidence-based model has been proven to be effective and sustainable.

Thomas's new creation, with Harvard Graduate School of Design trained Ana Pinto Da Silva as CEO, is Minka Homes and Communities. Minka makes small (330- to 640-square-feet), energy efficient, human-centered homes and communities that simplify independence so that people of all ages and abilities can live their best lives on their own terms. Modular, easy-to-assemble parts are made in Thomas's Upstate New York production facility and shipped for local assembly. With no interior load-bearing walls, the homes' floor plans are readily adapted to meet the needs of the person or people living in them. Minka homes employ principles of universal design "influenced by the clever use of space and materials in centuries-old Japanese architecture."[48] They can be standalone, serve as accessory dwelling units, or be erected in groups to form "pocket neighborhoods."

We've taken a pretty extensive "home tour" in this chapter: from relocating and renovating and roommates, to innovative communities for life in retirement and receiving care late in life, to the growing importance of care at home. All of the home-related services we've discussed are positioned to grow dramatically with the increasing number of retiree households: real estate and relocation services; technologies and services for home control, safety, transport, and health; construction, community living, and home care; and financial services to support the rest. Retirement often begins with unprecedented freedom in where and how to live, but the choices are shaped – and over time often constrained – by health, family, and as we'll discuss next, finances.

> **Actions and Opportunities for Organizations and Entrepreneurs in the Home Sector**
>
> 1. Help retirees live their dreams and exercise their freedom by introducing them to locations, communities, and living options they likely haven't thought about.
> 2. Recognize the variety of retirees' preferences and motivations; don't assume that they should move, or plan to downsize, or want to age in place.
> 3. Provide comprehensive relocation services patterned on those companies provide to their executives, including services for moving internationally.
> 4. Recognize retirees who prefer age-segregated living, but follow the trend toward intergenerational connection.
> 5. For new arrivals to the neighborhood or community, engage their sense of purpose with opportunities to contribute, collaborate, and volunteer.
> 6. Know your area's "successful aging" score in order to stress local strengths and compensate for weaknesses.
> 7. Offer integrated one-stop home repair and maintenance services, learning from how managed communities provide these services.
> 8. Educate retirees on how and when to make their homes "fit for life," recognizing that younger ones hesitate to make (especially exterior) changes that say, "Old people live here."
> 9. Follow universal design principles in renovation products and services to improve overall functionality and attractiveness as well as aging-friendliness.
> 10. Strive for additional socialization in home care (as communities provide), and additional customization of care in community settings (as home care provides).

9

Funding Longevity

Retirement Is the Biggest Purchase of a Lifetime – That Many Can't Afford

PEOPLE SAVE FOR RETIREMENT gradually, but if you think of the ultimate price tag, it's the biggest purchase of a lifetime. Retirement costs far more than all of life's other big-ticket items – buying a home, raising a child, paying for college. The average "cost" of retirement is over $1,000,000 (Figure 9.1). The cost keeps going up, not only with inflation, but also with longevity. As people spend more years in retirement, they'll need a lot more funds.

Most Americans are unaware of that price tag. A truly alarming eight in ten have reported that they have no idea how much money they'll need for a comfortable retirement. But they are beginning to realize that they are underprepared – in many cases by a great deal. Only 45% of Americans over the age of 60 feel their retirement savings are on track (Figure 9.2). In fact, the average 60-year-old pre-retiree has saved only about $135,000 toward their retirement.[1]

How far behind are Americans in funding their retirements? The answer depends on whom you ask and how it's measured. Using the rule of thumb that retirees need 75% of their pre-retirement

Figure 9.1   Retirement Is the Purchase of a Lifetime

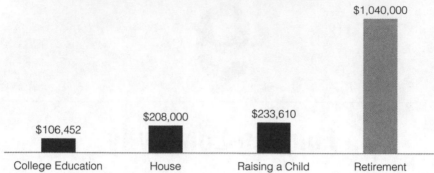

Sources: NCES 4 Year Institution, 2016–2017; USDA, 2017; Zillow, 2017; Retirement cost calculated from Consumer Expenditure Survey, National Center for Health Statistics, Social Security Administration

Figure 9.2   Retirement Savings Perceived to Be on Track

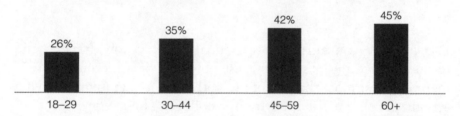

Source: Federal Reserve, *Report on the Economic Well-Being of U.S. Households in 2018*

annual income, the Center for Retirement Research at Boston College estimates that half of all working households are at risk of being unable to maintain their standard of living in retirement based on their current savings and retirement income sources. Half of the households age 65+ are in the same situation.[2] And half of all Boomers feel they need to catch up on retirement savings. They say they have fallen behind because of inadequate income, unexpectedly having to support family members, out-of-pocket health care costs, and having started saving for retirement far too late.[3]

Another rule of thumb says that total retirement savings should be at least eight times pre-retirement income. For the average household, that's almost a half-million dollars. That $135,000 average falls far short. And a significant number of households have no retirement savings at all, including 13% of those age 60+ and not yet retired (Figure 9.3).

This is a very serious problem. Are we heading to a new era of mass elder poverty, not seen since the 1930s, when one-third of older people were impoverished? Will the wealthiest generation ever also have unprecedented rates of retirees struggling to stay afloat financially? If nothing major changes, that may well become the case. As income inequality carries over into retirement funding inequality, there will in all likelihood be a public outcry.

The Funding Formula Is Changing: No More Three-Legged Stool

For the second half of the twentieth century, and thus for the Boomers' grandparents and parents, the retirement funding formula was for most a reliable and predictable three-legged stool: (1) personal savings and retirement accounts, (2) guaranteed employer pensions, and (3) Social Security. But the mix and certainty of those three components have shifted dramatically, and it appears that most people haven't made the necessary adjustments.

Figure 9.3   Non-retirees with No Retirement Savings

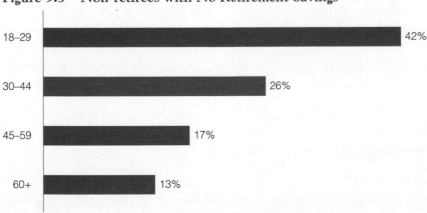

Source: Federal Reserve, *Report on the Economic Well-Being of U.S. Households in 2018*

Living for Today and Not Saving for Tomorrow

In our studies, Americans have told us they think they should be saving 15–20% of their income annually, and they know they should max out all tax-protected accounts such as 401(k)s. But that's not what's happening. The average annual savings rate (all savings, not just toward retirement) in the United States has risen a bit since the recession – largely due to the Millennial generation's savings activity – but is still only around 7%.

While roughly two-thirds of private-sector workers in the United States have access to an employer-sponsored retirement plan, only 13% of participants contribute the maximum amount allowed (currently $19,500). Incredibly, 26% of those eligible for plans do not contribute to them at all.[4] These accounts also suffer what is weirdly called "leakage," when people tap into them (and bear the tax and penalty consequences), before reaching age 59½. Three in ten have taken a loan or early withdrawal,[5] the latter common when people change jobs and fail to roll over their funds. The first leg of the stool is wobbly.

Guaranteed Pensions: Now You See Them, Now You Don't

At the same time, because most private-sector employers phased out guaranteed, or "defined benefit," pensions in favor of 401(k) and other forms of "defined contribution" accounts, the large majority of today's workers will not have employer-provided post-retirement income for life as their parents might have (Figure 9.4). Just 20 years ago, over half of Fortune 500 companies (59%) still had defined benefit pensions. Today it is only 16%.[6] There goes the second leg of the stool.

Social Insecurity

Social Security income can be significant but not sufficient. The average monthly payment is around $1,500. If each party in a couple receives that amount, that's $36,000 a year. Although today's older retirees rely heavily on Social Security, without much-needed adjustments in the program, the long-term viability of those benefits

Figure 9.4   Shifts in Pension Plans

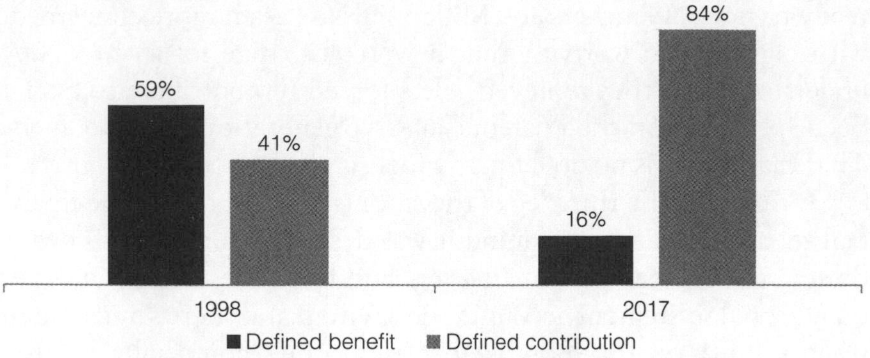

Source: Willis Towers Watson, *Retirement Offerings in the Fortune 500: A Retrospective,* 2018

is in question for future retirees. That's because the demographics, including the worker-to-recipient ratio, and the economics of Social Security have changed dramatically since the early days of the program (Table 9.1). Two-thirds of working Boomers now say they're

Table 9.1   The Changing Social Security Equation

	1940	2016
Life expectancy at birth	63.6	78.8
Additional life expectancy at age 65	12.7	19.4
Average retirement age	70	64
Population age 65+ (million)	9.0	49.2
Ratio: workers to recipients	40 to 1	2.8 to 1
Number of Social Security recipients	222,488	60,907,000
Average annual Social Security payout	$220	$16,320
Total Social Security payout (million)	$49	$916,000
% Federal budget for Social Security	0.03%	24%

Source: Social Security Administration, Center for Retirement Research at Boston College, U.S. Census Bureau, Congressional Budget Office, 2016

anxious about the availability of Social Security when they are ready to retire. Gen Xers and Millennials are even more concerned, with eight in ten worrying that it won't be there for them.[7] They understand that they're nevertheless forced to contribute to Social Security to support their parents' massive generation – the Boomers. That realization is no doubt partly fueling the #OKBoomer outcry.

As a result, the third leg of the stool is uncertain, and the financial security and peace of mind it was designed to provide is dwindling. So we're back to the first leg. Funding relies more than ever on personal retirement accounts and savings, and there's much more responsibility on the individual to fund one's potentially lengthy retirement.

Retirement Funding Variations Around the World

On average around the world, people now expect the government to provide almost half of their retirement income, their own savings to provide about a third, and employer pensions to cover one-fourth.[8] However, funding practices vary greatly. The Melbourne Mercer Global Pension Index rates retirement systems using more than 40 indicators grouped in three sub-indices: adequacy of support, sustainability of the system, and integrity of oversight. The top scores (As on an A to E scale) in 2019 went to Denmark and Netherlands. The United States received an unimpressive C for adequacy and C+ for sustainability and integrity.

Other countries have very different retirement funding mixes. In Belgium, about 85% of funding comes from public transfers. In nearby Netherlands, it's under 50% and a large share of the rest comes from occupational, or industry-wide, pensions. Canadians rely most heavily on private pensions and individual savings and retirement accounts. The pension rate, or coverage of pensions compared to working wages, also varies dramatically. Pensioners in the Netherlands receive on average slightly *more* than what their wages were while working. In the U.K., the pension rate is only 29%. The EU average rate is 71%, in China 83%, in the United States only 49%.[9]

A sample of the United States, Australia, and six European countries found that most workers were saving less than 10% of their income toward retirement. But again practices vary. The Netherlands

requires contributions of the equivalent of 20–25% of people's salaries, the bulk of it by the employers.[10]

Widespread Lack of Understanding, Confidence, and Trusted Advice

Most people, even those in their fifties who should be focused on
funding their retirements, don't understand the often-complicated
language and mechanisms of finance. Two-thirds of Americans age
50+ say they find financial industry language unfriendly and not
at all understandable. So their "financial IQ" isn't high. Only 60%
say they clearly understand the popular terms "IRA" and "401(k)."
(And who named it 401(k)? Talk about user-unfriendly – it sounds
like the name of a star system at the fringe of the Milky Way.) Even
fewer understand the problem of account "leakage" or the process of
asset "decumulation" in retirement. A mere 17% grade themselves
high on understanding how Social Security works.

That's unconscionable. How can a government put people in
charge of saving for their longevity and not educate them about how
to do it? Nearly two-thirds of retirees say they wish they had been
more knowledgeable about retirement saving and investing during
their working years.[11] Only 46% say they're doing a good job at
drawing income from their savings and investments in retirement.[12]

To compound these problems, most retirees don't discuss
financial matters as much as they probably should. That's in part
because, in the minds of many, discussing finances is still socially
taboo. Americans are near unanimous (92%) in saying that personal finances are a private matter, and nearly half of retirees say
they don't discuss retirement savings, investments, or finances even
with close family or friends.[13] Many people are more comfortable
talking about their end of life than about their finances.

Michelle Seitz, Chairman and CEO of Russell Investments,
says, "The industry has an obligation to redesign itself to more effectively provide for people's financial security." In a 2019 memo she
wrote: "We have an escalating societal crisis. . . . Today's worldwide
retirement savings gap has surpassed $70 trillion. According to the
World Economic Forum, that number is expected to reach $400
trillion by 2050."[14]

At the individual level, Seitz points out that given the magnitude of the shortfall, people deserve to understand their options. It needs to be their choice to work longer, reduce spending, leverage financial tools like reverse mortgages and annuities, or plan to rely more on family and friends. But her main message is a challenge: "Our industry's silence only serves to magnify the problem. As an industry, let's admit that none of us have a panacea product that completely solves this. . . . What can make a significant difference are savings levels and contribution rates. If a worker is significantly underfunded . . . they will either need to save more or their employers will need to contribute more, or both."

Retirees have told us repeatedly that they don't know who or what is a reliable source of advice on managing their assets for and in retirement. Less than 40% work with financial advisors. More than 40% say they have no dependable sources of advice at all.[15] And what sources do they trust? Most trusted are financial professionals, family, and friends. Least trusted are social media, the internet, and news media generally. In between are employers, financial institutions, and the financial news media.

More than a third of American adults (36%) say that financial decisions are the ones they second-guess the most (in second place at 18% is decisions about job and career). People may lack confidence in their financial decisions, yet they want to project financial confidence in front of family and friends. Sixty percent agree that, "It's important that others think I'm in control of my finances."

Digital Advice and Support on the Rise

Older Americans are not yet the heavy users, but financial services are becoming increasingly digitized and democratized. Enormous amounts of information and plenty of financial management tools and calculators are available online. Robo-advisors and hybrid robo-plus-human financial advising services are common. The number of options can be confusing, but retirees who want to learn and do more about managing their finances have resources at their disposal. And there's market opportunity for financial services firms that simplify and package services to meet retirees' needs. As Bessemer Venture Partners points out, today's proliferation of "fintech" products and services are aimed primarily at young "digital native" consumers, not at the older ones who have wealth, spend differently, and need different services and solutions. Technology platforms addressing their needs have appeared but we expect that will continue to evolve in the years ahead.[16]

David Tyrie, who heads Advanced Solutions and Digital Banking at Bank of America, shared his perspective on digital strategy: "Our digital platforms strive to bring never-before-possible convenience and personalization to our customers. For example, our virtual assistant, Erica, can proactively detect if there are duplicate charges on your account or notify you if your spending is higher than usual. While Gen Zs and Millennials are quick adopters of our digital platforms, we see adoption at every age and we believe our digital tools can make everyday banking experiences simpler and more convenient for everyone. Digital, however, is only half of our 'high-tech, high-touch' approach that relies on the expertise of our people and the relationships they build with customers."

Holistic Preparation for Retirement

It's hard to turn on the news in the evening without seeing ads from financial services firms offering to help you plan for your retirement. Most of the major ones have lines of business that help customers understand their financial situations, sort through their options, and manage their money and savings both in preparation for and during retirement. They all strive to advise and support customers in more comprehensive and holistic ways (and we hope this book helps the cause). Here's what a few of the executives we have spoken with and followed have to say about the industry's objectives and challenges today.

Andy Sieg, President of Merrill Lynch Wealth Management, recounts the recent evolution of financial planning: "For people to experience and achieve what matters to them in retirement, they need good financial planning in dollars-and-cents terms, but it has to be in the context of their plans for life. In this new environment, it's not just about money. Good advisors are trained in assimilating many perspectives. They go through a systematic process to identify what matters to retirees in non-financial terms.

To help them do an inventory of their personal values and objectives, as well as their financial objectives and tolerance for risk. Advising has grown more complicated over time because it's not just build a 60/40 investment portfolio, let it run, and hope for the best. It's an equation with many more dimensions that we're trying to solve."

His colleague David Tyrie adds: "We know that, whether big or small, financial decisions are about more than money; they are about living a better life. That is especially true during retirement, where financial wellness can have a major impact on one's overall experience. After all, for many of our clients, retirement will be the most significant expense they face during their lifetime. Financial advisors should help them navigate the retirement journey, whether it's projecting savings needs, building an investment strategy, helping them decide when to retire, or taking steps to downsize their home."

Ken Cella, who leads the Client Strategies Group for Edward Jones, told us, "Our clients' needs are complex and their expectations have never been higher. Given that complexity, they are looking to us to provide holistic solutions. Financial advisors are required to have the EQ and IQ – the emotional intelligence and empathy to understand the client's perspective, standing in their shoes to anticipate what they have not yet articulated."

Challenges Women Face

Women have greater need than men for financial planning both before and during retirement, for a variety of reasons. First, they are paid less than men – 82% for the same work. Over a lifetime, that adds up to a $400,000+ differential. Second, women have longer retirements, retiring on average two years earlier and then living an average five years longer than men.[17] Third, women tend to have less saved for retirement after spending more time out of the workforce as parents and then as caregivers.[18] The average American woman has a 401(k) balance that is only 68% of the average man's.[19] Fourth, given their longevity, women are more likely to need long-term care services. As couples grow older, the husband more often suffers health problems before the wife. She cares for him, sometimes for years, often depleting her energy and their finances along the way. Then when he dies, who will care for her? Women account for 61% of home health clients, 66% of nursing homes residents, and 71% of residential care community residents.[20]

Award-winning financial planner Ric Edelman says, "Longer lives, lower pay, less savings, more giving and receiving care – that combination makes financial planning really a women's issue. Women must engage in financial planning and management, and financial services firms must engage them. And to men who have traditionally been in the financial lead, I say encourage the women in your lives – mother, wife, sister, daughter – to get the financial planning support they need."

Women's pay gap while working carries over as a pension gap in retirement. Across the OECD, the average gender difference in pensions is more than 25%. In Denmark, it's only 10%, versus 40% in the U.K. and Netherlands. The pension gap in the United States is about one-third, in Japan almost one-half. If we add the pay gap, the effect of work interruptions, and the pension gap together, the "wealth gap" for an American woman in retirement can be over $1.2 million (Figure 9.5).

However, we're also seeing more financial independence among women retirees. They are coming into their own financially, thanks largely to how Boomer women differ from previous generations.

Figure 9.5   Women's Lifetime Cumulative Wealth Gap

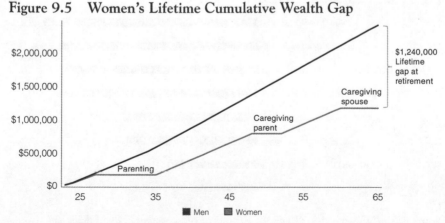

Source: Age Wave calculation[21]

They are twice as likely to have college degrees, more than half again as likely to have been working in their twenties, and twice as likely to be divorced, separated, or never married. They have more experience and confidence as investors, and more awareness of the challenges they face funding their retirement.

Course Corrections in Retirement

Well prepared or not, people retire and adjust to living on a new mix of spending habits and income sources. But most have three things in common. First, they worry about finances, starting with the potential expense of health problems (Figure 9.6). Other commonly cited concerns are rising costs, lack of money to do the things they want to do, and outliving their wealth.

Second, their objective is peace of mind, not wealth in itself. Given the choice, 88% say that they would like to save enough to have financial peace of mind, only 12% that they would like to accumulate as much wealth as possible. What constitutes financial peace of mind? For the majority (57%), it's simply being able to live comfortably within one's means. For many, it includes freedom to enjoy one's lifestyle, or confidence that unexpected expenses can be handled. What can disrupt financial peace of mind? Most

Figure 9.6   Financial Worries in Retirement

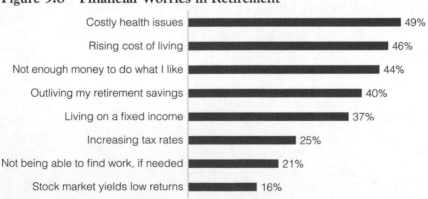

Source: Age Wave / Merrill Lynch, *Finances in Retirement: New Challenges, New Solutions*

commonly cited are health disruptions (87%), large unexpected expenses (84%), and loved ones needing financial support (57%).

Third, retirees are resilient and adaptable, willing to make lifestyle adjustments and course corrections (the less painful the better) during retirement in order to maintain their financial footing and enjoy this new stage of their lives. The most basic involve adjusting finances, working more, and spending less.

Adjusting Financial Structures

Some course corrections are directly financial. These include maximizing the tax benefits of retirement accounts, finding other ways to reduce taxes, and adjusting the timing (either accelerating or postponing) of initiating Social Security benefits. A strong majority of retirees (60% or more) would consider each of those actions. They are less willing (43%) to withdraw cash value from life insurance policies. One in four would consider declaring bankruptcy as a financial expedient.

Bankruptcy filings are "graying" with the population. The bankruptcy rate for age 65+ households has tripled over the last three decades.[22] Individuals age 65+ now account for over 12% of all bankruptcy filers, a dramatic rise from 2.1% in 1992.[23] Bankruptcy is a way to discharge medical and credit card debt while homestead exemptions can protect the primary home and savings in retirement plans are protected by law. Older household average debt (excluding mortgage) has declined to pre-recession levels, but at roughly $33,000 it is four times the 1991 level.[24] A growing source of debt is student loans taken out on behalf of children and grandchildren.[25]

Meanwhile, some retirees and pre-retirees hope for or expect inheritances to add to their retirement funds. Thirty-seven percent of Americans age 50+ have received an inheritance from a family member or someone else, and another 7% say they expect to.[26] A lot of money is in motion. Nearly two million inheritances are received each year, amounting for nearly $300 billion in transferred wealth. More than half of inheritances received are $50,000 or less, while only 2% are $1 million or more.[27] The likelihood of an inheritance peaks at around age 60, when parents are in their 80s. Not surprisingly, people in the top 10% of income distribution are twice as likely to receive an inheritance as those in the bottom half of the distribution.[28]

Working More

How do people try to catch up financially? The greatest impact comes from working a bit longer, even part time. That adds time to save and delays tapping into retirement savings. While working, people can maximize their contributions to 401(k) and other IRA accounts, and 60% of pre-retirees said they would delay their retirement to improve their finances.

As we detailed in Chapter 4, working part time in retirement is becoming the new normal. Seven in ten Boomers expect to work past age 65, are already doing so, or do not plan to retire at all.[29] Many retirees work out of financial necessity, but the majority work for a combination of both personal and financial advantage – staying active and socially engaged while supplementing their retirement income. Andy Sieg sees an increasingly important role for work: "Many retirees' income streams from savings and Social Security are insufficient. However, we've been very fortunate that, at the same time as the longevity wave has been building, the nature of work and the workplace have changed in ways that make it much more feasible and energizing and socially rewarding for people to continue working later into life. Retirees want to stay active and engaged, especially mentally, and the twenty-first century multigenerational workforce values skills and experience. So I'm optimistic about the overall Boomer financial journey through retirement because of the extent to which they're staying active and engaged and working."

Today's retirees are already working in a variety of formats – regular part time or seasonally, in their former occupations or trying something new, for their old employers or working for themselves, monetizing a hobby or starting a new business. The gig economy offers work-when-you-like options, from driving for rideshare services, to doing administrative or technical piecework online at home, to teaching English to children in China for VIPKids. If needed to improve their finances, three-fourths of retirees and pre-retirees say they would return to work part time in retirement, and 43% would consider working full time.

Spending Less

Cutting back on expenses is an obvious course correction. Nine in ten retirees say they'd do so if needed, and 60% say they spend less money now than when they originally retired.[30] Retirees have more time to do their homework and manage their budgets. Finding discounts and taking advantage of loyalty programs help the cause. But retirees want to maintain and enjoy their lifestyles, so general belt-tightening can definitely have a positive effect.

For some, thoughtful cost-cutting is the essence of a retirement plan. Edd and Cynthia Staton were undone by the economic crisis – careers, investments, home equity. Seeing no way to catch up, in 2010 they moved to Cuenca, Ecuador, where they could afford to live on the money they had. They write and blog about their experience and help others researching retiring abroad at their website eddandcynthia.com. Their bottom line: "Turns out it was one of the best decisions we've ever made. . . . Those financial nightmares are a thing of the past."

Another approach is extreme downsizing. Luxtiny is a tiny-house community in Lakeside, AZ. Custom-built or standard models range from 162 to 399 square feet. Options include a storage shed and a 144-square-foot guest house, and houses can be built in the community or anyplace in the state. Standard models start at $59,000, and custom houses can cost over $100,000. Owners save significant money across the board – purchase price, insurance, utilities, maintenance. Visitors are amazed on how much by way of both functionality and possessions can fit into a comparatively very small space.[31]

Some Additional Course Corrections

The retirees we surveyed indicated their willingness to make a variety of other course corrections with financial impact. For example, they say they'd sell possessions, perhaps the second car if no longer needed, perhaps as part of a decluttering process. Another way to make money is by turning a hobby into a source of income. *Next Avenue* has profiled a variety of retirees who make money and enjoy themselves by monetizing their hobbies. And it's not all woodworking, knitting, and other crafts. Examples include a contract bridge instructor, a purveyor of home-recipe gourmet nuts, and a travel-loving couple who hire out as fill-in innkeepers.[32]

Finally, one of the most beneficial actions retirees can take is investing in their health – exercise more, eat better, or stop smoking. The payback can't be precisely calculated, but better health means lower everyday medical expenses and the delay or better management of chronic conditions and their long-term costs. The value in terms of personal well-being can be felt even sooner than the financial value.

With all these potential course corrections, retirees need guidance assessing what moves will really make a difference for them. Expense-cutting may be straightforward, but major financial course corrections can be complicated. Some involve decisions, such as selling a house or purchasing an annuity, with long-term implications. Tapping the cash value of life insurance policies can sometimes be beneficial if the original need for the insurance has declined. Just deciding when to initiate Social Security benefits – early, at "full retirement age," or as late as possible – is puzzling for most Americans. Eight in ten retirees say they are willing to seek professional financial advice on these matters; however, as we mentioned, only about half as many actually work with advisors.

Spending and Decumulating in Retirement

The guideline we mentioned that retirees need 75% of their pre-retirement annual income seems a reasonable approximation in light of research from J.P. Morgan. However, spending doesn't always drop by exactly one-fourth upon retirement. The long-term pattern has household spending peaking when people are in their 50s, then gradually declining until leveling off around age 80. After age 60, the only cost category that increases is, as we would expect, health care. The short-term pattern has spending increasing measurably but not dramatically (about 5% on average) in the year *before* retirement. People may be investing in pre-retirement adjustments like home renovations or splurging on that retirement celebration trip. A year into retirement, spending is back to where it was a year before retirement.[33]

This analysis has good news for retirees. They may need less money in retirement than the retirement funding calculators typically suggest. But there's some bad news as well. They may be tapping into more of their retirement funds earlier than planned at the start of retirement. We can also conclude that a few years before retirement is a difficult time to still be playing catch-up financially.

Another common guideline is the 4% rule for drawing down, or "decumulating," retirement savings. Taking 4% of the total nest egg per year, adjusting for inflation (so the withdrawal amount grows a bit each year), can cover a 30-year retirement. The simple math works, but there are major variables, including the size of the initial nest egg, performance of investments, and the age when decumulation starts. An annual 4% withdrawal may do little to supplement Social Security and any pension income, and little to support the retiree's preferred lifestyle. In that case, adjustments are needed to income and outlay.

One of the biggest variables behind how much retirement costs and the pace at which retirees spend is location. GOBankingRates calculated how long a $1 million nest egg lasts on average state-by-state across America. It would last 25 years or more in Mississippi, Arkansas, Oklahoma, Michigan, or Tennessee, but only around 17 years in California, Alaska, New York, Connecticut, Maryland, or Massachusetts. In Hawaii, it would be consumed in a dozen years.

Guaranteed Paycheck for Life? The Potential Role of Annuities

Financial annuities got a major shot of awareness when the Alliance for Lifetime Income, the industry association of annuity providers, was the sole sponsor of the Rolling Stones recent North American tour. Annuities are insurance products that turn an initial lump sum premium into lifetime income, like a regular paycheck. They are typically purchased with proceeds from a 401(k), IRA, or other retirement savings account. An annuity provides income for life, thus serves as a form of "longevity insurance," with a minimum payment period's value guaranteed to the estate if the insured dies early in the annuity contract.

When asked to describe the ideal retirement investment, three-fourths of American adults said something that provides guaranteed income and something that is guaranteed not to lose value.[34] That's an annuity. However, annuities come in complicated variations, many consumers are wary of them, and they are underutilized. Todd Giesing of the LIMRA Secure Retirement Institute feels that the market is poised to grow: "The overall annuity market will thrive in an aging population. The number of people reaching age 65 or older will reach 60 million by 2023 – the target market for individual annuity products."[35] Abaris serves as a direct-to-consumer marketplace for retirement annuities from insurers such as AIG, Pacific Life, Guardian, Principal Financial Group, and Lincoln Financial Group.

The primary upside of an annuity is the security of guaranteed income. An insured person who lives long "comes out ahead." And for people who lack financial discipline, annuities prevent them from spending down their assets too fast. The downsides start with the money's no longer being in the insured's control – it takes a psychological leap to trade a lump sum for a series of payments in return. Inflation can reduce the spending power of payments (though cost-of-living riders are available). The insurance company could fail (though contracts are government-backed up to a limit). And if the insured dies prematurely, the estate can "come out behind."

Andy Sieg takes a measured view of annuities: "It's hard for the private sector to create a broad annuity market, from Boomers to Millennials, because what company wants to bet against longevity? There could be a breakthrough in genetic engineering that dramatically increases life expectancy, and that makes it challenging to be out there with an open-ended guarantee of lifetime income. For a program to scale in a big way, it would have to build on the bones of Social Security or reinvent Social Security for a new century."

Many financial experts recommend annuities or other guaranteed-return investments as *part* of the retirement funding mix. The idea is to establish a combination of annuity, pension, and Social Security income to meet retirees' baseline living expenses indefinitely, regardless of the performance of any other investments. If consumers are shy about annuities, that creates opportunities for financial services institutions that can simplify and more effectively explain and market them.

Cash Poor But Brick Rich: Ways to Monetize the Biggest Asset

Owning a home remains a solid part of the American Dream for 90% of adults of all ages.[36] But it takes time for most of us to accumulate a down payment and establish the cash flow to service a mortgage, then 20 or 30 years to pay it off. So homeownership and home equity naturally skew older. A majority of Americans have become homeowners by age 40. Among those age 65 and older, 79% own their homes (Figure 9.7), and seven in ten of those have paid off the mortgage. Their home equity, averaging nearly $300,000, may represent a significant portion of their total net worth, not to mention a big contributor to their financial peace of mind. The total home equity held by age 62+ American households reached a record $7.14 trillion in 2019.[37]

In the years ahead, one of the most significant financial moves in retirement for many people may be to monetize the value of an owned home. Sell and then rent, adding all the proceeds to the retirement fund. Or sell and buy a downsized home, pocketing the difference. And perhaps relocate in the process to someplace with lower housing, living, and property tax costs. For example, suppose a 62-year-old New Jersey couple sells their $325,000 house that still carries a $75,000 mortgage. They buy a $135,000 house in South Carolina, freeing up $115,000 to invest or spend, and leaving them mortgage-free. Over the next 15 years, their savings in cost of

Figure 9.7   Homeowners by Age

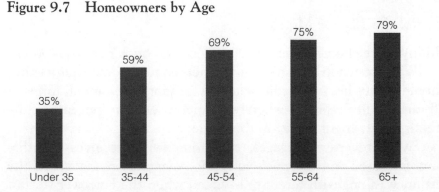

Under 35	35-44	45-54	55-64	65+
35%	59%	69%	75%	79%

Source: U.S. Census Bureau, Current Population Survey, 2017

ownership (mainly lower property taxes) and cost of living average $28,000 per year, or an aggregate of $420,000. If both live to age 90, the aggregate saving is $620,000.

Retirees we surveyed tell us that, though emotionally attached to their homes, they are willing to adjust. Three in four would downsize. Two-thirds would relocate to someplace less expensive or cut back on home improvements and repairs. Nearly half would consider selling and then renting.[38] And renting seems to have growing appeal. The number of age 65+ households that rent is projected to increase by a whopping 80% from 2015 to 2035.[39]

Especially if home equity is going to be a significant source of funding in retirement, most retirees need help considering all the variables – mortgage or rent payments, property taxes, insurance, utilities, and maintenance and repairs. They need help considering all the options – including stay-put alternatives such as home equity loans, reverse mortgages, and refinancing when rates drop. And then help determining what home equity actions make the most sense.

Selling or borrowing against it isn't the only way to monetize one's house. Older Americans have become the fastest growing segment as both hosts and patrons of Airbnb. In 2017, hosts over age 60 earned $2 billion from Airbnb by accommodating 13.5 million guests across more than 150 countries. Airbnb embraces the retiree market: "Airbnb is helping to redefine retirement by providing new ways to earn extra income, overcome loneliness and isolation, and travel the world in a truly local and authentic way."[40]

A Role for Reverse Mortgages?

Many retiree homeowners are cash poor and brick rich, thus potentially interested in ways to tap into their equity. Home equity loans, home equity lines of credit, and reverse mortgages are all forms of "home equity release," whereby homeowners can get cash while retaining the right to live in the home.

With reverse mortgages, the homeowner receives monthly income based on the home's value, no payments are made, and the balance (along with interest) is repaid when the borrower (or last borrower) sells the property, moves into permanent long-term care, or passes away. If the loan balance then exceeds the value of the property, the borrower or borrower's estate is usually not required to pay the difference.

Reverse mortgages are marketed as ways to supplement retirement income while having the security of owning a home. Retirees commonly use the money to cover everyday expenses, make home improvements, pay off other debt, or take trips and enjoy their leisure. Older homeowners have traditionally treated the mortgages as a last resort, but attitudes may be changing as both retirees and their heirs are focusing less on inheritances being passed down and more on enabling retirees to live comfortably.

Equity release has gained some popularity in the U.K., where retiree homeownership is high, and the market is approaching £4 billion a year. The Equity Release Council finds that nearly a half million homeowners have released equity with the help of their member institutions over the last three decades. Retirees trust the products because the industry is regulated, lenders are conservative regarding loan size, and sales are predominantly through financial advisors.[41]

In the United States, reverse mortgages are less popular – the market is not much larger than in the U.K. despite almost five times the population. Reverse mortgages are increasingly promoted by television ads featuring celebrity spokespeople, but consumer uncertainty remains high. The products can be complex and difficult to understand. Some retirees take out the mortgages too early, draw down all their home equity, and find themselves in financial trouble paying property taxes and maintenance. When the loans are paid off, borrowers or their heirs can be taken by surprise by the settlement complications and how little equity remains.

Ric Edelman, founder of Edelman Financial Engines and three times ranked the country's top financial advisor by *Barron's*, says: "In principle, reverse mortgages are a wonderful idea. Unfortunately, current products fail to serve the best interests of most homeowners, so anyone interested in generating income from their home equity should proceed with caution."

Reverse mortgages could become a useful part of more retirees' financial plans. However, as with the annuities market, we believe it will likely take the combination of simpler and more transparent products and better consumer protections for the market to really take off. Until then, independent advisors can help retiree homeowners make sure the products are clearly aligned with their financial interests.

Coping with Health Care Costs

Health care cost is many retirees' greatest financial worry for good reason – the costs are high, increasing, and uncertain. Most retirees are willing to spend what they can afford to regain or maintain their health. But for those of modest means, sudden and unanticipated health care expenses can be financially disastrous. This concern is ubiquitous, as Andy Sieg points out: "Health care funding is not a niche topic or niche market. When you talk about it, everyone tunes in. Everyone is thinking about longevity and the need for caregiving and the worry about dementia. Look how quickly Alzheimer's became a dominant health concern. More people are trying to balance caregiving to their parents with the needs of their immediate families, and it's something they have to engineer on their own for the first time."

Longer retirements naturally mean more accumulated out-of-pocket health care costs (Figure 9.8). Even with some recent reforms, medical costs have continued to outpace inflation. Since 2000, they have risen an average of 3.41% per year, half again the

Figure 9.8   Out-of-Pocket Health Care Costs if Your Retirement Lasts . . .

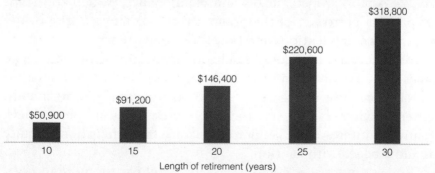

Source: Dale H. Yamamoto, *Health Care Costs – From Birth to Death*, Health Care Cost Institute Report, 2013

2.12% rate for total consumer categories.[42] Adding to the financial challenge is that retirees are largely on their own paying for Medicare supplement programs and other out-of-pocket costs. And like guaranteed pensions, "now you see it, now you don't." As recently as 1988 two-thirds of large employers provided retiree health care benefits. Today it's only 18%.[43]

Fidelity Investments estimates that a 65-year-old couple retiring in 2019 can expect to spend $285,000 out-of-pocket in health care and medical expenses in retirement.[44] That's more than the average home equity and more than the median household net worth of Americans 65 and older.[45] And that estimate does not include long-term care.

Only 37% of Americans anticipate that they may need long-term care at some point, when informed estimates put it at about double that (70%).[46] In 2018 the average annual long-term care costs in the United States were $45,800 for a home health aide for 40 hours/week, and $89,300 for a semi-private nursing home room.[47] Total out-of-pocket expenditures were $9.6 billion on home health care and $46.1 billion on nursing home and continuing care facilities. The average lifetime costs for an individual's paid long-term support services is $266,000, more than half of it not covered by insurance and thus out-of-pocket.[48] Aggregate national spending on home health care is expected to nearly double in the next 10 years.[49]

Retirees can protect themselves from the high cost of long-term care. But the market for traditional long-term care insurance hasn't taken off because it's perceived as an expensive "use it or lose it" proposition. That is changing with the availability of hybrid life-and-care insurance. LIMRA reports that sales of annuity/long-term care combinations have surpassed sales of individual long-term care policies for the last five years.

Retirees need help understanding, anticipating, and managing the costs of their health care, balancing the objectives of quality care and financial asset protection. But many don't really understand their health insurance coverage to begin with. Over 40% erroneously think that Medicare will cover nearly all their health care and long-term care costs.[50] Part of the problem is that many find information on insurance and costs to be complicated, often overwhelming. Among people age 55–64, only 7% say they feel knowledgeable about Medicare and its options.[51] That only rises to 19% of those over 65 who are currently covered. It's perhaps one of the reasons that AARP and UnitedHealthcare's partnership leads the market. Millions of people, unable to figure out the whole crazy world of Medicare Supplements, think, "Well, I can't tell the difference, but if AARP is supporting United-Healthcare, it must be good." They're probably not aware of the more than $600 million that AARP receives each year through the arrangement.

Anticipation and preparation should start well before retirement, yet health care is often a missing link in retirement planning. Only 15% of pre-retirees say they have ever attempted to estimate their health care and long-term care expenses in retirement.[52] Nearly all would welcome guidance on Medicare and supplemental plans, long-term care, other insurance and funding options, and how much money they may need for health care. However, as with financial advice generally, few say they have a trusted source for answers on financing health care.[53] As we discussed in the chapter on health, they could use something like a personalized "Health Waze" app.

At the point of retirement, most people also need to play catch-up with how they'll fund their health care. A retiree we spoke with shared her sticker shock: "I read the numbers on what health care can cost. I didn't even think about that when saving for retirement." Another put the challenge bluntly: "Uncertainty is the real problem. If only I had an expiration date, I'd know how much I need to save."

Avoiding Elder Fraud: A Hidden Menace

Financial fraud and abuse are a scourge on older Americans. True Link Financial estimates the losses at over $36 billion annually across three categories. Exploitation accounts for about $17 billion in losses, as when people use misleading language and pressure tactics to get seniors to pay for things that are marked up, unneeded, or worthless. These include subscriptions, quack products and services, work-from-home schemes, and hidden shipping and other fees. Individual amounts lost may be small, but the number of incidents is uncountable.

The second category, criminal fraud, includes email and phone scams to obtain financial information and money directly. Nearly $10 billion is lost to scams, $3 billion to identity theft. And the third category is caregiver abuse, where $6.7 billion is lost, mainly through theft, to trusted people – family members, paid helpers, friends, lawyers, or financial managers.

The National Adult Protective Services Association describes the common ways family members and other trusted people exploit vulnerable adults. Direct financial abuse often involves misuse of powers of attorney, withdrawing funds from joint bank accounts, or using the victim's ATM card or checks to take funds. In-home caregivers may overcharge for services or simply not perform them, or "keep the change" from errands. Family members may not arrange for medical care the recipient needs in order to keep the money available to themselves. And financial abusers may resort to threats to abandon or harm the victim if they don't get their way.

Financial institutions are increasingly vigilant, and the number of "elder finance exploitation" (EFE) "suspicious activity report" (SAR) filings is rising steadily. But it's estimated that the 63,500 SARs in 2017 may represent less than 2% of actual incidents, and more than 3.5 million older adults were victimized that year. The banks tend to report the larger losses. The slight majority of SARs are associated with strangers, and the median loss is $8,500. Those associated with persons known to the victim have a median loss of $23,300. The likelihood of incidents increases with age, and the highest average losses are incurred by people in their seventies.

Preventing financial fraud and abuse also requires vigilance by individual retirees, with some technological help. For instance, EverSafe is a subscription service that monitors activity and patterns of bank, credit card, and investment accounts and issues suspicious activity alerts and warnings about unusual withdrawals, missing deposits, and unpaid bills. EverSafe was created by Howard Tischler after his aging mother received an unusually high credit card bill with fraudulent charges including an auto club membership. His mother was legally blind and didn't own a car. Tischler says, "Baby boomers control trillions of dollars in wealth, much of it in retirement funds. And as that big generation gets older, a treasury of life savings will increasingly beckon predators who are cunning with computers."[54]

Tools and Resources to Help Keep Affairs in Order

There's one more financial matter to attend to in retirement – keeping one's formal "affairs in order." Retirees care very much about the legacies they leave. They want to remain in control in their final years, including in control of their late-in-life health care. And they want to enrich rather than burden the lives of their loved ones and heirs.

So they need three essentials: a will or trust to control distribution of assets not already covered by beneficiary arrangements, a durable power of attorney to make financial decisions if one is incapacitated, and health directives specifying treatment preferences and who can make medical decisions if one is incapacitated. In addition, their key documents (including insurance policies, real estate titles, family medical history, and account passwords) need to be organized and secure but accessible.

Unfortunately, the overwhelming majority of older Americans cannot claim to have their affairs in order. Only 55% of those age 55+ have a will, and only 18% have the trifecta of a will, power of attorney, and health directive (Figure 9.9). One-fourth of those age

Figure 9.9   Possession of the Essentials among Ages 55+

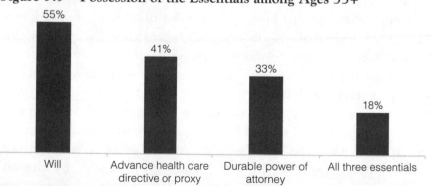

Source: Age Wave / Merrill Lynch, *Leaving a Legacy: A Lasting Gift to Loved Ones*

75+ still lack a will,[55] and an estimated 23% of wills in force are out of date.[56] Best prepared are widows, who have learned from the experience of dealing with their deceased spouses' end-of-life and legacy matters.

What does this mean for the unprepared and their families? The unprepared are increasing the odds that they *will* be financial and caregiving burdens on their families. And they risk diminishing their personal legacies, because heirs recognize that dying without having the formal affairs in order is irresponsible. The heirs inherit disarray and headaches as part of the estate.

Some of these preparations begin early in life – executing a will upon marriage or buying life insurance upon becoming a parent. However, a concerted effort to get one's affairs in order is usually triggered later in life by a health scare in the family, a life event like retirement, or the influence of family, friends, doctors, or financial advisors. A lot is already changing at the point of retirement, and that can make it a good time to get some affairs in order, to consider the still-distant as well as the immediate future.

We're seeing online services and tools to help retirees with rudimentary estate planning and organization of their affairs. For example, Future Vault is a "digital safety deposit box" that enables people to share with financial advisers their financial, legal, and personal as well as small business documents. Genivity is a similar service that also incorporates family health information so financial advisers can consult with clients about health risks in conjunction with financial and estate planning. Both tools support clients' relationships with their planners. Whenever assets are significant, family structures are complex, or life and health circumstances are complicated, keeping affairs in order requires the help of financial, legal, and estate planning professionals.

Funding retirement rightly focuses on saving and preparing well in advance. But even if retirees have attained their "magic number" of funds accumulated, other factors – starting with family and health – can disrupt their plans. "Easy Street" is a bit of a myth. Many people need closer attention to – and more help with – their finances during retirement than before.

Actions and Opportunities for Organizations and Entrepreneurs in the Financial Services Sector

1. Advise retirees holistically on all the financial implications and options at the intersections of housing, health care, and managing assets through a potentially lengthy retirement.
2. Demystify complex financial options like annuities and reverse mortgages to make them more accessible, attractive, and useful.
3. Help retirees at all asset levels develop specific, disciplined, and understandable plans for both catchup accumulation and then decumulation of assets in retirement.
4. Customize Fintech products and services to fit the needs, priorities, and preferences of older customers. And provide the choice of technology-based or personal service.
5. Be informed and empathetic to the specific financial circumstances and challenges common to women retirees.
6. Bundle in fraud and abuse prevention technologies and services wherever possible. Make them seamless and easily understood.
7. Provide integrated services for getting and keeping all affairs in order, not just the financial side.
8. Connect retirees with complementary services for home relocation, renovation, and maintenance; finding interesting and suitable jobs; and managing their health and health care.
9. Educate customers in financial management at every turn, starting with things as simple as "click here to learn more." The act of consuming financial products, services, and advice should raise retirees' knowledge and confidence.

10

The Giving Revolution

Living with Purpose and Leaving a Legacy

Across our decades of study, we've noticed that today's retirees want to be *useful* even more than they want to be *youthful*. They very much want to avoid becoming irrelevant. Having a strong sense of purpose keeps them more active, healthier, happier – and, yes, feeling more youthful. But the sources of purpose shift in retirement, and many retirees are seeking a new and even stronger sense of purpose in their lives than when they were younger. For others, a decline in sense of purpose can be one of the most debilitating conditions of age.

The Power of Purpose

Earlier in life, people find purpose in a variety and combination of places. Supporting and nurturing a family provides the strongest purpose for many, especially on becoming parents. Work is often central to purpose, on its own merits or with companion motivations around career and financial success. Purpose can be largely internal, rooted in self-knowledge, self-improvement, and self-actualization. Or it can be largely external and social, focused on

227

achieving success, fulfilling goals, or contributing to the welfare of others. And for many, purpose is spiritual, based on one's faith and usually combining elements of inner and social purpose.

A sense of purpose in retirement is both individual and subjective, as Paul Irving, JD, chair of the Milken Institute Center for the Future of Aging, observes: "I think of purpose as this intersection between the skills, motivations, talents, and passions that one has and some void in the universe that those qualities can fill. Could it be time with grandchildren? Yes. Could it be a great golf game? Yes. Could it be leading a social movement? Yes. Could it be working in a meaningful job? Yes. Without a sense of purpose, in many ways we lose our humanity."

With our increasingly long lives, purpose changes and often intensifies in retirement. Retirees find that their family and friendship connections become even more important and valuable. This might include aging parents on one hand and grandchildren on the other. Work and career recede into the past for most retirees, but remain front and center for a significant segment. Inner purpose grows as people reinvent themselves in retirement, focused on learning and doing new things, staying healthy, and being more of their best selves. Social purpose expands as retirees have more time to volunteer and support activities and causes they care about. And as people mature, they also report becoming more reflective, philosophical, and spiritual. Late in life, retirees focus on their last gifts, the legacy they want to leave behind to loved ones and heirs. Along the new retirement journey, giving back supplants getting ahead.

Dr. Charlotte Yeh is the Chief Medical Officer for AARP Services, Inc. Her experience spans medical practice, the health insurance industry, and public sector health services. She was instrumental in the development of the City of Boston's Age Strong campaign (which we described in Chapter 3). She shared some of the insights she garnered from the campaign:

With older people, we've traditionally chased after the failure to thrive and its social determinants – transportation, housing, education, nutrition, and so on. But thriving also depends very much on the personal determinants – what makes two 80-year-old women in similar circumstances completely different at that stage of life? We pivoted and created the Age Strong campaign to see if we could uncover the secret sauce of the thrivers. Our hypothesis was that it has to do with resiliency, the ability to adapt with change. There are many things that go into resiliency, but three stood out.

The first is a positive view of aging and the possibility of your future. Why can't you be 80 and have a vision for tomorrow or the next day? If you have a positive view of aging, you live seven-and-a-half years longer.

The second is social connections. Isolation is an objective number, how big your network is. But loneliness is how you feel, and we found that loneliness was the strongest predictor of dissatisfaction with health care. That was an industry wake-up call. We have all these measures for improving the experience of care and we're dancing around the biggest factor by not talking about loneliness.

The third is purpose. If you have a strong sense of purpose that gets you up in the morning, and people to do it with, your possibilities become endless. You also have fewer heart attacks, fewer cases of dementia, better cholesterol, lower stress hormones, better blood pressure, and you make use of more preventive services. On the business-of-medicine side, 61% fewer nights in the hospital, 31% fewer doctor visits, and a lower per member per month health care cost. Purpose, people, possibilities – those are core to the Age Strong campaign.

Encore.org founder and CEO Marc Freedman helped to establish the Purpose Prize in 2006. Now run by AARP, the prize annually recognizes extraordinary people age 50 and older who tackle the world's urgent problems as social entrepreneurs, innovators, and change-makers. You could say that purpose is Marc's purpose. He shared some of his reflections with us:

Older people want to stay engaged in life and connect with other generations, and they're rolling up their sleeves and finding ways to do that all over the country, all over the world. We're trying to build a movement of older people who want to put purpose front and center, purpose beyond our own lives that helps to create a better future.

So we elevate the stories of people who are already living lives like that, who are using their life experience to solve important problems. We want to shift the norm for this period of life so that people feel like it's an honor to live with purpose. At the same time, we have to make it easier for people to go from aspiration to action. It's not enough just to feel like you'd like to live a life that still matters. We're finding ways to make that life possible. We're creating better "pathways to purpose." Purpose can then become a springboard for an encore career, a second act focused on the greater good but anchored in what people have learned and honed over all their years of work and experience.

We've explored numerous elements of retirees' sources of purpose in many sections of this book. In this chapter, we focus on two more: direct giving/volunteering and leaving a legacy.

The Longevity Bonus: The Upside of Aging

The influx of Boomer retirees holds the potential to take giving and volunteering to new heights. The Boomers have always been a cause-oriented, change-the-world generation. Now that they have far more free time in retirement, we envision a revolution in giving and volunteering for decades to come. And Boomers want to contribute not just with time and labor, but with their talents and experience. They want their giving to have impact in causes, global and local, that matter a lot. And they are ready to use technology and social media to determine where to give and to band together for greater impact.

Surveys by Gallup and the Charities Aid Foundation find the United States to be one of the most generous nations in the world, based on rates of giving, volunteering, and helping others.[1] America's retirees are especially generous. Two-thirds of them say that retirement is the best time of life for giving back, and they overwhelmingly define success in retirement as being generous (85%) rather than being wealthy (15%). Retirement gives people the opportunity to expand their generosity – with more time, more savings to donate, and more accumulated skills and experience.

Charitable giving has been steadily increasing for the last quarter century, with only brief dips in times of recession, and over three-quarters of that giving comes from individuals and families – not foundations and corporations, as people often think.[2] Older Americans are especially generous, as charitable contributions tend to increase as people grow older (Figure 10.1). In 2018, Boomers contributed the most in aggregate, averaging over $1,000 each and accounting for 41% of all individual donations.[3]

Americans also contribute nearly seven billion hours of time annually through volunteering, worth an estimated $167 billion in economic value, assuming a modest $23 per hour. In 2018, the Baby Boomer generation accounted for the most volunteer time, a cumulative 2.2 billion hours with an estimated value of $54.3 billion.[4] That will only grow with the number of retirees and their desire to give with impact.

Retirement transforms how and how much people can give. Retirees often view giving in a new light, as one explained: "I never really thought about giving and what it meant to me. I just did it. And now in retirement, it means a great deal to me. There are

Figure 10.1   Percent Who Reported Donating to Charity in the Past Year

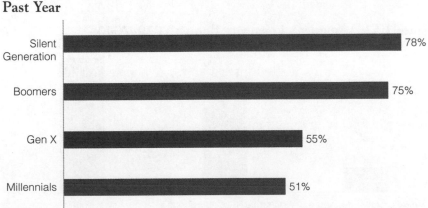

Source: Blackbaud Institute, *The Next Generation of American Giving*, 2018

values that I didn't really recognize, and in some ways I feel like I'm paying myself when I'm giving."

Retirees have the key ingredients. They have *more time*. No longer working full-time means dramatically more discretionary time – an average of over 70 hours per week for those 65 and older. That's time available for volunteering and purposeful charitable giving. They have *more wealth*. Older Americans hold more savings and other assets than younger age groups do. That accumulated wealth funds their retirement years, but part may be available for charitable causes. And they have *more skills and experience*. Retirees bring a lifetime of experience to their volunteer work and their decisions to donate. Eighty-four percent say that enables them to give more in retirement than they could when younger.[5] As Nancy Henkin, Senior Fellow at Generations United, puts it, "Volunteering is not just coming in and serving soup. It might be that if you have some executive skills maybe you organize a recruitment campaign, or maybe you take care of marketing, or maybe you manage other volunteers."

How large is the potential for retirees to give back? As the ranks of Boomer retirees swell and they enjoy lengthier retirements, their aggregate capacity for giving time and money over the next two decades totals nearly $9 trillion in value (Figure 10.2) in the United States alone. We anticipate enormous growth in financial donations – an estimated total of $7.2 trillion over that time. Then add in an estimated 63 billion hours of volunteering, which translates into about $1.6 trillion worth of services. We call that enormous

Figure 10.2   America's Longevity Bonus: 2020–2040

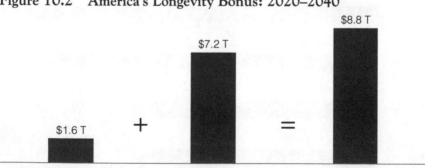

| Value of volunteer hours | Charitable contributions | Total |

Source: Age Wave calculation[6]

opportunity to do social good "America's Longevity Bonus." When we imagine this as a global phenomenon, the World's Longevity Bonus might approach $100 trillion over the next two decades!

Economic conditions may grow or shrink the bonus. The economy has a direct effect on donations but can have an inverse effect on volunteering. When generous people have less money to donate, they often compensate by increasing their volunteer work. But we see enormous potential for the amount of volunteering to exceed our estimates regardless of economic conditions. Generous though they may be, older Americans spend only a small fraction – under 4% – of their discretionary time as volunteers.[7] Charitable and community organizations need to crack the code of better engaging retiree volunteers.

Giving with Purpose and a Desire for Impact

Boomer retirees are more purposeful in giving than their parents were or they themselves were when they were younger. They have the inclination and time to be more hands-on. They research charities online and focus on those where the impact of their giving is greatest. More than three-fourths of retirees tell us they have more time to determine what charities they really care about. They have the freedom and control to give as they want, rather than following the expectations of, for example, their employers. Overall, they feel they have better strategies for giving and believe they are having more impact (Figure 10.3). As one retiree related, simply but eloquently, "Before I retired, I just wrote checks to charities. I didn't have time for anything else. In retirement, I give of my money, my time, and myself. Now I can really feel the difference I am making."

In giving, as with many other facets of life in retirement, Boomers learn from their grandparents and parents and then do things differently. Boomers say they are much more likely than their parents to research how charities use donations, to give significant thought to where to donate, to specify how their donations are used, and to try to gauge the impact of their donations. As one retiree told us, "My parents were very generous, but my sister and I have a very different attitude toward giving. We are much more hands-on, and want to

Figure 10.3   Compared to How I Gave Before I Retired, in Retirement . . .

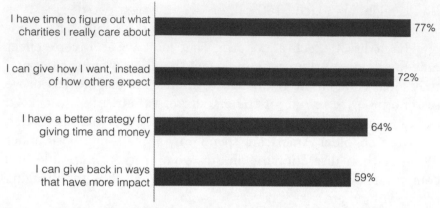

I have time to figure out what charities I really care about — 77%

I can give how I want, instead of how others expect — 72%

I have a better strategy for giving time and money — 64%

I can give back in ways that have more impact — 59%

Source: Age Wave / Merrill Lynch, *Giving in Retirement: America's Longevity Bonus*

see how our giving makes a difference." Boomers have less faith than their parents that charities spend donations well, and they tend to give to fewer charitable organizations and often smaller ones. When volunteering, they're more motivated to challenge themselves and put their acquired and honed skills and experience to work. One in five retirees expresses interest in becoming a "philanthropreneur" by starting their own nonprofits to meet needs they really care about.

Where is today's retirees' generosity directed? They give to a variety of causes, with worship groups, local social services, health-related charities, emergency relief, and charities supporting children the most common recipients.[8] And what motivates them to give and volunteer? By far, the greatest reason is simply "making a difference in the lives of others," as over 80% tell us (Figure 10.4). We heard many examples like this: "I volunteer at the homeless shelter. It has an immediate impact for me, because I can see directly where I'm helping and how I'm helping. If you just write a check, you often don't know what the impact is." Serving others has the reciprocal effect of giving meaning and purpose to our own lives. Those who volunteer cite the desire to stay mentally and physically active, and to develop and deepen friendships and relationships. One in three cites being motivated by religious or spiritual beliefs. Only 16% mentioned the charitable tax deductions – doing good for others carries five times the motivational power.

Figure 10.4 Retirees' Motivations for Charitable Giving or Volunteering

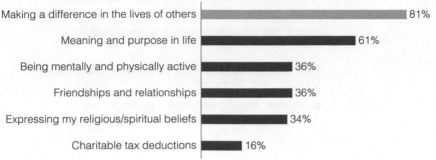

Making a difference in the lives of others	81%
Meaning and purpose in life	61%
Being mentally and physically active	36%
Friendships and relationships	36%
Expressing my religious/spiritual beliefs	34%
Charitable tax deductions	16%

Source: Age Wave / Merrill Lynch, *Giving in Retirement: America's Longevity Bonus*

At a more emotional level, retirees are most often driven by gratitude. Grateful for what they have in life, they want to share. Many look back upon help they've received throughout their lives and want to "pay it forward" to those in need today.

How Giving Gives Back

We've discussed how retirement can transform giving. The reverse is also true. For many retirees, giving plays a major role in their new lives and reforged identities. With the yardsticks of career advancement, job status, and paycheck size out of play, retirees are developing new definitions of success through new pursuits. Helping people in need brings happiness to far more retirees (76%) than spending money on themselves (24%) does. Winston Churchill was right: "We make a living by what we get. We make a life by what we give."

Retirees' generosity is amply rewarded in greater emotional and physical well-being. Retirees who give or volunteer have a stronger sense of purpose and higher self-esteem, and they report being happier and healthier (Figure 10.5). Seven in ten say that giving is a major source of happiness, and research has demonstrated that giving and volunteering are even associated with lower rates of depression, blood pressure, and mortality. Volunteering is also correlated with greater longevity.[9]

Volunteering and being active in causes also carry social benefits in new connections and friendships, according to 85% of retiree volunteers. Volunteering alongside similarly interested and committed

Figure 10.5   How Retirees Who Give/Volunteer Describe Themselves

Strong sense of purpose	59%	43%
High self-esteem	57%	51%
Happy	66%	52%
Healthy	50%	43%

■ Gives or volunteers   ■ Does not give or volunteer

Source: Age Wave / Merrill Lynch, *Giving in Retirement: America's Longevity Bonus*

colleagues can make up for workplace connections lost in retirement. As one retiree put it, "Volunteering is a chance to build relationships with other like-minded people. The chemistry of giving becomes very important." It's also been known to bring romance.

Giving money and volunteering effort each pays back. But retirees tell us that the most fulfilling experience comes from doing both – combining financial generosity with volunteering for a charity, nonprofit, or cause they really care about. Another retiree put it simply: "I'm giving more of myself and find it more fulfilling when I volunteer my time in addition to giving money."

Some forms of giving are impersonal – writing a check to a major charity with which the donor has no direct experience. For Boomers, the greatest fulfillment and satisfaction come from giving that is close to the heart. People are passionate about causes that have touched their lives or the lives of loved ones – fighting Alzheimer's for example. They are passionate when they give something of value to them and to their recipients, as one retiree shared with us: "It's so important to give back using the skills that you've acquired in your life. I'm using my artistic skills in helping younger people. Because being an artist is not just about painting. It's about expressing your emotions."

The most meaningful and engaging giving and volunteering experiences are often local and hands-on, with tangible and visible impact – helping the hungry through food banks or community gardens, helping young people through mentoring and community organizations, helping people in crisis. The common denominator, as we have emphasized, is making a difference in the lives of others.

Intergenerational Connections

Contributing to future generations, especially by volunteering in schools, is central to the lives and purpose of many retirees. Over 90% of Generations United survey respondents believe that elders benefit from building relationships with children and vice versa.[10] Encore.org's Marc Freedman says, "Older people have an important role to play in society. There's a reason we've been accumulating all of this experience and understanding and ability to see the patterns. It's to pass on what we've learned from life to the next generations, and in the process learn from those younger people. The real fountain of youth is the fountain *with* youth."

Many of the new careers people launch with Encore.org's help involve mentoring and teaching, with the goal of mobilizing people age 50+ "to stand up for – and with – young people today." Collaborating with more than 250 partner organizations and thousands of activists, Gen2Gen helps youth-serving organizations tap experienced talent and "tells a new story" about the benefits of intergenerational connection.[11] One such organization is "Grandpas United" in White Plains, NY. The group's founders wanted to counter the stereotype of grumpy old men and show how older men are caring and community minded. Partnering with schools and libraries, the men serve as role models and mentors for children without enough caring adults in their lives.[12]

In the U.K., Now Teach brings experienced professionals into the classroom by lowering the barriers to entry to teaching jobs and offering part-time and flexible work schedules. Lucy Moore wasn't ready to simply retire from her roles as doctor and CEO in the National Health Service. Now she is teaching math and loves learning how the younger generation learns. She says, "Throughout my life I've always tried to make a difference to disadvantaged communities. That's why I originally made the change from practicing physician to public health, and it's why I've made the decision to become a teacher." Others changing careers with the help of Now

Teach come from law, civil service, financial services, journalism, and a variety of other fields.

Marc Freedman again shares his insight: "One of the things I learned from Experience Corps 25 years ago is that once you get enough older people into schools, things start to happen that aren't part of the program. The older adults aren't just working one-on-one with kids to help them read. They're forming ties with the teachers and with parents, becoming part of the central fabric of the institution. Older and younger people are made better by working, learning, and living side-by-side and having contact in the central institutions of daily life."

Recently Ken was a speaker at a conference that also featured actor and climate activist Harrison Ford. During his speech, Ford repeatedly emphasized the need for young people to go outside and plant trees – lots of trees. After his talk, Ken enjoyed a private meeting with Ford and asked him, "Since there are nearly 70 million retirees in our country with 20 years of free time on their hands, why not ask them to go outside and plant trees?" Ford took a few minutes to digest this idea and then responded, "I had never considered that." He's not alone. Ageism can cause us to overlook many great opportunities that are hiding in plain sight.

Women: The More Generous Gender

Studies repeatedly show that women are considerably more generous than men, including during retirement. They donate more and volunteer more, and because they outlive men by an average of six years, they more often control bequests and inheritances.[13] And generosity is a bigger part of their identities in retirement. Women are more likely than men to define success by their generosity (versus their wealth), to say they get happiness from helping people in need (versus spending on themselves), and to agree that retirement is the best time in life to give back.

Women retirees are also more likely than men to make charitable donations (81% vs 71%) and volunteer (29% vs 22%). And they have stronger – and we might say purer – motives in giving. They more often give out of gratitude, faith, or passion. Men are more likely to say they give out of obligation or pride. Very significantly, women retirees increasingly control decisions around giving. And single older women hold the power of numbers. For every 100 men over age 65, there are 121 women. Among Americans age 85 or older, there are almost twice as many women as men. With women being three times more likely than men to be widowed in later life, they therefore often decide how and where to pass on money and assets – both to family and to charitable causes. Among people age 55+, single women, including those who are widowed, divorced, or never married, already contribute nearly half (49%) of all charitable bequests (Figure 10.6).

Colleges are taking note of the potential for wealthy older couples and single women of all ages to be highly engaged donors. Duke University has a Women's Impact Network (WIN) of donors who have given $100,000 or more. The initiative grew from examining women's giving patterns and recognizing their underrepresentation on Duke boards. Similarly, in early 2014, a small group of dedicated alumnae set an ambitious goal to recruit 100 Dartmouth women to make gifts of $100,000 or more to honor the 100th anniversary of the Dartmouth College Fund. The response was extraordinary: in less than three months, 114 women joined the Centennial Circle and raised almost $15 million to support female students through financial aid. Alumnae leaders then set a more ambitious target of 100 women donors each pledging $1 million or more. To date, the count of those commitments is over 75.

Figure 10.6   Who Leaves Charitable Bequests? (Among Age 55+)

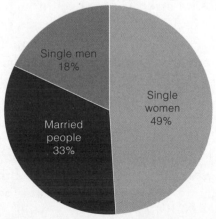

Source: American Charitable Bequest Demographics, 2013

New Ways of Giving

A variety of new opportunities and formats for donating and volunteering are emerging. For example, communities in Jiangsu province in China have piloted a "senior citizen support bank" wherein people who volunteer to assist older citizens "bank" the same number of hours of support for themselves, family members, or friends to be used in their later years in the future. Volunteers sign up for specific duties, such as doing laundry, grocery shopping, and reading newspapers to elderly people in need of support. While people of all ages, including students, are encouraged to volunteer, about two-thirds of the volunteers are comparatively young senior citizens. This is another way that communities in China are innovating with crowdsourcing assistance in the face of a looming extreme shortage of care workers.[14]

More and more websites facilitate giving and volunteering. In the first 30 days following Hurricane Harvey in 2017, initiatives on the GoFundMe crowdsourcing donation platform delivered over $27 million directly to people affected by the storm. A growing array of volunteer projects can be done online, including consulting projects needing specific skills, tutoring children who live in a different country, and promoting fundraisers via social media. Open Humans is a nonprofit site that enables individuals to share personal data for projects of their choosing. For example, they can upload Fitbit activity or 23andMe genetic data and donate it to a research project trying to tackle a particular disease.

Many retirees feel they make a difference through social impact investing. They invest in a company or fund based on its social or environmental practices and commitments. Financial returns are valued, but more important to many is influencing businesses to do good and getting results for causes the retirees care about. A 2018 Fidelity study found that three in ten investors age 54 and older had made an impact investment.

Sites like MicroPlace.com and Kiva.org crowdsource funds for microlending, small loans typically given to support the business ambitions of people without access to banks and other resources. For example, on Kiva.org Anna was looking for a loan of $500 to buy fertilizer and seeds for her farm in Kenya. Multiple people can donate as little as $25 to fund the full $500. Loans are not guaranteed; however, Kiva has a historical 97% repayment rate.

Finally, as mentioned in the chapter on Leisure, voluntourism is becoming increasingly popular, with people contributing to the places they are visiting. Projects-Abroad.org helps travelers find volunteering opportunities and arrange their accommodations and travel almost anywhere in the world. Initiatives are as focused as a one-week trip to Costa Rica to work on bird, butterfly, and bat conservation. Thami Bhakanava, a Volunteer Advisor for Projects-Abroad, says, "Our older volunteers find a sense of purpose in their contributions. They are willing to share a part of what they know to make a difference in the lives of the community and the people that they meet on their project. But the exchange usually surpasses their expectation as they get to experience different food, cultures and sentiments of what life is like on the other side of the world."

Waze Needed to Precisely Match Interested Givers with Potential Recipients

Many retirees are interested in giving more but frustrated in their efforts. The most commonly cited barriers are worries about the trustworthiness of charities, having too many charities to choose from (GuideStar counts 1.8 million organizations registered as tax-exempt in the U.S.), and their own financial limitations (Figure 10.7). Persistent fundraising by charities can also turn people off, and fundraising scams often target older people.

Retirees would like more targeted and trusted advice in evaluating charities and causes, finding causes they can be passionate about, and assessing the impact of their giving. But it can take a lot of research to determine how to donate and volunteer with maximum effectiveness. Various websites and services offer a hand. CharityNavigator gives objective ratings on thousands of nonprofits based on their finances, accountability, and transparency. Similarly, GreatNonprofits collects reviews and testimonials from donors and volunteers as "community stories." Each year Givewell recommends a limited number of thoroughly vetted charities that are deemed to be highly effective and underfunded. Animal Charity

Figure 10.7 Why Retirees Limit Their Giving

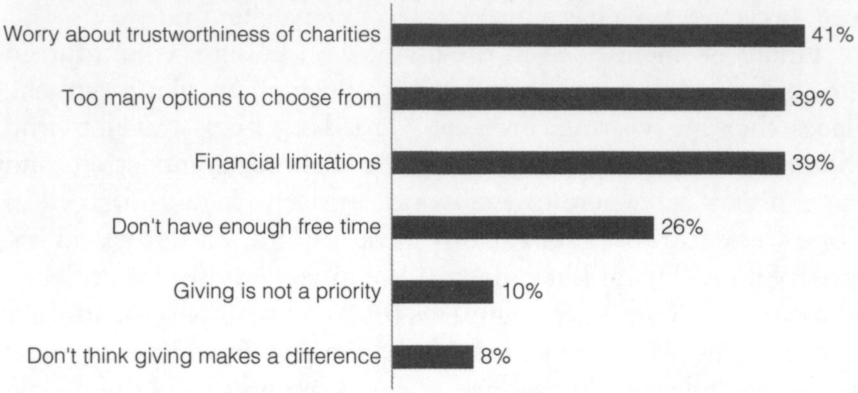

Worry about trustworthiness of charities	41%
Too many options to choose from	39%
Financial limitations	39%
Don't have enough free time	26%
Giving is not a priority	10%
Don't think giving makes a difference	8%

Source: Age Wave / Merrill Lynch, *Giving in Retirement: America's Longevity Bonus*

Evaluators provides reviews of charities and advice for donors who are passionate about animal rights.

Maybe what Boomer retirees need is not only a Health Waze app, as mentioned in Chapter 6, but a Giving Waze app that can assess a giver's deepest intentions and match them with the perfect organization.

Many counties and large municipalities have websites dedicated to local volunteer opportunities, but few are focused on retirees and even fewer offer consultative services. An exception is Bergen County, NJ, where Louisa Hellegers helped to found the Redefining Retirement program that matches retirees with skills-based volunteer opportunities. They train "matchmakers" to interview volunteers about their past experience and how they'd like to give back, then introduce them to local nonprofits based on their skills and interests.

Some nonprofit organizations are discovering the special advantages of older volunteers. AVID works with two million underserved students to encourage college and career readiness. They often engage college students to serve as volunteer tutors, but college students have high turnover rates and aren't always accessible in some communities. So they conducted a trial of 25 volunteers age 50 and older. Nearly all of them continued on to the next program year, and AVID is recruiting more 50+ volunteers. To engage and accommodate these older volunteers, AVID adjusted the length and timing of training sessions, provided opportunities for tutors to connect with one another for peer support and socializing, and did regular check-ins through the school year to provide support and get feedback. Perhaps most importantly, AVID directors and teachers were briefed on the value of older tutors and intergenerational connections, and they received coaching on strategies for recruiting and managing older tutors.

Innovative organizations and websites also assist people in finding suitable volunteer opportunities. For example, VolunteerMatch enables recruiting organizations to post their needs and volunteers to find them. Opportunities can be local or virtual and focused on specific needs and causes – children, education, arts, human rights. Since its founding in 2010, Catchafire has matched more than 7,000 volunteer professionals who have donated roughly 358,000 hours of pro-bono work. Volunteers can donate one-hour blocks of time as advisors or take on pre-scoped projects based on skills, interest, and availability. One recent retiree was able to use his 25+ years in management at IBM and Xerox to help a small educational technology nonprofit in Minnesota develop its volunteer recruitment strategy.

While 7,000 volunteers is a lot, we believe there's an opportunity to match 100 million men and women worldwide with organizations that could benefit from their smarts and goodwill. For over three decades, Ken has been envisioning that when the Boomers migrate into retirement, the timing would be right for the creation of a global Elder Corps. Two parallel problems exist: One is the growing wasteland of so many older people sitting idle in their homes, and the other is the fact that we have hundreds of millions of young people considered at risk, without enough funding or human support to help them. What if we took these two dynamics and brought them together through a Global Elder Corps? The seeds for such a social invention were planted in 1963 by President Kennedy as he envisioned a National Service Corps, and since then, many wonderful programs such as Foster Grandparents, Green Thumb, Service Corps of Retired Executives, and Retired and Senior Volunteer Program have grown. However, progress has been hamstrung by an absence of an overarching vision and strong international leadership. If the public and private sectors joined forces worldwide to recruit and sponsor retirees in order to create a full-blown Elder Corps, tens of millions of elders could become mentors in the workplace, friends to latchkey children, teachers' helpers in our schools, and leaders in their communities. With the retiring of the Boomers, there have never been so many high-spirited, motivated men and women who, with their deeds and values, could clear a new and more hopeful path to our future.

Giving Within Families: The Four Pillars of Legacy

Groucho Marx famously asked, "Why should I care about posterity? What's posterity ever done for me?" Fortunately, that's not the attitude of today's new retirees. They tell us that a lot of their purpose in life involves the legacy they leave for loved ones and heirs.

Back in 2005, Allianz Life Insurance Company asked Age Wave to conduct an in-depth investigation of how people related to giving or receiving an inheritance. We were intrigued by the issue and got to work. However, when the focus groups began, in preparation for constructing a major national survey, we were stymied because most participants said they didn't like thinking about or even talking about inheritance. They felt it was a negative subject and had to do with dividing up the loot after people died. Ken suggested that the focus group moderator replace the word "inheritance" with the word "legacy." When people were asked if they wished to either leave or receive a legacy, the room exploded with lively discussion. The results of the study were picked up by media outlets from *Fortune Magazine* to ABC's World News Tonight, and it appears to have changed the public narrative about this subject.

That study developed and tested the notion that one's personal legacy has four major components, or "pillars." First, and the one that seems to get most of the media attention, is financial assets, real estate, and other possessions of significant value. These are conveyed through wills, trusts, and beneficiary assignments. Ninety percent of financial inheritances go to immediate family members,[15] and leaving financial affairs in good order is an additional gift to them. Dying intestate, and often without arrangements for funeral costs, places an extra burden on them.

Second is personal possessions of emotional value or special significance in one's life. These may include family heirlooms passed down many times, items that have come to represent the individual in the minds of children and grandchildren, and items that invoke a stage of the individual's life – education, military service, high points of a career. Specifying clearly how these are passed along is another gift to heirs; otherwise, valued possessions can become objects of contention among family members.

Third is those instructions or wishes to be fulfilled, plus other directions related to the end of life. Most important are living wills or advance health directives that state what kinds of medical care an individual does and does not want to receive if incapacitated, as well as who is authorized to make medical decisions on behalf of the individual. Lack of those instructions can throw family members into turmoil. Other instructions cover funeral arrangements, preferences to die at home if possible, and the distribution of those personal effects. Ideally, the instructions are not only on paper, but also shared and discussed with family members. And they can go far beyond wills and such. They can include whether the elder might want to see her grandchildren go to college or how she might wish for the family to stay connected.

The fourth pillar is the values and life lessons passed on to others, the wisdom that helps heirs and loved ones navigate through their own lives. These are communicated in conversations and shared experiences throughout one's lifetime. They can also be captured in legacy projects – ethical wills or legacy letters, and collections of photos, videos, personal documents, and social media artifacts. A legacy project can provide closure to heirs and loved ones, and for those inclined to review and reflection late in life, building a legacy project can be meaningful, enjoyable, even celebratory.

What Matters Most Regarding Legacy

When asked to choose the most important of the four pillars of legacy, six in ten older Americans said, "values and life lessons," and to our surprise, younger generations felt the same way. And when we asked what people would most like to be remembered for, 69% said the memories shared with loved ones. In second place was the quality of their marriage or partnership. Only 4% cited the amount of wealth accumulated, and those responses were consistent across people at all levels of wealth.[16] As one retiree told us, "I want my legacy to be that I was a good husband and father. I want to leave this world knowing that I've made a positive impact on my family's life."

High among those values is generosity, and retirees know that the best way to instill it is by being a role model – both by giving and by explaining why that's so important. As another retiree told us, "What I most want to leave my grandchildren is my values, starting with the importance of being generous." Some families have giving traditions such as donating together over the holidays, volunteering together, and creating a family giving fund.

Ethical wills are growing in popularity, making a comeback of sorts. They have deep roots in Judeo-Christian tradition from biblical examples of prophets leaving instructions to their disciples. The oldest surviving ethical will dates to medieval times, and the documents grew more elaborate through the eighteenth century. Ethical wills can mix in memoirs, blessings, apologies, explanations about the disposition of physical goods, and requests about how the departed would like to be remembered. Most fundamentally, they pass on values and instructions to the next generations, including advice on how to live and requests for taking care of one another.

One retiree told us, "I would like to leave a hologram filmed with me playing the piano and telling all sorts of stories about my life for my kids and grandkids – who today are far too young to appreciate the crazy life I've lived. However, after I'm long gone and they're grown up, they can ask questions and then the holograph of me would tell them my stories. That way they could really get a sense for how and what I am – or I should say, who and what I was." A growing variety of services help people to record their memories, lessons, and stories. Some are directed at the individual, others at families and professional caregivers helping their loved ones or care recipients record their legacies.

"History is a chorus of voices! The greatest body of wisdom in history is going extinct as millions of our elders pass away." That's the impetus behind the Living Legacy Project, founded by Dennis Stack and Tom Cormier in 2008 to provide families with free education and tools to record and pass down legacy stories. The idea originated in a booklet by Stack of 200+ questions he wished he had asked his parents before they died. After working with elder-care professionals to determine the best ways to elicit reminiscent stories, they developed an interview and recording process that reveals the values as well as the most important legacy stories of the subjects. LegacyStories.org and a companion mobile app guide people to record and share their stories in multimedia.

Financial Inheritances

Legacy, of course, is also about money. For most people, more assets go in motion upon their death than at any time in their lives. Over the next 30 years, an estimated $30 trillion will be passed down from aging Boomers to the next generations in the United States alone.[17] People are motivated to leave inheritances for a variety of pragmatic reasons, but the most commonly cited is simply that it's the right thing to do for one's family and heirs (Figure 10.8).

It's a good thing to do, but is it a parent's *duty* to leave their children a financial inheritance? Only a little more than a third of Boomers think so, but 44% of GenXers and 55% of Millennials do. More fathers (39%) than mothers (30%) feel obliged to leave their children financial inheritances, and Latinos (49%), Asians (45%), and African Americans (38%) feel far more obligated than Caucasians (30%) do. Feeling obliged or not, nearly six in ten Americans say they do plan to leave inheritances to their heirs.[18]

Figure 10.8   Reasons for Leaving an Inheritance

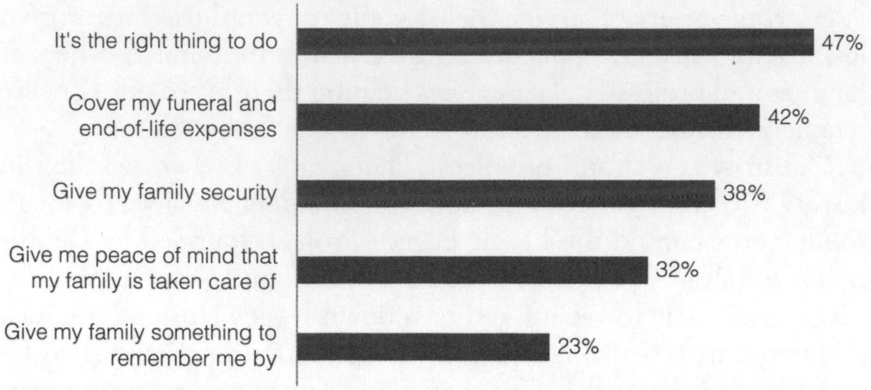

Reason	Percentage
It's the right thing to do	47%
Cover my funeral and end-of-life expenses	42%
Give my family security	38%
Give me peace of mind that my family is taken care of	32%
Give my family something to remember me by	23%

Source: Age Wave / Merrill Lynch, *Leaving a Legacy: A Lasting Gift to Loved Ones*

In many cultures throughout history, the bulk of an inheritance traditionally or legally went to the first-born son. That was still the default in Scotland until 1964. There were many variations, however. In parts of Africa and Asia, for example, the youngest son would inherit as compensation for the designated responsibility of caring for the parents in their old age.

Under common law today, inheritances can be directed however one wishes. The United States and other Western societies tend toward equal distribution among children, with gender and birth order no longer determining factors. Slight favoritism may even go to daughters and younger sons.[19] But other factors are increasingly coming into play. Two-thirds of Americans now say that a child who provided them care should receive more than children who did not, and nearly one-fourth would favor a child with children of their own over one who is childless. Blended families have another variable, and 60% say that stepchildren should receive the same portion as biological or adopted children.

Probably the biggest continuing shift in attitude and preference is that two-thirds of Americans now favor "giving while living," dispensing some of their assets to heirs while they're still alive (Figure 10.9). Assuming that's a responsible decision in terms of retirees' own financial status, that provides the opportunity to

Figure 10.9   Timing Preference for Giving Financial Inheritances

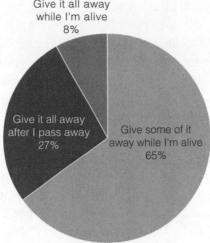

Source: Age Wave / Merrill Lynch, *Leaving a Legacy: A Lasting Gift to Loved Ones*

control the distribution and see how the assets are put to use and benefit the heirs. It can also provide financial support to heirs when they most need it, for example, in raising children or covering college costs. Women, and thus many widows, tend to be more interested in giving while living than men are. As Chuck Feeney, founder of Atlantic Philanthropies, puts it, "If you give while living, the money goes to work quickly – everyone gets to see and feel good about the action and the results."

A Good Death and Dying with Purpose

Beyond leaving a strong and positive legacy, what do people want late in life? Dying can be a sensitive topic, shaped by personal and religious beliefs and cultural traditions. The topic is often avoided because awkward, yet 90% of older Americans say they are open to discussing their end-of-life preferences with family and often friends. About 40% of those 75 and older say they are not afraid of dying. Of greater concern is how they fare approaching death.

The notion of a "good death" is not an oxymoron, but a subject of ongoing study among health academics. *The Economist's* Quality of Death Index ranks 80 nations on a variety of indicators covering the palliative and health care environment, affordability of care, quality of care, and other factors. The top-ranking countries in quality of death are the U.K., Australia, New Zealand, Ireland, and Belgium. The United States ranks ninth with its score hampered most by the reimbursement environment, especially for palliative treatment.

We asked Americans age 55+ what would constitute a good death, and their answer was many-faceted: being surrounded by loved ones, experiencing minimal pain, maintaining dignity, maintaining mental capacity, and being at home or in a location they prefer. Only 6% said it included receiving all possible medical treatments (Figure 10.10). What most worries them about the end of life? For themselves, having dementia and being in pain. Regarding their families, they want to avoid becoming a caregiving or financial burden.

Most Americans approve of assisted dying, but it remains a sensitive question. Overall, 72% believe that doctors should be legally allowed, at a patient's and a family's request, to end a terminally ill patient's life using painless means. This drops to 66% among those 50 and older, and among those who attend church weekly, the majority (60%) oppose the practice.[20] Suffice it to say that attitudes toward death vary widely.

Figure 10.10   Meaning of a "Good Death"

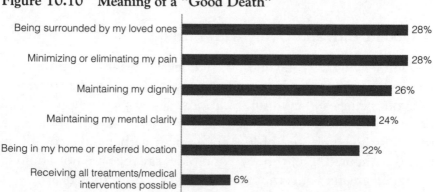

Source: Age Wave / Merrill Lynch, *Leaving a Legacy: A Lasting Gift to Loved Ones*

The Future of Dying

The $16 billion U.S. funeral industry is being disrupted in a variety of ways. In a *Washington Post* article, "The Funeral as We Know It Is Becoming a Relic – Just in Time for a Death Boom," Karen Heller writes, "An increasingly secular, nomadic and casual America is shredding the rules about how to commemorate death, and it's not just among the wealthy and famous. Somber, embalmed-body funerals, with their $9,000 industry average price tag, are, for many families, a relic."[21] Funerals are instead celebrations of the departed's life, with food, drink, activities and themes near and dear to the departed. Attendees can wear any color but black. Celebration-of-life planners, like Final Bow Productions, operate in a fashion similar to wedding planners. Funeral homes have hired event planners, remodeled to include dance floors and lounge areas, even acquired liquor licenses. To save distant friends and relatives the travel expense, funerals are live streamed.[22]

Cremation is becoming the rule rather than the exception.[23] Cremations have outnumbered traditional burials in recent years, and the national cremation rate in the United States is projected to approach 80% (or 2.8 million cremations per year) by 2035. More cremated remains are returned to families than are buried in cemeteries. Among the 61% of Americans who would choose cremation for themselves, more than half would prefer to have their remains scattered in a sentimental place. That makes ash scattering a growing business. Captain Ken Middleton's Hawaii Ash Scatterings performs 600 cremains dispersals a year. Up to 80 passengers sail on a scattering cruise that may feature a ukulele player or a conch-shell blower, and a release of white doves or monarch butterflies. "It makes it a celebration of life and not such a morbid affair," says Middleton.[24]

Green funerals and cemeteries are also on the rise – with no use of embalming chemicals and caskets that must be bio-degradable. Natural burials, where the body is buried without a casket, are legal in the U.K. In Italy, an eco-friendly, egg-shaped container from Capsula Mundi is buried where it will nourish a sapling planted above. Greener still, human composting is allowed in Sweden and recently in Washington state. The Recompose service turns remains into top soil that can be used, for example, "to fertilize a garden, or a grove of trees, the body literally returned to the earth."[25]

In South Korea, the deceased's ashes can be converted into colorful beads for display in glass containers. A U.K. company will now press one's ashes into a vinyl LP album (yes, we know that sounds crazy).[26] In Ghana, craftsmen make "fantasy coffins" shaped as cars, boats, and planes to "transport" the departed, or as favored objects or product containers. In Japan, where space for traditional burial is limited, there's a temporary timesharing solution – urns are stored in a columbarium where they can be visited for 33 years before burial in a communal site.[27]

These things are happening as Boomers age and death is steadily losing its taboo. Death Cafes are an international movement of pop-up guided discussion groups "to increase awareness of death with a view to helping people make the most of their (finite) lives." Death doulas, modeled after the popular use of doulas for childbirth, serve as personal guides who support individuals and their loved ones as they reach the end of life. On the theory that death is less frightening if contemplated regularly, the fledgling website wecroak.com sends subscribers messages at five random times a day with quotes on dying from poets, philosophers, and other thinkers.

The recent HBO documentary "Alternate Endings: Six New Ways to Die in America" traces the stories of six terminally ill people. Their choices ranged from peaceful green burials and eco-friendly caskets to launching remains into space, from drive-thru funeral viewing to living wakes (with the not-yet-deceased there to hear what people have to say). Filmmaker Matthew O'Neill says, "The baby boomer generation has had a greater degree of control over their lives than any other generation before them. . . . Every topic that's taboo – be it sex, be it drugs – it's all on television and it's all being talked about. And death is the last taboo."[28]

In dying as in living, tomorrow's retirees will have an expanded and unprecedented range of choices.

Actions and Opportunities for Organizations and Entrepreneurs in the Nonprofit Sector

1. Leverage the skills and experience of Boomer retiree volunteers, not just their time and simple labor. And give them opportunities to innovate in your organization, not just fill predefined slots.
2. At the same time, make the volunteering experience collaborative and egalitarian. Retirees may have had their fill of corporate or organizational hierarchies.
3. Recognize the power and potential of women retirees as givers and volunteers, and appeal to their priorities, sensibilities, and social skills.
4. Be listed on the trusted charity evaluators, be transparent, earn their seal of approval, and display the seal proudly.
5. Report tangible results – not just how donations are used but the impact they have. Boomer retirees are after outcomes, not just the satisfaction of giving.
6. Devise engaging "insider" communications for regular donors, such as webinar briefings with your organization's leaders talking frankly about results and challenges ahead.
7. Offer opportunities with future-generations appeal. Children's causes and mentoring roles can engage givers in wonderful ways.
8. Be easy to find and deal with online, work with the volunteer "matchmaker" sites, and become a local matchmaker if there is a void to fill.
9. Showcase your retiree donors and volunteers and the impact they have (noting that some may prefer to avoid the fanfare). Prospective givers relate to real examples.
10. Expand your social reach – on social media, by recruiting groups of givers, and by enlisting givers to enlist their friends and family.

11

Retiring Retirement

The Rise of Life's Third Age

IN THE FIRST chapter of James Michener's captivating 1959 book *Hawaii*, he talks about how for millions of years, large tectonic plates were slowly moving and grinding against each other far below the sea that we now call the Pacific Ocean. As these forces converged, masses of land started to rise up from those plates and ultimately surfaced as beautiful Polynesia.

And so it is with the future of retirement. For thousands of years, medical, economic, social, and demographic forces have been shifting and often grinding against each other. From this interplay a new stage of life has been emerging and morphing.

Earlier in our book, we reviewed the modern history of retirement. During what we've called the first era, which lasted throughout history until the early twentieth century, retirement was for all intents and purposes nonexistent. People worked throughout their relatively short lives and they worked until they died.

Then in the 1930s, with economic disruptions and profound shifts in demography and sociology, a second era of retirement emerged. In this one, the safety nets such as Social Security were

255

created and, at the same time, a new point of view took root that suggested that older men and women would be happier if they stopped working and, by so doing, made room for the young.

By the 1970s, employer pensions had proliferated, as did guaranteed health benefits, with Medicare front and center. Longevity was steadily increasing, as was the financial well-being of retirees. So retirement-focused leisure industries began popping up from senior housing to cruise excursions. This new version of retirement looked delightful and appeared to be a very good arrangement for a couple of generations of retirees.

With today's demographic liberations and pressures, retirement has become far more lengthy and more complex. Worldwide, nearly a billion people are in or near retirement and there are many more options and opportunities for how to spend this newfound time affluence. However, in many parts of the world and in many communities, there is both more longevity and far less financial security, which necessitates far more reliance on oneself and one's family – something for which most are unprepared.

Should we be calling this new stage of life the "fourth era of retirement"? In 2004, we wrote an article in the *Harvard Business Review* titled "It's Time to Retire Retirement," for which we were proud to earn the McKinsey Award (tied with the legendary Peter Drucker). Clearly we believe the word "retirement" is reaching the end of its line. It's far too small and narrow for what is now emerging. Its positive connotations – freedom, leisure – tell only part of the story. Its negative connotations – withdrawal, decline – are increasingly problematic. The words "retirement" and "retiree" will most likely linger for another decade or so, but their meanings will evolve as the lifescape of retirement keeps expanding, disaggregating, and diversifying.

We believe it's time to re-identify the "Lifestage Formerly Known as Retirement" to mean something far bigger and worthy of a new name.

The Third Age: Life's New Frontier

It is from outside the realm of traditional psychology that we find a pivotal perspective on the new possibilities – and lexicon – of maturity. A compelling philosophy has emerged from the European tradition of adult education that provides a simple yet visionary orientation. Referred to as "Le troisième âge" – the third age – this point of view has three "ages" of man, each with its own special focus, challenge, and opportunity.

In the *first age*, from birth to approximately 30 years of age, the primary tasks of life center around biological development, learning, and survival. During the early years of history, the average life expectancy of most men and women wasn't much higher than the end of the first age, and as a result the entire thrust of society itself was oriented toward these most basic drives.

In the *second age*, from about 30 to 60, the concerns of adult life focus on issues pertaining to the formation of family, parenting, and productive work. The years taken up by the second age are very busy and filled with social activity; the lessons gathered during the first age are applied to the social and professional responsibilities of the second. Until the last century, most people couldn't expect to live much beyond the second age, and society at that time was thus centered on the concerns of this age.

However, with the rise in longevity and the coming of the age wave, a new era of human evolution is unfolding, the *third age*. There are new purposes to this third age of life. First, with the children grown and many of life's basic adult tasks either well under way or already accomplished, this less pressured, more reflective period allows the further development of the interior life of the intellect, memory, imagination, of emotional maturity, and of one's own personal sense of spiritual identity. This is akin to Erik Erikson's concept of the achievement of ego integrity and to Abraham Maslow's concept of self-actualization.

The third age has another dimension: there's plenty of time and opportunity to try new things. Not just to be reflective but to explore new facets of life. Not just to relax in front of the TV but to seek out new transformative adventures. Not just to share wisdom but to contribute directly to society in new ways. Not just "retire," but maybe have an encore career, another modified go-round of life's second age. The third age is now full of potential for individuals, families, and society. The scope of this potential is enormous and unprecedented. And from this perspective, modern elders are seen not as social outcasts, but as a living bridge between yesterday, today, and tomorrow – a critical evolutionary role that no other age group can perform. According to Monsignor Charles Fahey, the Founding Director of Fordham's Third Age Center, "People in the third age should be the glue of society, not its ashes."

Of course, this is not an entirely new or novel perspective, just one that years of youth-focus have obscured. In other cultures, and at other times, elders have been revered for their wisdom, power, and spiritual force. In ancient China, for example, the highest attainment in mystical Taoism was long life and the wisdom that came with the passing of years. According to social theorist Simone de Beauvoir in her classic *The Coming of Age*, "Lao Tzu's teaching sets the age of sixty as the moment at which a man may free himself from his body and become a holy being. . . . Old age was therefore life in its very highest form." Among the Aranda, hunters and gatherers of the Australian forests, old age brings with it a transition to near-supernatural status. De Beauvoir writes: "The man whom age has already brought close to the other world is the best mediator between this and the next. It is the old people who direct the Aranda's religious life – a life that underlies the whole of their social existence."

A Glimpse into the Future

Throughout this book, we've attempted to share some of the enormous variety of retirees in every facet of life – work, leisure, health, family, home, finances, purpose. Tomorrow's elders won't be one big homogeneous group. One-size-fits-all products, services, and marketing will fail. We can, nonetheless, step back and anticipate what will be different in tomorrow's Third Age.

More Learning

There will be more learning and more of the personal development, fulfillment, and untapping of potential that goes with it. Paul Irving makes an eloquent case for lifelong learning: "While I'm an advocate for education across our lives, the old adage about education being wasted on the young is to an extent true. We should all go back to school at some point later in life. There's something magic about being on a campus. It starts with feeding intellectual curiosity, challenging oneself, and realizing the joy of learning. Then there's the opportunity to reinvent, reskill, update. Continuing one's productivity requires lifelong learning. And returning to school can be a huge confidence builder – confidence both in what you know and in how much you can learn."

Paul himself went back to school. After a successful career serving in and leading a major law firm, he applied and was accepted as a fellow at Harvard's Advanced Leadership Initiative for experienced leaders. The latest act of his career, in his third age, includes chairing the Milken Institute Center for the Future of Aging. When we asked him to elaborate on why he shifted gears, he said, "While I loved my time as a lawyer, I felt that there was something else ahead. It was a sense that I wasn't done. Part of it was love of learning and challenge. I've long been an advocate of lifelong learning. I think democratizing learning, spreading and scaling up opportunities for people to learn throughout life, just couldn't be a more important priority. Wise and knowledgeable populations will distinguish countries and societies in the decades to come. Those countries that figure out ways to reeducate, reskill, and continue to challenge and engage their older populations are the countries that will succeed."

More Intergenerational Contribution

Intergenerational connection and contribution will go far beyond Boomers making donations, volunteering, and leaving personal and financial legacies – important though they are. Encore.org founder and CEO Marc Freedman reflects: "We need to create more and more opportunities for people to find encores later in life in roles that give back and benefit society. One of the most beautiful ways we can experience purpose in this phase of life is by forming deep connections that nurture the next generation. In the process, we not only alleviate social isolation and loneliness among older people, but also provide a deep sense of living a worthwhile life."

Fernando Torres-Gil puts things in perspective: "We hear how great it can be to grow old and be independent and do whatever you want. That's a good thing. However, the way I see it, the real ideal is *interdependence*, because we're all going to need each other at some point, and none of us will ever grow old and be truly independent."

More Activism

We recounted some of Ken's adventures with Maggie Kuhn – visionary, author, founder of the Gray Panthers – in Chapter 3. Her third age career was activism on behalf of both youth and age. In 1978, Ken was interviewing her for *New Age Magazine* and she told him: "We're the elders of the tribe, and the elders are charged with the tribe's survival and well-being. We who are older have enormous freedom to speak out, and equally great responsibility to take the risks that are needed to heal and humanize our sick society. We can and should try new things and take on entirely new roles."

She went on to list what she thought were the most important of those roles: Testing new lifestyles, including living in more cooperative modes. Building new coalitions across ethnicities and economic conditions, because age is a universal. Serving as watchdogs of public bodies and guardians of the public interest. Advocating for consumer rights and blowing the whistle on fraud and corruption. Monitoring corporate power and responsibility on behalf of workers and society. In short, using the power of wisdom and experience and attention to assess society, heal what ails it, and plan for its future. Maggie's challenge and agenda were and remain ambitious – but they seem to be even more relevant and needed today than when she outlined them decades ago.

A Great Age?

Will the Boomers use their experience and assets to help shape a future based on mindfulness and generosity of spirit? Or will they act only to promote their own interests #OKBoomer-style? If we are to live longer, on average, than humans have ever lived before, and if the global center of gravity is to shift from youth to age, should this be regarded as good news or bad? As we have seen, the answer is, "It depends." It depends on whether or not we can:

- Uproot the ageism and gerontophobia that cloud our hopes for the future and replace them with a new, more positive image of aging
- Replace the limiting confines of the linear life plan with a flexible, cyclic plan – with periods of education, work, and leisure throughout life – much more appropriate to the shifting needs of a longer life
- Create a new spectrum of family relationships that are matched to the companionship, sexuality, friendship, and caregiving needs of older adults
- Discover ways to grow old well, in the absence of debilitating illness, and especially the diseases of the aging brain such as Alzheimer's
- Create products, services, housing, and programs that will treat older men and women with respect and provide comfort, convenience, pleasure, peak experiences, and purpose
- Foster a new era of cooperation and interdependence among people of all ages while creating a social system that is fair and equitable for everyone

Time's Up

Dr. Robert Butler coined the terms "ageism" and "gerontophobia" in the late 1960s. Maggie Kuhn founded the Gray Panthers in 1970. Pat Moore published *Disguised*, recounting her experience passing – and being disrespected and mistreated – as an old lady in 1985. Ken published *Age Wave* in 1989. Betty Friedan published *The Fountain of Age* in 1993. Mary Furlong founded Third Age Media in 1996.

The destructive problems of ageism, the impacts of the age wave, the necessity to reframe aging – these are not "breaking" news. Very capable people, including many whom we interviewed for this book, have been working and making progress on these issues for a long time, both battling ageism and guiding government groups, organizations, and companies to be better prepared for the demographically driven changes to come. What's different today? Why this book now? Because about half of the massive Boomer generation are now "retired." The cohort that proclaimed "never trust anyone over 30" will soon all be over 60. The age wave is no longer coming. It's here, and it's the future. By 2050, there will be more than two billion people over the age of 60 worldwide.

A few years ago, when we interviewed renowned psychologist and author of *Emotional Intelligence* Daniel Goleman, PhD, he reflected, "The legacy of the Boomer generation won't be the 'me first' image of their early years, but rather the potential huge surge in volunteerism that might characterize their later years. It's not how you begin the act, it's how you leave the stage that people remember."

It's time to write the next act – about reframing aging and enabling people to thrive in the Third Age.

Acknowledgments

WE'D LIKE TO EXPRESS our deepest gratitude to the firms that have partnered on our studies and their forward-thinking leaders who helped us to discover what dwells in the hearts and minds of people regarding retirement all over the world. Special thanks to Andy Sieg, David Tyrie, Lorna Sabbia, and Surya Kolluri at Bank of America Merrill Lynch, Sir John Bond and Steve Troop at HSBC, Jay Wintrob at SunAmerica, Kim Sharan at Ameriprise, David Poltrack at CBS, Greg Gable at Charles Schwab, and to the leadership of Allianz, Chrysler Motors, Edward Jones, General Motors, Genworth Financial, Johnson & Johnson, LPL Financial, Merck, Searle, and Vi Senior Living.

We'd like to thank all of the experts and industry leaders who so generously agreed to be interviewed for this book, including: Michael Adams, Jim Bendt, Lori Bitter, Ken Cella, Chip Conley, Christine Crosby, Ric Edelman, Richard Eisenberg, Marc Freedman, Mary Furlong, Lisa Genova, Geoffrey Godbey, Kerry Hannon, Mike Hodin, Paul Hogan, Paul Irving, Karyne Jones, Don Mankin, Colin Milner, Andy Seig, Michelle Seitz, Percil Stanford, David Tyrie, Fernando Torres-Gil, Nadia Tuma-Weldon, Matthew Upchurch, and Charlotte Yeh. They shared their experience and insight and pushed our thinking at every turn.

We are also grateful to the teams of pollsters, researchers, gerontologists, sociologists, psychologists, economists, and academics who, with the Age Wave team, have collectively contributed more than 75,000 hours investigating the new lifescape of retirement. Special thanks to the professionals at The Harris Poll and Kantar TNS.

This book would not be here without the extraordinary research contributions of Katy Flick and the collaboration, support, and friendship of all the superb professionals of Age Wave, including Maddy Dychtwald, Elyse Pellman, Dan Veto, Robyn Reynolds, Kathleen Chau, Stacy Cranston, Neil Steinberg, Luke Van Meter, and Thi Truong. They collaborated on the research, shaped our thinking, reviewed the drafts, and kept our efforts on track. And thanks to talented former Age Wave research staff members David Baxter, Erin McInrue Savage, and Janna Goldberg.

Thanks to our editors and the marketing and production staff at Wiley, in particular Richard Narramore, Michael Friedberg, Peter Knox, Vicki Adang, Victoria Anllo, and Sharmila Srinivasan for their guidance and support in developing and launching our book.

Finally, posthumous thanks to two very special individuals who inspired our pursuit of this topic – Dr. Robert Butler and Maggie Kuhn.

About the Authors

Ken Dychtwald, PhD
Over the past 40+ years, Dr. Ken Dychtwald has emerged as North America's foremost visionary and original thinker regarding the lifestyle, marketing, health care, and workforce implications of the age wave.

Ken is a psychologist, gerontologist, and best-selling author of 16 previous books, including *Bodymind*, *Age Wave*, *Age Power: How the 21st Century Will Be Ruled by the New Old*, and *A New Purpose: Redefining Money, Family, Work, Retirement, and Success*.

Since 1986, Ken has been the Founder and CEO of Age Wave, a firm created to guide companies and government groups in product and service development for Boomers and mature adults. His client list has included over half the Fortune 500. He has served as a fellow of the World Economic Forum and was a featured speaker at two White House Conferences on Aging. Ken has twice received the distinguished American Society on

Aging Award for outstanding national leadership, and *American Demographics* honored him as the single most influential marketer to Baby Boomers over the past quarter century. He was honored by *Investment Advisor* as one of the 35 most influential thought leaders in the financial services industry over the past 35 years. Ken has received the Esalen Prize for his outstanding contributions to advancing the human potential of aging men and women worldwide. And in 2018 he received the Inspire Award from the International Council on Active Aging for his exceptional contributions to the active-aging industry and for his efforts to make a difference in the lives of older adults globally.

During his career, Ken has addressed more than two million people worldwide in his speeches to corporate, association, social service, and government groups. His strikingly accurate predictions and innovative ideas are regularly featured in leading print and electronic media worldwide. He and his wife, Maddy, live in the San Francisco Bay Area.

Robert Morison

Robert Morison is a researcher, writer, speaker, consultant, and authority on what happens at the intersections of business, technology, and people management. He has been leading breakthrough research for more than 30 years, collaborating with eminent academics, thought leaders, and management innovators. He has written on topics ranging from business innovation, reengineering, and analytics to workforce management, demographics, and retirement.

Bob has been collaborating with Dr. Ken Dychtwald and Age Wave for twenty years, including managing – on behalf of a consortium of major corporations – the research projects "Demography is De$tiny" and "The New Employee/Employer Equation." He co-authored with Ken Dychtwald and Tamara Erickson the McKinsey Award–winning *Harvard Business Review* article "It's Time to Retire Retirement" and the book *Workforce Crisis: How to Beat the Coming*

Shortage of Skills and Talent. He is also co-author, with Thomas Davenport and Jeanne Harris, of *Analytics at Work: Smarter Decisions, Better Results.*

Earlier in his career, he held management and research leadership positions with General Electric, CSC Index, and the Concours Group. He has spoken before hundreds of corporate, industry, research, and government groups, and he has been a commentator on workforce issues on *Nightly Business Report* on PBS. Bob currently serves as Senior Advisor with Age Wave and Lead Faculty for the International Institute for Analytics. He holds an AB from Dartmouth College and an MA from Boston University. Bob and his wife, the author Lynne Barrett, live in Miami, Florida.

Notes

Chapter 1

1. Gary Burtless and Joseph Quinn, "Retirement Trends and Policies to Encourage Work Among Older Americans," Brookings, 2000.
2. Patrick Seburn, "Evolution of employer-provided defined benefit pensions," *Monthly Labor Review*, 1991.
3. AARP, *The Longevity Economy Outlook*, 2019; Age Wave calculation of household wealth from the Survey of Consumer Finances, 2016, and Financial Accounts of the United States, 2018.
4. Wealth-X, *Billionaire Census 2019*.
5. U.S. Bureau of Labor Statistics, Consumer Expenditure Survey, 2018.
6. AARP, *Longevity Economy*.
7. Survey of Consumer Finances, 2016, and U.S. Census Bureau, Current Population Survey, 2018.
8. United Nations, Department of Economic and Social Affairs, Population Division, 2017; World Population Prospects: The 2017 Revision; StatCan, Survey of Financial Security, 2018; Australian Bureau of Statistics, Household Income and Wealth, 2017–2018; Office for National Statistics, Individual wealth by age band: Great Britain, July 2014 to June 2016; Statistics Bureau of Japan, Statistical Handbook of Japan, 2019.
9. James Ellis, "Generational Wealth Gap Is Greater Than 20 Years Ago," MagnifyMoney, July 17, 2019.

10. "Baby Boomers Possess the Majority of US Household Wealth," Marketing Charts, April 12, 2019.
11. Dr. Rita Smith, *Empty Nest, Empty Desk, What's Next? How Boomer Professional Women Are Reinventing Their Retirement* (Outskirts Press, 2018).
12. The initial version of this segmentation was developed in Age Wave / SunAmerica, *Re-Visioning Retirement*, 2001.
13. The initial version of this stages model was developed in Age Wave / Ameriprise Financial, *New Retirement Mindscape*, 2006.

Chapter 2

1. Increase Mather, *Dignity and Duty of Aged Servants of the Lord* (Boston: B. Green, 1716).
2. William Osler, M.D., "Valedictory Address at Johns Hopkins University," March 4, 1905. Available at: jamanetwork.com/journals/jama/article-abstract/465107.
3. Libby DeLana, "Are we there yet? How ageism is holding back our industry," Campaign US, April 9, 2019.
4. AARP, "Media Image Landscape: Age Representation in Online Images," September 2019; "AARP and Getty Images Announce Collaboration to Change the Look of Aging" press release, September 23, 2019.

Chapter 3

1. Survey results cited in this section are from: Age Wave / Merrill Lynch, *Leisure in Retirement: Beyond the Bucket List*, 2016.
2. "L'Oreal, The Non-Issue," McCann.com.
3. Tina Seelig, "The Power of Possibility – My Experience at the Modern Elder Academy," *Medium*, December 27, 2018.
4. Nellie Bowles, "A New Luxury Retreat Caters to Elderly Workers in Tech (Ages 30 and Up)," *The New York Times*, March 4, 2019.
5. Richard Eisenberg, "Modern Elder Academy: The Cool School For Midlifers," *Next Avenue*, September 23, 2018.
6. "OXO: Getting a Grip on Usability and More," Disability-Marketing.com.
7. "Oxo International Becomes a Universal Design Icon," The Center for Universal Design case study, North Carolina State University, 2000.
8. Kelly Greene, "12 People Who Are Changing Your Retirement," *The Wall Street Journal*, February 16, 2008.
9. Laura Beck, "Changing Aging with Dr. Bill Thomas," The Eden Alternative, April 24, 2018; drbillthomas.org.

Chapter 4

1. Nonprofit Transamerica Center for Retirement Studies, *19th Annual Transamerica Retirement Survey*, 2019.
2. OECD, Labor Force Participation Rate, 2018.
3. Zarla Gorvett, "How elders can reinvigorate the workforce," BBC Generation Project, November 14, 2019; Richard Eisenberg, "How These 3 Countries Embrace Older Workers," *Next Avenue*, May 10, 2018.
4. Julian Birkinshaw et al., "Older and Wiser? How Management Style Varies With Age," MIT *Sloan Management Review*, Summer 2019.
5. Unless otherwise cited, all survey results in this chapter are from Age Wave / Merrill Lynch, *Work in Retirement: Myths and Motivations*, 2014.
6. Nonprofit Transamerica Center for Retirement Studies, *18th Annual Transamerica Retirement Survey*, 2018.
7. TD Ameritrade, *Unretirement Survey*, 2019; Age Wave / Merrill Lynch, *Work in Retirement*.
8. Diana Kachan et al., "Health Status of Older US Workers and Nonworkers, National Health Interview Survey, 1997–2011," Centers for Disease Control and Prevention, 2015.
9. Jeff Haden, "A Study of 2.7 Million Startups Found the Ideal Age to Start a Business (and It's Much Older Than You Think)," Inc.com, July 16, 2018.
10. Chris Farrell, "Coming Soon: 2 New Encore Career Programs at Colleges," *Next Avenue*, March 22, 2018.
11. U.S. Bureau of Labor Statistics, 2014.
12. Transamerica, *19th Annual.*
13. Ibid.

Chapter 5

1. "Study: A Record 768 Million U.S. Vacation Days Went Unused in '18, Opportunity Cost in the Billions," U.S. Travel Association press release, August 16, 2019.
2. Blair Decembrele, "Your Workplace Guide to Summer Vacation," LinkedIn blog, July 11, 2018.
3. Nielsen Total Audience Report, Q3 2018.
4. Unless otherwise cited, all survey results in this chapter are from Age Wave / Merrill Lynch, *Leisure in Retirement: Beyond the Bucket List*, 2016.
5. AARP, 2019 Boomer Travel Trends.
6. Ibid.
7. Mark Strauss and Brian Kennedy, "Space tourism? Majority of Americans say they wouldn't be interested," Pew Research Center, June 7, 2018.

8. G. Oscar Anderson, "Video Games: Attitudes and Habits of Adults Age 50-Plus," AARP Research, June 2016.

9. Kelsey Ogletree, "Virtual Reality Offers the Ability to 'Travel,'" *Next Avenue*, December 19, 2018.

10. Lynn Langway, "Boomers Took Fitness and Made It Their Own," *Next Avenue*, January 30, 2017; Dorene Internicola, "New fitness centers cater to aging baby boomers," Reuters, May 13, 2013.

11. Serenitie Wang, "Beijing gets tough on dancing grannies," CNN, February 28, 2017.

12. Vittoria Traverso, "The cities designing playgrounds for the elderly," BBC Generation Project, October 29, 2019.

13. Michael Anderson, "Bike Use Is Rising Among the Young, But It Is Skyrocketing Among the Old," PeopleforBikes.org, June 19, 2014.

14. Heide Raschke, "Whom Do Arts Benefit Most? Older Adults," *Next Avenue*, November 28, 2016.

15. Abraham Maslow, *Toward a Psychology of Being*, 1962.

16. AARP, 2019 Boomer Travel Trends; "Celebrating Airbnb's 60+ Host Community," Airbnb.com, 2015; "RV Business Indicators," Recreation Vehicle Industry Association, 2015.

17. Abby Ellin, "Goodbye, Golf Clubs. Hello, Hiking Boots and Kayak," *The New York Times*, January 15, 2016.

18. 2019 Virtuoso Luxe Report.

19. "Overseas Adventure Travel Reports Rise of Solo Travelers Aged 50 and Older, Especially Women," PR Newswire, February 4, 2015.

Chapter 6

1. Eric Niiler, "An AI Epidemiologist Sent The First Warnings of the Wuhan Virus," *Wired*, January 25, 2020.

2. Angela Chen, "As tech companies move into health care, here's what to watch in 2019," *The Verge*, January 3, 2019.

3. World Population Review, Heathiest Countries 2020.

4. Axios, "Poll: How many people want to live to 100," May 9, 2019.

5. World Health Organization, World Health Statistics 2018.

6. Age Wave / Merrill Lynch, *Health in Retirement: Planning for the Great Unknown*, 2014.

7. Gallup, "Trends Show Bathing and Exercise Up, TV Watching Down," 2000.

8. International Health, Racquet & Sportsclub Association, *2019 IHRSA Health Club Consumer Report*.

9. U.S. Bureau of Labor Statistics, Consumer Expenditure Survey, 2017.

10. The Harris Poll, ASCO 2018 Cancer Opinions Survey, 2018.
11. Grand View Research, Complementary and Alternative Medicine Market Size, Share & Trends Analysis Report by Intervention, 2018.
12. Age Wave / Merrill Lynch, *Health in Retirement*.
13. Population Reference Bureau, "Are Baby Boomers Healthy Enough to Keep Working?" 2018.
14. Age Wave / Merrill Lynch, *Health in Retirement*.
15. "Top 15 Ad Campaigns of the 21st Century," *Advertising Age*, 2015.
16. Ibid.
17. "Baby Boomer Beauty: Marketing to Female Boomers," *Medium* Infographic, April 4, 2017.
18. Andrew Joseph, "A hilarious Twitter thread roasted peloton's absurd commercials," *USA Today*, January 29, 2019.
19. Coherent Market Insights, CRISPR & CAS Gene Market Size Research Report 2026.
20. Donald H. Taylor et al., "Benefits of Smoking Cessation for Longevity," *American Journal of Public Health*, 2002.
21. K. L. Pellegrin et al., "Potentially preventable medication-related hospitalizations," *Journal of the American Pharmacists Association*, 2017.
22. National Institute on Aging, "Social isolation, loneliness in older people pose health risks," April 23, 2019.
23. National Center for Health Statistics, Health United States, 2017; World Health Organization, "Hypertension Fact Sheet," 2019.
24. National Health and Nutrition Examination Survey (NHANES) 2003–2010.
25. Statista, eHealth Report U.S., 2018.
26. Age Wave / Merrill Lynch, *Finances in Retirement: New Challenges, New Solutions*, 2017.
27. Age Wave / Merrill Lynch, *Health in Retirement*.
28. Alzheimer's Association, *2019 Alzheimer's Disease Facts and Figures*.
29. National Institute on Aging, "Social isolation, loneliness in older people pose health risks," April 23, 2019.
30. Kantar Health, *The Global Health and Wellness Report 2018*.
31. Grand View Research, Cannabidiol Market Size, Share & Trends Analysis Report 2019–2025.
32. Harvard Medical School Division of Sleep Medicine, "Healthy Sleep: Sleep and Disease Risk," 2007.
33. American Sleep Apnea Association, "Sleep Apnea Information for Clinicians."
34. Statista, "Sleeping aid OTC revenue in the United States from 2011 to 2018."
35. Brand Essence Research, "Sleep Aids Market: Global Size, Trends, Competitive, Historical and Forecast Analysis, 2019–2025," 2019.

36. National Institute on Deafness and Other Communication Disorders.

37. C. S. Florence et al., "Medical Costs of Fatal and Nonfatal Falls in Older Adults," *Journal of the American Geriatrics Society*, 2018.

38. OECD, Health at a Glance 2017.

39. Judy A. Stevens and Robin Lee, "The Potential to Reduce Falls and Avert Costs by Clinically Managing Fall Risk," *American Journal of Preventative Medicine*, 2018.

40. Statista, eHealth Report U.S., 2018.

41. Age Wave / Merrill Lynch, *Health in Retirement*.

42. U.S. Census Bureau, American FactFinder, 2018.

43. National Resident Matching Program, *Results and Data: Specialties Matching Service 2018 Appointment Year*.

44. Association of American Medical Colleges, *The Complexities of Physician Supply and Demand: Projections from 2015 to 2030*, 2017; Physician's Foundation, *2018 Survey of America's Physicians*.

Chapter 7

1. D'Vera Cohn and Jeffrey S. Passel, "A record 64 million Americans live in multigenerational households," Pew Research Center, 2018.

2. Generations United, "A Place to Call Home: Building Affordable Housing for Grandfamilies," 2019.

3. David Brooks, "The Nuclear Family Was a Mistake," *The Atlantic*, March 2020.

4. Age Wave / Merrill Lynch, *Family in Retirement: The Elephant in the Room*, 2013.

5. Patricia A. Thomas, Hui Liu, and Debra Umberson, "Family Relationships and Well-Being," *Innovation in Aging*, 2017.

6. AARP, *2018 Grandparents Today National Survey*; Sabi, *The BOOMer Report 2015*.

7. Marketing Sherpa, "How To Market To Grandparents – Q&A on Tips, Tactics and Results," February 3, 2009.

8. Lynda Laughlin, "Who's Minding the Kids? Child Care Arrangements: Spring 2011," U.S. Census Bureau, 2013.

9. Patty David and Brittne Nelson-Kakulla, "Grandparents Embrace Changing Attitudes and Technology," AARP Research, 2019.

10. Age Wave calculation based on TD Ameritrade, *Millennial Parents Survey*, 2017, and Sabi, *The BOOMer Report 2015*.

11. TD Ameritrade, *Millennial Parents Survey*, 2017.

12. Suzanne Rowan Kelleher, "The Grandparent's Planning Guide to Walt Disney World," Trip Savvy, June 26, 2019.

13. "MassMutual Significantly Expands Suite of Employee Benefits," MassMutual press release, January 9, 2019.
14. Patrick Coffee, "Volkswagen Looks for America, With Help From Simon & Garfunkel, in This Poetic Cross-Country Trip," *Adweek*, May 1, 2017.
15. Opheli Garcia Lawler, "Oprah Gives Loving Toast to Ralph Lauren," *The Cut*, September 7, 2018.
16. Emilia Petrarca, "Ralph Lauren Expands Its Definition of 'Family' in a New Campaign," *The Cut*, March 28, 2019; Rosemary Feitelberg, "Ralph Lauren Unveils New Global Campaign, 'Family Is Who You Love,'" *WWD*, March 28, 2019.
17. Age Wave / Merrill Lynch, *Family in Retirement*.
18. HBSC, *The Power of Protection: Facing the Future*, 2017.
19. Age Wave / Merrill Lynch, *Family in Retirement*.
20. Renee Stepler, "Led by Baby Boomers, divorce rates climb for America's 50+ population," Pew Research Center, March 9, 2017.
21. General Social Survey, NORC at the University of Chicago.
22. U.S. Government Accountability Office, *Retirement Security: Women Still Face Challenges*, 2012.
23. Susan Brown interviewed by David Baxter of Age Wave, July 17, 2013.
24. National Alliance for Caregiving and AARP Public Policy Institute, *Caregiving in the U.S. 2015*.
25. "How Much Care Will You Need?" LongTermCare.gov, 2017.
26. Judith D. Kasper et al., "The Disproportionate Impact of Dementia on Family and Unpaid Caregiving to Older Adults," *Health Affairs*, 2015.
27. Nonprofit Transamerica Center for Retirement Studies, *A Precarious Existence: How Today's Retirees Are Financially Faring in Retirement*, 2018.
28. *Caregiving in the U.S. 2015*.
29. Nonprofit Transamerica Institute, *The Many Faces of Caregivers*, 2017.
30. Ibid.
31. SAGE, *Out & Visible: The Experiences and Attitudes of LGBT Older Adults, Ages 45–74*, 2014.
32. AARP, *Family Caregiving and Out-of-Pocket Costs: 2016 Report*.
33. Unless otherwise noted, survey results in this section are from Age Wave / Merrill Lynch, *Journey of Caregiving: Honor, Responsibility and Financial Complexity*, 2017.
34. Gary Koenig, Lori Trawinski, and Elizabeth Costle, "Family Financial Caregiving: Rewards, Stresses, and Responsibilities," AARP Public Policy Institute, 2015.
35. Transamerica, *The Many Faces*.
36. Holmes and Rahe, Life Change Index Scale.

37. U.S. Census Bureau, Historical Marital Status Tables, 2106.
38. U.S. Census Bureau, American Community Survey, 2016
39. U.S. Census Bureau, Current Population Survey, 2018.
40. Unless otherwise noted, survey results in this section are from Age Wave / Merrill Lynch, *Widowhood and Money: Resiliency, Responsibility and Empowerment*, 2018.
41. "The world of the widow: grappling with loneliness and misunderstanding," *The Guardian*, October 5, 2015.
42. Sarah Wilcox et al, "The Effects of Widowhood on Physical and Mental Health, Health Behaviors, and Health Outcomes: The Women's Health Initiative," *Health Psychology*, 2003.
43. Charlie Jordan, "Widows with wealth: Managing money after losing a spouse," CNBC, October 31, 2017.
44. Susan B. Garland, "A To-Do List for the Surviving Spouse," *Kiplinger*, September 1, 2011.
45. *Survey of Widows and Widowers Topline Report*, The American College State Farm Center for Women and Financial Services / Greenwald and Associates, 2016.
46. Ibid.

Chapter 8

1. National Coalition on Aging, The 2015 United States of Aging Survey National Findings.
2. Unless otherwise cited, survey results in this chapter are from Age Wave / Merrill Lynch, *Home in Retirement: More Freedom, New Choices*, 2014.
3. William Frey, "How migration of millennials and seniors has shifted since the Great Recession," Brookings Institute, 2019.
4. Clare Trapasso, "Reverse Migration: How Baby Boomers Are Transforming City Living," Realtor.com, May 16, 2016.
5. Perkins Eastman, "The State of Senior Living. An Industry Grappling with Autonomy," 2019.
6. Andy Smith, "The Next Wave of Mixed-Use Senior Housing Development," Senior Living Innovation Forum, May 3, 2018.
7. Andy Smith, "7 Leaders Share Predictions for the Future of Senior Living," Senior Living Innovation Forum, February 9, 2018.
8. Sindhu Kubendran and Liana Soll, *Best Cities for Successful Aging*, Milken Institute, 2017.
9. World Health Organization, "Global Age-Friendly Cities Project."
10. Social Security Administration.

11. Perkins Eastman, "The State of Senior Living"; Angie Hickman, "Meet the 2018 Largest Providers in Senior Living," Argentum.

12. Don Mankin, "5 Cheap and Easy Places to Retire That You've Probably Never Thought About," *MarketWatch*, September 28, 2019.

13. Rodney Brooks, "Baby Boomers Are Retiring to College Towns," *U.S.News*, August 31, 2018.

14. National Association of Realtors Research Group, *2019 Home Buyers and Sellers Generational Trends Report*.

15. D'Vera Cohn and Jeffrey S. Passel, "A record 64 million Americans live in multigenerational households," Pew Research Center, April 5, 2018.

16. Audrey Hoffer, "Homes with Multigenerational Family Members Are a Growing Trend," *The Washington Post*, April 12, 2018.

17. Melissa Stanton, "Two Houses in One for a Home Within a Home," AARP, 2016.

18. Joanne Binette and Kerri Vasold, "2018 Home and Community Preferences Survey," AARP.

19. Shaun Keeley, "100 Most Popular Active Adult Communities for 2018," 55Place.com, May 30, 2018.

20. Mallory Hackett, "Best 55+ community rankings released," McKnight's Senior Living, August 9, 2019.

21. Kate Santich and Adelaide Chen, "Fastest-growing metro in the nation? The Villages," *Orlando Sentinel*, April 18, 2019.

22. latitudemargaritaville.com/daytona-beach.

23. "CoHousing Is. . ." Cohousingco.com.

24. Tim Parker, "What Is a Naturally Occurring Retirement Community?" *The Balance*, January 31, 2019.

25. Alix Langone, "These Real-Life 'Golden Girls' Moved in Together in Their 60s. Here's How They Make it Work," *Money*, March 27, 2019.

26. "Silvernest Raises a $3 Million Series A Round to Help Boomers Find Roommates," Silvernest press release, September 6, 2018.

27. World Health Organization, "Innovation@Home: A Contest and a Call for Age-Friendly Housing Practices that Work," October 25, 2018.

28. "Dutch nursing home offers rent-free housing to students," PBS News Hour, April 5, 2015.

29. Langone, "Real-Life 'Golden Girls.'"

30. Harvard Joint Center for Housing Studies, *The State of the Nation's Housing 2017*.

31. Marianne Cusato, "2017 Aging in Place Report," HomeAdvisor.

32. Harvard Joint Center for Housing Studies, *Housing America's Older Adults 2018*.

33. Brittne Nelson Kakulla, "Older Americans' Technology Usage Keeps Climbing," AARP Research, 2019.
34. CDC, "*Quickstats*: Percentage of Adults With Activity Limitations," Morbidity and Mortality Weekly Report, January 15, 2016.
35. Harvard Joint Center for Housing Studies, *Projections and Implications for Housing a Growing Population: Older Households 2015–2035*, 2016.
36. Centers for Medicare & Medicaid Services, "National Health Expenditure Projections 2018–2027," 2019.
37. CDC National Center for Health Statistics, "Long-Term Care Providers and Services Users in the United States: 2015–2016," 2019.
38. 2019 Top 100 Home Healthcare Providers, LexisNexis.
39. Stephen Campbell, "New Research: 7.8 Million Direct Care Jobs Will Need to Be Filled by 2026," PHI, January 24, 2019.
40. Sarah Varney, "Private Equity Pursues Profits in Keeping the Elderly at Home," *The New York Times*, August 20, 2016.
41. "China pilots internet-based nursing program for the elderly," PR Newswire, July 11, 2019.
42. CBRE, *Senior Housing Market Insight*, 2018.
43. National Center for Assisted Living: Facts and Figures: Residents.
44. Garden of Palms, "Assisted Living and Memory Care demand increasing quickly in the United States," July 14, 2017.
45. Belmont Village Senior Living, "Belmont Village Santa Fe Stands Out for Its Mixed-Use Development," April 11, 2018.
46. Chris Weller, "Inside the Dutch 'dementia village' that offers beer, bingo, and top-notch healthcare," *Business Insider*, August 2, 2017.
47. The Green House Project, ChangingAging.org.
48. myminka.com.

Chapter 9

1. Ann Brenoff, "Here's How Long $1 Million in Retirement Savings Will Last in Your State," Huffpost, August 25, 2017; Darla Mercado, "Here's the Number 1 reason why seniors work well into retirement," CNBC, October 9, 2019.
2. Anqi Chen, Alicia H. Munnell, and Geoffrey T. Sanzenbacher, "How Much Income Do Retirees Actually Have? Evaluating the Evidence from Five National Datasets," Center for Retirement Research at Boston College, 2018.
3. TD Ameritrade, *2019 Retirement Pulse Survey*.
4. U.S. Government Accountability Office, *The Nation's Retirement System: A Comprehensive Re-evaluation Is Needed to Better Promote Future Retirement Security*, 2017; Vanguard, *How America Saves 2019*.

5. Nonprofit Transamerica Center for Retirement Studies, *19th Annual Transamerica Retirement Survey*, 2019.
6. Brendan McFarland, "Retirement Offerings in the Fortune 500: A Retrospective," Willis Towers Watson, 2018.
7. Transamerica, *19th Annual*.
8. Aegon Center for Longevity and Retirement, *The Aegon Retirement Readiness Survey*, 2019.
9. OECD, *Pensions at a Glance 2017*.
10. European Commission, "Country Fiche on Pensions for the Netherlands – The 2017 Round of Projections for the Ageing Working Group."
11. Nonprofit Transamerica Center for Retirement Studies, *A Precarious Existence: How Today's Retirees Are Financially Faring in Retirement*, 2018.
12. Society of Actuaries, 2017 Risks and Process of Retirement Survey, 2018.
13. Transamerica, *A Precarious Existence*.
14. World Economic Forum, "Investing in (and for) Our Future," 2019.
15. Transamerica, *A Precarious Existence*.
16. Charles Birnbaum and Tali Vogelstein, "Roadmap: Fintech for the aging," Bessemer Venture Partners, September 27, 2019.
17. Center for Retirement Research at Boston College, *Frequently Requested Data*, 2018; Centers for Disease Control, National Vital Health Statistics: Life Expectancy, 2016.
18. Age Wave / Merrill Lynch, *Women & Financial Wellness: Beyond the Bottom Line*, 2017.
19. Vanguard, *How America Saves 2019*.
20. CDC National Center for Health Statistics, "Long-Term Care Providers and Service Users in the United States 2015–2016," 2019.
21. Age Wave calculation compares a man who works full-time uninterrupted and a woman who works full-time except for periods of caregiving, each earning average wages for their gender, based on U.S. Bureau of Labor Statistics, Economic News Release, Usual Weekly Earnings Summary, January 17, 2020.
22. Anne Tergesen, "Bankruptcy Filings Surge Among Older Americans," *The Wall Street Journal*, August 7, 2018.
23. Deborah Thorne et al., "Graying of U.S. Bankruptcy: Fallout from Life in a Risk Society," Indiana Legal Studies Research Paper, 2018.
24. National Coalition on Aging, "Older Adults and Debt: Trends, Trade-offs, and Tools to Help," 2018.
25. Lynn Stuart Parramore, "Why Bankruptcy Has Become a Rite Of Passage for Many of America's Seniors," NBC News, August 9, 2018.
26. Associated Press-NORC Center for Public Affairs Research, "The Impact of Intergenerational Wealth on Retirement," 2017.

27. Laura Feiveson and John Sabelhaus, "Lifecycle Patterns of Saving and Wealth Accumulation," Federal Reserve System, 2019.
28. Laura Feiveson and John Sabelhaus, "How Does Intergenerational Wealth Transmission Affect Wealth Concentration?" Federal Reserve System, 2018.
29. Transamerica, *19th Annual*.
30. Transamerica, *A Precarious Existence*.
31. Kerri Fivecoat-Campbell, "Will Tiny-House Communities Help Middle-Class Homebuyers?" *Next Avenue*, April 29, 2019.
32. Nancy Collamer, "How to Make Money from a Hobby in Retirement," *Next Avenue*, July 3, 2018.
33. Katherine Roy and Yoojin Kim-Steiner, "Three retirement spending surprises," J.P. Morgan, January 21, 2019.
34. Age Wave / Merrill Lynch, *Americans' Perspectives on New Retirement Realities*, 2013.
35. "Fixed & Indexed Annuities Poised For Growth Amid Volatility In Equity Markets," *Advisor Magazine*, April 4, 2019.
36. Samantha Smith, "Most think the 'American dream' is within reach for them," Pew Research Center, October 31, 2017.
37. "Senior Housing Wealth Reaches Record $7.14 Trillion," National Reverse Mortgage Lenders Association press release, June 24, 2019.
38. Age Wave / Merrill Lynch, *Home in Retirement: More Freedom, New Choices*, 2014.
39. Harvard Joint Center for Housing Studies, "Housing America's Older Adults 2018."
40. Greg Greeley, "Ageless Travel: The Growing Popularity of Airbnb for the Over 60s," Airbnb Newsroom, October 1, 2018.
41. "Equity release market rises 8% in Q3," Equity Release Council press release, October 28, 2019.
42. U.S. Bureau of Labor Statistics Consumer Price Index, 2000–2019.
43. Kaiser Family Foundation, 2018 Employer Health Benefits Survey, Section 11.
44. "Health Care Price Check," Fidelity Investments press release, April 2, 2019.
45. U.S. Federal Reserve System, Survey of Consumer Finances, 2016.
46. Age Wave / Merrill Lynch, *Finances in Retirement: New Challenges, New Solutions*, 2017.
47. Genworth Cost of Care Survey 2018.
48. Melissa Favreault and Judith Dey, "Long-Term Services and Supports for Older Americans: Risks and Financing Research Brief," U.S. Department of Health & Human Services, 2016.
49. Centers for Medicare & Medicaid Services, "National Health Expenditure Projections 2018–2027," 2019.

50. Age Wave / Merrill Lynch, *Finances in Retirement.*
51. Age Wave / Merrill Lynch, *Health in Retirement: Planning for the Great Unknown*, 2014.
52. Ibid.
53. Ibid.
54. Howard Tischler, "2017 Data Breaches Are a 2018 Danger and Beyond," EverSafe, February 15, 2018.
55. Age Wave / Merrill Lynch, *Leaving a Legacy: A Lasting Gift to Loved Ones*, 2019.
56. Tim Hewson, "Are there even fewer Americans without wills?" USLegalWills.com, 2016.

Chapter 10

1. Gallup, *The 2018 World's Most Generous Countries Report*; Charities Aid Foundation, *World Giving Index 2018.*
2. *Giving USA: The Annual Report on Philanthropy*, 2019.
3. Blackbaud Institute, "The Next Generation of American Giving," 2018.
4. The Corporation for National and Community Service, *2018 Volunteering in America.*
5. Unless otherwise cited, all survey results related to giving in this chapter are from Age Wave / Merrill Lynch, *Giving in Retirement: America's Longevity Bonus*, 2015.
6. Calculation based on data from the Center for Wealth and Philanthropy at Boston College, U.S. Census Bureau, U.S. Corporation for National Community Service, and *Giving in Retirement: America's Longevity Bonus* survey.
7. U.S. Bureau of Labor Statistics, *Volunteering in the United States 2015.*
8. Blackbaud, "Next Generation."
9. Caroline E. Jenkinson et al., "Is volunteering a public health intervention?" *BMC Public Health*, 2013.
10. Generations United and The Eisner Foundation, *I Need You, You Need Me: The Young, The Old and What We Can Achieve Together*, 2017.
11. generationtogeneration.org
12. Sarah McKinney Gibson, "These grandpas are uniting to make a difference with community youth," generationtogeneration.org.
13. Women's Philanthropy Institute, Indiana University – Purdue University Indianapolis, "Do Women Give More?" 2015.
14. Wang Xin and Cang Wei, "Volunteers pilot care 'bank' for elderly," *China Daily*, August 4, 2015.

15. National Bureau of Economic Research, "Expected Bequests and Their Distribution," 2002.

16. Unless otherwise cited, all survey results in the remainder of this chapter are from Age Wave / Merrill Lynch, *Leaving a Legacy: A Lasting Gift to Loved Ones*, 2019.

17. Accenture, "The Greater Wealth Transfer: Capitalizing on the Intergenerational Shift in Wealth," 2016.

18. HBSC, *The Future of Retirement*, 2015.

19. Catherine A. Salmon, Todd K. Shackelford, Richard L. Michalski, "Birth order, sex of child, and perceptions of parental favoritism," *Personality and Individual Differences*, 2012.

20. Megan Brennan, "Americans' Strong Support for Euthanasia Persists," Gallup, May 31, 2018.

21. Karen Heller, "The Funeral as We Know It Is Becoming a Relic – Just in Time for a Death Boom," *The Washington Post*, April 14, 2019.

22. Ellen Scott, "These Are 2018's Biggest Funeral Trends," Metro, September 26, 2018.

23. National Funeral Directors Association, "2018 NFDA Cremation and Burial Report."

24. Heller, "The Funeral."

25. Ibid.

26. Steve Palace, "'Rest in Vinyl' – A Company Will Press Your Ashes into a Working Vinyl Album," *Vintage News*, February 14, 2019.

27. Rochelle Rietow, "6 Funeral Trends Happening In Different Cultures Around The World (And What We Can Learn From Them)," funeralOne blog, July 29, 2019.

28. Ann Oldenberg, "Can We Talk . . . About Death?" *Next Avenue*, September 30, 2019.

Index